HIGH GALDR
RUNES & RUNE SECRETS

By Frank A. Rúnaldrar

HIGH GALDR SERIES
Book One: The Breath of Oðin Awakens (2nd Ed)
Book Two: The Spirit of Húnir Awakens (Part 1)
Book Three: The Spirit of Húnir Awakens (Part 2)
Book Four: The Blood of Lóðurr Awakens
Book Five: Roadmap to High Galdr Rune Work
Book Six: High Galdr: Runes & Rune Secrets

ARTS OF SEIDR SERIES
Spirit Walking for the Rune Mystic

QUESTIONS & ANSWERS SERIES
The Breath of Oðin Awakens - Questions & Answers
The Spirit of Húnir Awakens - Questions & Answers

HIGH GALDR: RUNES & RUNE SECRETS

The Book of Runes
&
Divine Speech

by
Frank A. Rúnaldrar

Part of the High Galdr Series
www.highgaldr.com

Published in 2021 by:
Bastian & West
www.bastianandwest.com

Copyright © 2021 Frank A. Rúnaldrar

The moral right of the author has been asserted.

All rights reserved. No part of this publication may be reproduced or transmitted in any form or by any means, electronic or mechanical, including photocopying, recording, or by any information storage and retrieval system, without permission in writing from the copyright holder. Reviewers may quote brief passages.

Part of High Galdr Series
www.highgaldr.com

ISBN: 978-0-9955343-8-4

A CIP catalogue record for this book is available from the British Library.

Editor: James Millington
In-book illustrator: Ben Hansen

Book typeset in Niva Light by PeGGO Fonts, Norse font by Joël Carrouché and runic elements in Felt-Tip Futhark by Thomas Kaeding

Copyright Notice: All rights, title and interests in the copyrights to all materials (including but not limited to any proprietary knowledge, data, information, manuals, illustrations, diagrams, flowcharts, marks or other information therein contained or thereby disclosed and representing the author's original works), are hereby reserved and to be considered the exclusive property of and belong exclusively to the author. The purchase of this book by any person(s), and its usage by any other party, shall not be construed as granting or conferring any rights by license or otherwise to the purchasing party or any other party who may come in possession of the book and/or its materials. No part of this publication or its materials may be reproduced, distributed, disseminated, or transmitted in any form or by any means and for any purpose, including but not limited to photocopying, recording, or other electronic or mechanical methods, without the prior written permission and consent of the author, except in the case of brief quotations embodied in critical reviews and certain other non-commercial used permitted by copyright law. In the event any reader or third party submits to the author or the publisher, either jointly or severally, any questions, then any questions based on, derived from or incorporating any of the author's materials in this publication, together with any answers provided by the author, if any, shall be deemed to be works derived from the author's copyrighted materials and accordingly such reader or third party in submitting its questions irrevocably agrees to the exclusive and royalty free world wide transfer and assignment (free of costs) of all or any rights, title or benefit in such questions to the owner for its discretionary use in any format and by any medium.

Usage Disclaimer: It is expressly agreed and acknowledged by all and any reader(s) and any parties that come into possession of the materials that all materials, information, techniques, methods, processes or statements made in this publication, and all and any associated materials as may be derived therefrom and distributed from time to time in any written or tangible forms and in any media (including electronic media), as the case may be, by the author or its publisher(s), are for to be used strictly for educational purposes only (the "Permitted Purpose") and not for any other personal or commercial purpose. All materials reflect the author's personal views and opinions, and no method or process or statement or anything else said in the materials is to be treated as having any scientific value, validity or status. Under no circumstances whatsoever or howsoever are any materials in this book, in whole or in part, intended to operate as scientifically proven methods, processes or statements, or intended to offer any medical or other advise, or be used in substitute for medical advise of and/or treatment by physicians for any matters. Neither the author nor its publisher(s) make any statement, representation, guarantee or undertaking howsoever or whatsoever as to the usefulness of any materials. The use of the materials for any other purpose, including any personal or commercial purposes other than for educational purposes, contrary to the Permitted Purpose, is not promoted and strictly prohibited. The author and its publisher(s) accept no risk, responsibility or liability for any unsanctioned use, which shall be at the user's sole risk, and shall, together and severally (the "Released and Indemnified Parties"), be held harmless and indemnified by any users engaging in any unsanctioned use contrary to this disclaimer from all and any claims, rights, liabilities, demands, obligations, conditions, promises, acts, costs, expenses, accountings, damages or actions of whatsoever kind or nature, whether in law or otherwise, whether known or unknown, which they made have or may thereafter have against the Released and Indemnified Parties for or by any reason of any occurrence, matter or thing which arise or are claimed to have arisen out of or in connection with any such unsanctioned use of the materials.

This book and the wisdom contained within I gift to mankind, to any who seek it and desire knowledge of creation through the ancient mysteries and heritage of the West.

For too long have all seekers of ancient wisdom had to look afar, across continents and times to other sources, to other people's heritage due to the 'loss' or rather inaccessibility of their own.

Nothing is ever lost or locked away forever. It is always hidden until the time comes for it to resurface, for it is and has always been all part of Creation, and part of Us.

In these pages I gift you the knowledge, the keys to power, the path to the wisdom of our proto-European ancestors. Honour them, and use this gift wisely, for the fates smile upon the wise and the fools the fates drown in their own foolishness.

And with these words let me share with you some of the deepest mysteries of the West.

May Mjötvið nourish you well in your journey.
– F.A.Rúnaldrar

Table of Content

High Galdr: Runes & Rune Secrets
- Definitions of Norse Terms I
- Introducing... High Galdr VII
- The Norse Tradition - Heritage of the Indo-Europeans XI
  - The Eddas XI
  - The Saga(s) XIV
- The Tradition of The Warrior XVII

Rune Practices & Hávamál Rune Teachings
- Preliminary Requirements 1
- Into the Runes! 3
- Dangers 5
- Effects of the Runes (Be Prepared) 11
- Why Use the Elder Futhark 19
- Numerological and Phonetic Significance of the Ættir 22
- Rune Energy, Power and Force 27
- Instructions Within The Hávamál 31
  - Know How to Carve (Cut) Them 32
  - Know How to Interpret Them 36
  - Know How to Tint (Colour) Them 37
  - Know How to Prove Them 39
  - Know How to Ask Them 41
  - Know How to Sacrifice Them 44
  - Know How to Send Them 49
  - Know How to Discard (Send) Them 52
- Runic Energy Learning 59
  - Energy to Information: Using the Rune Energy for Information 64
- Dangers of Correspondences 67

Fundamentals of Rune Vocalisations 71
Runic Energy Sensations 77
Using High Galdr – The Technique 79
    Using High Galdr – The (Non-Self) Technique 92
High Galdr – Breathing the Runes 97

The Runes
The Rune Fehu – Fé 103
The Rune Uruz – Úr 113
The Rune Þurisaz – Þurs 123
The Rune Ansuz – Óss 133
The Rune Raiðo – Reið 143
The Rune Kenaz – Kaun 151
The Rune Gebo – Gjöf 161
The Rune Wunjo – Vin 169
The Rune Hagalaz – Hagal 177
The Rune Nauþiz – Nauð 185
The Rune Isa – Íss 195
The Rune Jera – Ár 203
The Rune Perþo – Perð 213
The Rune Eihwaz – Jór 223
The Rune Elhaz – Ýr 231
The Rune Sowilo – Sól 239
The Rune Tiwaz – Týr 249
The Rune Berkano – Bjarkan 259
The Rune Ehwaz – Eykur 269
The Rune Mannaz – Maður 279
The Rune Laguz – Lögur 291
The Rune Ingwaz – Ing 303
The Rune Dagaz – Dagur 313
The Rune Oþala – Óðal 325

Hávamál Rune Songs
Insights into the Hávamál Rune Songs 339

Appendixes
Appendix A: Table of Runic Names in
    Icelandic & Germanic 351
Appendix B: References & Footnotes 355

Forthcoming Titles...359

Publisher Notes

During the editing and production of *High Galdr*, we have had to make a number of changes to the original manuscript (all with the approval of the author) in order to ensure the best quality of this book. We would like to apologise for any confusion this might cause and would like to inform you, his readers, what these changes were and clarify why they were made.

As you will see, we have had to change the usual rune-naming convention used in Frank's books. He usually mentions each rune in the following manner: the rune itself – Rune Icelandic Name (Rune Germanic Name). Because of the increased frequency of rune use, we have had to change this for legibility purposes and have opted for the Rune Glyph (Rune Germanic Name) form instead. In addition to this, we have also had to reduce the use of names in parenthesis for various parts of the self: spirit (Odr), physical body (Lik), shadow self (Sal), energy body (Hamr), mind (Hugr) and memory (Minni) have had their Norse terms removed to assist with legibility.

A further change was necessary in order to make this book possible. The original manuscript was definitely one of the most comprehensive practical works on the runes ever to be written – it exceeded 1,200 pages, which just made it far too large for a single publication. After a lot of work, we have managed to section off the content without taking away from the author's original goal, which was to make this a solid and complete foundation for learning how to work with the runes practically.

The manuscript had large unbroken paragraphs, which have been structured under headings to improve accessibility for reference purposes and to enable us to split the work into multiple volumes. This resulted in individual sections for the rune effects and theories divided across parts of the self and what the author referred to as 'levels of reality'. In this volume, you will find the following: Archetypal, Spirit and Spiritual Reality, Mind and Mental Reality, Energy body and Energy Reality, Physical Body and Reality.

The original manuscript had content for a further 19 sections: Shadow Self and Reality, Biological and Healing Galðr, Sexual Galðr, Bindrune Uses, Hamingja Uses, Fylgja Uses, Effects on the Spark of Self, Runic Polarities, Dream Uses, Cosmic Galðr and one additional section for each of the nine worlds. We have agreed with the author to move these into existing forthcoming titles and to add several new titles to the series. Please rest assured we will do our best to make these available to you as soon as possible.

Bastian & West

Author Notes

It is important, when dealing with the runes, to keep in mind that what we understand of them and perceive in terms of their influences will always be very personal. As we grow so does our understanding, and sometimes exactly the same words read in a new light, from a new perspective, can have a different meaning when placed in a new context, which in turn unleashes entire waves of insight into not only the nature of the runes, but our own natures and those of the reality we are in.

The information given on each rune here and in my other work should always be used as a foundation to build on, a springboard to leap forward into yet a deeper understanding and a widening of insights. Some things might not make sense, no matter how hard and carefully I try to explain them. Do not worry; keep those in mind for later discovery., Other things might not be relevant, and that is fine as well, ; we all have our areas of interest and they do not always match. If they did we would be all unidirectional and creation would become bored of us.

My view on the runes can seem rather abstract, even when I deal with their applications to daily life. Keep this in mind when you read through this. Use it as a signpost, a guide pointing you in the direction of where the runes lead., Your journey might be a little different, but these differences are to be expected; they are often subtle variations along the same road. Always analyse and question all you experience, validate your experiences over and over again, and reproduce them time and time again, – that is ultimately the best gage on whether you are succeeding or not.

I have included both the Galðr and Seiðr elements of the runes in their respective descriptions. I am well aware that the purists are going to heavily criticise me for doing so, to them all I have to say is that my aim was to provide as complete an overview of each rune as possible. Ignoring the Seiðr understanding and uses of the runes would have provided a large gap in knowledge. When both are combined, we get a more complete picture and gain access to concepts that would have otherwise never been mentioned. Use them if you want to or ignore them if you do not; the methods are all Galðr based (except for the breathing ones given at the end) and the Seiðr- specific uses are noted in the text for those of you who wish to stick to the purist approach.

Before we head into the text, I would like to mention one final thing. When discussing some of the runes, there is mention that they some should not be used directly within yourself by men and others should not be used directly within yourself by women. It is not my intent to prohibit anyone from using any rune. Quite to the contrary: them being universal manifestations means they can be used by anyone irrespective of sex, ancestry or gender, or any other characteristic for that matter. The only reason I do make those comments (for Þ Thurisaz, ᛏ Tiwaz and ᛒ Berkano) is because when those forces are unleashed within us, they have a very masculinising or feminising effect on the energy bodies and physical body. This in turn can cause disruption of both the energetic and physiological metabolisms, leading to problems down the road. The theoretical and practical knowledge of the energy, shadow and physical bodies are based on traditional teachings and understandings and are subject to those views in terms of biology and sex; they are different across the sexes and those parts of us have different configurations as well as different techniques for each sex to use. It is very much advisable to avoid using those runes within yourself when instructed to, according to the rune teachings, or you could do yourself harm. Ultimately, whether you do or do not is entirely up to you – the choice is yours, as is the responsibility for their use (or the use of any rune for that matter).

Definitions of Norse Terms

All terms used refer to their original Old Norse or Proto-Germanic meanings not their modern day derivatives in the Scandinavian, German or Icelandic languages.

Önd – Part of the psycho-spiritual construct of the Self as viewed in Norse mysticism and mythology, the Önd sits at the apex of the spiritual level of the Self and can be loosely described as 'The Breath of Oðin' or luck / Megin-fulled breath.

Óðr (or Óðr, or Óð) – Part of the psycho-spiritual Self- sitting at the apex of the mental part of the Self, it can be loosely thought of as the conscious awareness or totality of the spirit.

Hugr – The Hugr is often thought of as the reasoning or logic part of the mind, sometimes as the mind itself and often as the intellect or intellectual capacity of the mind. Essentially it is the manifestation of the active characteristics of the Spirit (Óðr).

Minni – The polar opposite of the Hugr and often thought of as the root of memory, the Minni is actually the individual record of one's experiences and acts as an anchor point for those events.

Hamr – The Hamr is the energy body, often described as the blueprint of the physical.

Lik – Part of the psycho-spiritual Self sitting at the apex of the energetic part of the Self, the Lik is the complete physical body as a result of the fusion of matter and spirit via the medium of energy. When talking about the Lik we include everything which is part of it, including the energetic and spiritual elements as well as the typically physical ones such as blood, DNA, nervous system and so forth.

Sal – Part of the psycho-spiritual self sitting at the bottom of the energetic part of the Self, the Sal is often loosely translated as the 'shadow'. In effect, it is the complimentary opposite of the Hamr.

Heimdall – One of the principle Gods in Norse mythology, Heimdall was described as the white god or whitest of the gods. He is linked to light and the pure power thereof. He possesses the resounding horn Gjallarhorn, which he will sound at the time of Ragnarök. He is the God responsible for originating the various classes of mankind and imbuing these with increasing degrees of divinity.

The Æsir – This refers to the clan of Gods from Ásgarð, typically associated with the divine aspects of spiritual origin. They are wielders of the Galðr sciences (use of runes and their correct applications) and have strong connections with the spiritual, awareness, intellect, mind, knowledge and the sciences.

The Vanir – The Vanir refers to the clan of Gods from Vanaheim, typically associated with the natural order of things and having strong connections with nature, the world and the physical as it moves towards the spiritual. They are wielders of Seidr crafts (sorcery, divination, soothsaying, shamanistic practices, herbal medicines and so forth).

Yggdrasil (Mjötvið) – The mythical Ash tree that is home to the nine worlds in Norse cosmology. It is also thought of as being the foundation of the cosmos itself and everything within it.

Egil's Saga – Otherwise termed in Iceland as the Egla, this is an Icelandic Saga dating back to 1240 AD, which details the life of Egil Skallagrimsson a farmer, Viking and poet.

Muspelheim – Muspelheim was the first world to be formed out of the great emptiness called Ginnungagap. It is a realm of flame, fires, light and explosive power unreachable by any not native to it.

Húnir (Hœnir) – One of the Æsir Gods, he helped create mankind along with Oðinn and Lóðurr. He gave the first man and woman Óðr and hence imbued them with spirit. He is also one of the Gods who survives Ragnarök and gains prophetic powers thereafter.

Njörðr – Vanir god of the Sea, he is the father of Freya and Frey and was one of the hostages exchanged in the Æsir-Vanir war. It is said he will return to head the Vanir after Ragnarök.

Lóðurr (Lóð or Lóðr) – Lóðurr is a mysterious God, whom academics seem unable to accept other than trying (and failing) to identify him with Loki or even Freyr. He gives the first man and woman blood and hence health, in other words flesh or physicality.

Ragnarök – Also known as the Twilight of the Gods, this final battle was foretold in the Völuspá (stanza 41). It describes the ultimate fate of the Gods themselves.

Ætts – Meaning 'clan', it can also refer to related grouping of concepts, individuals or sets of people. It is sometimes referred to as kin-Ætts which would be used in terms of a grouping of related people. For instance, Ætts in terms of individuals would include related individually such as family, whereas kin-Ætts would expand this to a wider set of relations such as an entire clan.

Norns – This typically refers to the Jotun (giantess) sisters Urð, Verðandi and Skuld who weave the threads of fate for men and gods alike. They also draw water from the Well of Urð and collect sands from around it to pour on the Yggdrasil to prevent it from rotting. The word Norn can also refer to the concept of the fate weaver attached to individuals at birth which could be either good or bad, weaving either a fortunate or unfortunate fate for that individual.

Niflheim – One of the Nine Worlds in Norse Cosmology, Niflheim is a world of primordial ice and cold, sometimes also called the mist world.

Fylgja – Part of the archetypal level of the Self, the Fylgja is a spirit which binds to the individual, becoming a part of him or her upon birth. It is always inherited down the ancestral lines and carries experiential essence and memories and powers of the former Self's embodiment. The Fylgja forms into either animal, humanoid or geometric form depending on evolutionary progress of both the individual and itself.

Kin-Fylgja – Similar to the Fylgja, this overarching spirit carries the experiential essences of the entire family line, the sum resulting from the entire ancestral lines up to the current point. It attaches to the eldest male of the family line and communicates primarily through the females of the line.

Hamingja – The Hamingja is part of the archetypal level of the Self. It manifests as an energetic organ in the individual which stores the Megin (power) it produces from various runic and life energies.

Wyrd and Ørlǫg – This refers to fate or rather threads of fate as they flow through creation. Cosmically, Ørlǫg is seen as infinite fibres of energetic substance flowing throughout all existence. From a human perspective, these fibres appear to flow through Creation but also through individuals, Gods and all life forms, setting the path they will follow over the course of their existence. However, when viewed from a Cosmic perspective, all things in Creation flow through the fibres. The Wyrd refers to these threads on a larger scale such as for humanity as a whole, individual races and clans while Ørlǫg refers to how these threads manifest on the individual level. The Wyrd is formed by the Norns and the Ørlǫg is build from the Wyrd based on individual's power, fate and evolutionary needs by the Fylgja.

Óðrerir (Odhrærir, Óðrørir) – This refers to the container or cauldron which holds the sacred mead. Its equivalent is the legend of the 'Holy Grail' in Arthurian mythology and the 'Holy Chalice' in Christian mythology. The Óðrerir may well have been the inspiration for these later myths.

Introducing... High Galdr

High Galdr: Runes and Rune Secrets is entirely focussed on the runes. It provides foundational knowledge and training allowing you to not only embark upon using the runes to their full potential but also in deepening your training and specialising with your selected rune(s) should you desire to do so.

What is Galdr?

The practice of Galðr is fundamental to the Æsir and was 'taught' to humankind by Heimdall when he revealed the runes to humanity. Subsequently, other teachers from the realms of Ásgarð came forth to various gifted individuals, to teach them more advanced applications of runic practices. Oðin himself came to amplify those teachings throughout his travels and interactions with our ancestors, leading to various written sources being made available, the most notable of which is the Hávamál. Long ago, he even undertook teaching Galðr to the Vanir in exchange for knowledge of the arts of Seiðr. Interestingly, this exchange is an excellent illustration of the practical applications of ᚷ Gebo (the principle of a gift requiring a gift) even at that divine level!

So what is Galðr? One can define it as the uttering of runes, runic formulae, runic chants, runic vocalisation and bind-runes accompanied by their tracing/carving.

In Midgard (Earth), and specifically in relation to humans, these arts were used in a severely limited fashion, which essentially reduced Galðr to vocalisation and writing of the runes. It became a meagre chanting, visualising and tracing of the runes (for the sake of brevity, formulae, chants and bind-runes are herein included when mentioning 'runes'). Worse yet, the concept of Galðr itself has been fused with that of Seiðr. This merging was not done through a harmonious blending of the two arts, but rather aspects of the one were muddled into the other. The underlying fundamentals of Galðr gradually shifted from pure mysticism to those of ritualistic application. In the process, it lost the true power of Galðr itself, which wound up as a shadow of its former potential.

Some might argue that elements of Seiðr are needed in Galðr, such as the induction of trance states found within Seiðr as being essential to the effective use of Galðr. This is both partly correct and incorrect. While it is true that trance mastery is essential to Galðr, it is incorrect to assume that Seiðr is required or was the only means of achieving the trance (or ecstatic) states. Galðr itself is used to induce a trance state, which can at times even surpass those achieved via Seiðr (in terms of practicality, not potential). This stems from the mystical aspects of Galðr and is the reason why it was deemed, in days long past, to be the sacred science of the Gods.

The 'High Galdr' series seeks to bring back the knowledge and the tools to practice the sacred aspects of Galðr. Due to its nature, many will flock to it. Some will seek to master it and others will seek to abuse it. To the former, all that remains to be said is be persistent and practice; even partial success and minor achievements expand the Self, providing phenomenal gains: new perceptions, skills and abilities, as well as pure wisdom, knowledge and most importantly, the ability to influence reality in a very formulistic (scientific) manner. It becomes the equivalent of coding but in this case, we are coding reality itself! Once fully mastered, there will be nothing left that anyone in Midgard can teach. To the latter, those who seek to abuse High Galdr, a warning: even though High Galdr can be misused, it is vital to remain aware that the Gods protect their mysteries and they themselves throw hurdles in the path and practices of those who are seeking to harm their people, their creation and the cosmic order of things for which they are responsible. Not much else needs to be said on that subject, other than to confirm that no matter how hard those who would abuse them try, these sacred mysteries will always evade full mastery.

In these pages, you will find instructions to take your first steps in actual rune work and take you all the way to solid mastery. They will assist in uncovering the mysteries of and awaken the runes, their powers and forces within your Self and out.

The Norse Tradition - Heritage of The Indo-Europeans

It is impossibly difficult to determine the full extent of or to search out all sources of the Norse tradition. Most pre-date the widespread availability of writing, while others were passed exclusively from one generation to the next orally. The main sources of knowledge left to us in this modern day and age are found in the Eddas and the Sagas.

The Eddas

The term 'Eddas' comes from Old Norse and it is used by modern-day students and academics to refer to two main Icelandic literary works that serve as the basis of our knowledge of Norse mythology, tradition, teachings and history.

There are two primary Eddas, both written during the 13th Century in Iceland. The first set is grouped under the label 'Poetic Eddas', which predate even the Viking Age, and come from an unknown source.

They are divided into two sections; the first is a narration of the creation, destruction and rebirth of the world and provides the mythology of the Norse deities as well. The second is a set of legends relating to Norse heroes, kings and wise men.

The Poetic Eddas were incorporated into the Codex Regius written during the 13th century. Unfortunately, it was not until the mid-1600s that the Codex resurfaced in the hands of Brynjólfur Sveinsson, a bishop to the Church of Iceland in Skálholt. Brynjólfur was also a scholar at heart, hence his fascination with the old myths and legends! It is he who collected and produced this compilation of Old Norse mythology and heroic poems into the Eddas. However, it is widely accepted that he was not their author and so they were not labelled after him. He gifted his findings to King Christian IV of Denmark in manu-script form, thus earning it the name Codex Regus, which was then preserved in the Royal Library until 1971 when a formal return was made to Iceland.

The second Eddas were compiled from traditional oral sources and (theorised to be derived from) an unknown set of Eddas often referred to as the Elder Eddas by Icelandic scholar Snorri Sturluson (dated from the 14th century). He collated these literary works under the label of Prose Eddas. Like the Poetic Eddas, the Prose Eddas also describe in detail the creation, destruction and rebirth of the world, Norse mythology and life. Due to his background and the time period in which Snorri lived, the 'Christianisation' of certain concepts and legends are to be found in this text. Nonetheless, it does provide an invaluable and rich account of the Norse tradition and, just as importantly, how it was recounted over the generations.

Scholars have long held the view that the Poetic Eddas, and therefore the Prose Eddas, came from a much older source. The rediscovery of what is known as the Elder Eddas helped confirm that suspicion. The Elder Eddas are comprised of the Pagan poems and teachings that were later hinted at in Snorri's Prose Eddas.

Many translations from Old Norse can be found and the number thereof seems to increase steadily over time. One key point to keep in mind is that the Eddas are complex literary works detailing the Norse tradition through poetry and prose. Accordingly, when reading various translations, different terms and words are often found to express the same underlying concept or similar words are used to describe totally different ones. Add to this the fact that many Old Norse terms have no equivalents in modern day languages, and it becomes vitally important to read in between the lines, so to speak, referring back to the concept rather than relying strictly on the words themselves. A literal, legalistic reading that has become completely engrained in the modern readers' minds will fail to capture the actual meanings, concepts and knowledge held within the Eddas.

Aside from those mentioned, other so-called Eddas can be found. These are typically adaptations in use by specific groups based on either the Prose or Poetic Eddas. The key point to note, however, is that those are adaptations.

The translations of the Prose and Poetic Eddas that have been used as source materials for this work can be found in both the references and further reading sections. Modern day adaptations and/or derivatives are not used.

The Saga(s)

Unlike the Eddas, the term Saga (story) refers to one of the many stories, poems, legends and so forth. Not all the Sagas made it into the Eddas. Individual Sagas might have not been discovered until a much later, post-Eddas compilation period.

These Sagas are individual tales in prose or poetic form detailing historical events of heroic deeds, tales or important persons (a great many of them Vikings, Pagans or even sometimes Christians), bishops, saints and even legendary heroes. Many of the Sagas include tales of kings, special individuals (such as the Egil Sagas used in this text), and even territorial historic events ranging from the Nordic countries to the British Isles, France and even North America (Canada in particular)[1]. Their main characteristic is that they are a historical statement or tale (that is the literal meaning of the term Saga). This has raised much speculation as the intellectual machinery attempts to digest material that is these days considered to be supernatural or metaphysical.

This range of subject matter is simply due to the fact that these records were, more often than not, kept within individual families, transmitted orally or simply brought from a different territory. Remember, the Old Norse people (Indo-Europeans) existed long before the Viking age and had to survive forced Christianisation, dispersion of territories, hostile natural environments, and so forth. In other words, these Sagas provided additional insights into the traditions, mythology, legends and teachings that were initially transmitted orally and then, once writing became widely available, were from time to time published. Even to this date, however, many of the Sagas have never been published and are kept from public view for a variety of reasons. Some of these reasons are of a very practical nature. In Iceland, for instance, these stories are considered to be part of the national heritage, hence books or manuscripts that are valued as family heirlooms, if known about, would be confiscated by the state on the basis of it being a national treasure. This is somewhat of an over-simplification but is an example of one of the many reasons why a lot of these Sagas never have (and most probably never will) see the light of public accessibility or dissemination. Others might hold deep-seated hereditary knowledge, which, more often than not, requires specific genetic and energetically transmitted capabilities to be of any use. This is the case with the higher mysteries bestowed upon the Jarls by Heimdall.

Fortunately, many Sagas are available for public consumption, and they do provide an exceptional insight into the wisdom and traditions of our ancestors. In this work, the Sagas are used to illustrate and gain further insights into teachings from older sources, be they part of the oral tradition or those in the Eddas[2].

This seeming endless diversity of sources is what makes studying the Old Norse tradition wildly exciting and fascinating beyond expectation, yet also insanely frustrating. Each Saga and Edda can expand our understanding, yet finding the relevant ones can be a most noteworthy challenge, in addition to actually understanding the knowledge therein once it is found! Nevertheless, gaining a reasonably solid foundation into the tradition is key; it is after all part of our heritage and is what empowers us. The appendices will provide more references and recommended reading. Fear not, however — all Eddas and Sagas relevant to the topics and teachings in this book have been included; for without basing such teachings in the actual texts and other sources of heritage they would hold no validity per se. It is of vital importance to work with these Eddas and Sagas as the foundation upon which we build our spiritual heritage.

# The Tradition of the Warrior

Before diving into rune work itself, it is important to understand one fundamental distinction between the Norse tradition and a wide range of others. We work from the basis of a warrior tradition. What does this mean? Simply that the tradition and our ancestors all recognised one basic fundamental fact: that life, the universe and the cosmos are all predatory in nature. This might come as a surprise or even shock to people because of our modern-day obsession with personalising every impersonal force we perceive, in such a manner that we delude ourselves into believing they are all out there to help poor old us. They are not. Everything outside the human sphere of being is fundamentally predatory. This is why our ancestors adopted the path of the warrior. As we shall see, this is very prominent in Galðr (Rune work), but be not mistaken – it features prominently in Seiðr (sorcery/arts of the seers) as well. They are simply two different types of warrior approach, and who traditionally used each was based on gender (with men using Galðr and women Seiðr). In today's 'modern' age, these gender foundations have blurred, with more and more crossover found across the two fields of practice. It is not something new, even as far back as the time of the Eddas report of Oðinn learning and practicing Seiðr. However, it was not common. Other than for a very specific group of Seiðr work (mostly dealing with sexual mysteries), it no longer matters. The same runs true of Galðr work. The only distinction left which one should be aware of is that the type of energy manifested by men and women will at its core be different in HOW they function, but the end results should nevertheless be on par, irrespective of the gender of the rune mystic. There are a few exceptions found with certain runes – these will be mentioned when dealing with the appropriate runes.

With the rune work, we will look at what is a very logic-driven, deductible approach. With (proper) Galðr, one's methodology is very reason-based and scientific, as it is driven by reason, logic and a straightforward, universally legal manner of manifestation. In some oddly ironic sense, one can think of it as far more scientific than the human sciences most are familiar with. We will see later on that Seiðr practices are biased towards work involving intuition, instinct, and feeling everything about Seiðr is far more ephemeral in terms of practical work. With Galðr, logic and deductive planning are emphasised. With each step of how and when something manifests, how this leads to the next step and how it is set in motion, and so forth, one observes from a detached distance as the events unfold. With Seiðr, you unite and go with the flow, and you become part of the energetic wave of power. It is highly intuitive rather than detached, in terms of interactions. Here we have more of the Hamr (soul) and a lot of the Sal (shadow), whereas with Galðr, is it more of the Hugr (mind-spirit) which is the driver. The two compliment each other perfectly, and I would encourage everyone to study and master both. Opting for a way of working opposite to how you are accustomed opens up new possibilities and new avenues of growth and knowledge acquisition. That in itself justifies switching between the two. Combining them is key, but doing so by preserving the uniqueness of each is a must. Ideally, at some point you will have both in play simultaneously. When the two modes of functioning are in perfect balance, a third state is awoken (as their effects interact) and unleashed.

The warrior characteristics are also essential here. Galðr for all of us is primarily involved in how we grow ourselves, our reality and how we battle these predatory universal forces (both within and without ourselves). At its core, you have a rune or set of runes (think of it as a mathematical formulae where *rune1+rune2 = desired effect*), which is applied through the Self in a precise manner, and this produces a very specific directed end result. Logic and reason are used as springboards into the archetypal levels to unleash the Galðr with such laser precision that for a skilled mystic, it is even possible to reprogram the 'codes' of existence themselves. In all High Galðr work, you will notice that the steps of the practices are very specific: each part is purposefully used in a given order to produce a given result. In more complex workings, you would take the resulting effects of one part of your practice and chain it into another, and so forth.

When you unleash a rune (or rune set), you are always striking at something; you are in full-blown battle mode where the strength and power of your runes determine victory or failure. With each victory your power grows, and with each failure you experience a setback. This is where the mentality of the warrior is essential: you NEED to be strong enough to pick your Self up each and every time and continue with your 'onslaught'. Whether you are using the runes to counter something in life, to cause an event or so forth, you will be fighting against something or someone. Even when causing so-called beneficial end results, you are still in battle fighting against the status quo, against your Ørlǫg or Wyrd (fate) or creation itself. This is why it was essential to grow your Self before embarking on practical Galðr.

In the previous books, you have strengthened and trained your Self, prepared your senses, your bodies, and your very Spark of Self. Now that you have a strong YOU, it is time to start working on the warrior skills: High Galdr itself! This is going to be a long path to walk but each step you take will make the next easier and will give rise to many beneficial developments, as well as a deepening of understanding of your Self and creation. Someone who walks this path will grow to incredible heights, providing he or she has the strength to keep moving forward no matter what. Remember, stasis is the ultimate enemy of life. Some runes will be easy to work with and others will be hard; some might seem impossible but in any of these cases, those who persist and prove strong enough will be victorious! And once you are victorious with the runes, many new wonders and challenges open up, with many more battles to enjoy! There are not only nine worlds (realms) to explore, but also the nine heavens found above Ásgarðr! Arise now Rune Warrior, wield that sword of yours (your sharpened mind) with the intensity of your spiritual resolve, and unleash your actual true Self!

RUNE PRACTICES
&
HÁVAMÁL RUNE TEACHINGS

Preliminary Requirements

In order to ensure nothing is left out, here is a quick rundown of what is an absolute must before starting with the actual High Galdr practices. As you will see from the rune's individual descriptions, the effects of each rune are categorized into five sections:

Physical and energetic: for background on the physical body, energy body and shadow, *The Blood of Lóðurr Awakens*[3] is your guide. The practices within will have given you an in-depth practice and theory on these parts of the Self.

Mental and Spiritual: *The Spirit of Húnir Awakens*, both parts I and II[4], will have covered in-depth information on the Hugr (mind), the Minni (memory) and the Óðr (spirit).

Additionally, *The Breath of Oðin Awakens*[5] covers the Hamingja and Megin, including teachings on how to infuse your High Galdr with megin to increase its effectiveness.

The Fylgja and Archetypal use are mentioned in the rune descriptions in this volume, but those parts of the Self are covered in much greater detail in forthcoming titles, which will compliment this one.

Those of you who have worked through these existing titles will have all the basic skills and quite a large number of advanced ones in readiness for High Galdr work. The other option was to follow the training provided in the *Roadmap to High Galdr*[6], which provides all the essential skills in order to get you to the point where you are prepared to dive into High Galdr. It will not give you the same in-depth background but it will definitely include everything you need to get started with this work.

A final note on these books. Once you have started working through High Galdr and developed the ability to use it, it is well worth the effort to revisit these previous titles using your newly gained skills in Galðr rune work. Adding this new skill set to those practices can prove to be a major boost in their effectiveness, especially when combined with those you have practiced the most and are very familiar with.

 Into the Runes!

Runes, runes and more runes! Finally it is time to take an in-depth look at the runes themselves. Do keep in mind that although we are going to go into quite some depth, it is impossible to cover everything about each rune or you would end up with multiple book sets per rune! The goal here is to give you the information you need to master the general abilities and powers of each rune in the key areas. This includes the mental and spiritual level, in terms of effects on mind, memory, spirit, senses, and your perceptions; the energy body and its realm of operation: namely the energy body, the shadow self, your emotions, states of being, desires, energy systems and interactions with energetic realities as well as awareness; and the physical, including the physical body, everyday life, social interactions, life's circumstances and so on.

One might ask, why bother with the runes in the first place? The answer is simple: because the runes embody the initial outpouring of abstract meanings and their respective forces into creation. Working with them, you are tapping into fundamental forces in operation everywhere and in everything. Even in realities where the runes are unknown or ignored, they still affect the fundamental forces which make those realities exist. This is why we can use the runes to affect any system of any tradition. It is also why it is written that Oðinn liked them so much that he wrote them on everything in existence – that is a symbolic description of their impact and scope. Another good way to think of them is in this way: they are the keys or language with which the genetics of existence and life are programmed. Because of this, we can re-code any part of existence (based on our power and ability, of course) to fit our own intended patterns. Naturally, those who are skilled in using the runes in this fashion do so very sparingly; it is not an issue of not wanting to demonstrate power but rather of not wanting to make a mess of things. Each rune casting will cause certain effects and creation will rebalance accordingly. Sometimes, those instances of rebalancing can take us away from our original aims and goals faster than not having unleashed the runes in the first place. Knowing when to use them and when not to is where wisdom comes into play. One big exception to this rule is when it comes to developing the Self; in that scenario, they are used extensively. Why? Because quite honestly, there are only so many life experiences you can have as a physical life form here and now. Once you have worked through the main set of them, there is nowhere else to seek the truly new other than in the unknown.

Dangers

It is worth a few words of warning before embarking on any practical work with the runes. One of the unique dangers faced when using the runes is unlike those found in any other system or tradition. When using the runes in the proper way, you are for all intents and purposes tapping into universal forces and bringing those forces to bear down upon you and your environment to cause change. What level of effect and how far reaching those changes may be depends entirely upon you, but some effect will occur regardless of skill or experience. Remember the words of the All-Father:

> 'All will prove true that thou askest of runes –
> those that are come from the gods,
> which the high Powers wrought, and which Odin painted:
> then silence is surely best.'[7]

This places a massive amount of responsibility upon each rune user's shoulders because each and every one of us is responsible for whatever we unleash, irrespective of whether it is intended or not, desired or not, planned or not. This is one of the reasons why it was so important to work through the various parts of your Self, to get familiar with all those impulses and desires that come from within, and more often than not completely escape your awareness. It is also one of the reasons why you have had to improve your concentration, sharpen your intent and become used to shifting your awareness. All those small exercises have a cumulative effect; they all result in greater knowledge and control of one's own Self. Additionally, they all provide you with the strength (or power) and balance needed to stand firm when coming face to face with universal forces. Make no mistake, those forces are not to be toyed with, nor trifled with – they can be helpful and just as devastating. It is the wisdom of those calling upon them that determines which. Yes, sometimes the destructive is needed; it is after all one of the two coins of the laws of balance, but a skilful rune mystic or master will achieve its effects with a surgeon's scalpel precision, while an unskilled user will cause havoc and all sorts of unnecessary destruction, which ends up being harmful rather than helpful. Always ensure you protect yourself and be extremely aware of what thoughts are your own and which are externally projected into you; always be on the lookout for fantasy or imaginings, and cut through them with the sword of your trained mind. Using these simple rules of thumb will ensure you avoid overstepping your capabilities (thus harming yourself) and ensure that you will act from a genuine place within (and do not cause harm or 'splash' damage to those around you accidentally).

    Always be sure you understand what you are about to do. Using a rune is like opening a door or a floodgate for that runic force. If it is not the correct one, or is not used correctly, it will be just as capable of harm as it is of help. Remember, here you are about to embark on actually manipulating or rather learning to manipulate the very codes of creation, the universal and cosmic forces responsible for existence itself. Always be thorough with your practices, do not skip any and do not leave things open (such as calling upon a rune's power but never discarding it). Whilst learning, avoid being too creative at all costs; there will be time for that later on when you are familiar with High Galdr and can experiment on the basis of your own mastery. Everything in its time, and in its place. It is worth remembering the warning from the *Hávamál* found just after Oðinn outlines the instructions on rune use:

> 'Better is not to have asked
> than to have over-blóted,
> [...]
> better is not to have sent a sacrifice
> than to have over-killed.'[8]

Here we have guidance and instruction on rune power use and the proportionality of sending with respect to the cost of doing that sending. It's a lesson in balance and the harmonisation of energy and action. He is warning us not to overcommit our resources when doing a sending and making sure the results of the work will yield a proportional outcome to what is being used (sacrificed).

You will always start working on yourself – in other words, inner work and work which improves your own life. You need to ensure first and foremost the survival of the Self. Only when you have gained a strong degree of mastery should you proceed to doing rune work for others, starting with those of the same biological sex as you, then gradually moving to those of the opposite sex (because in these cases, you also need to master runic polarities). Having mastered all of these, only then should you start working on larger-scale rune work. Typically, I would recommend after working through all the runes, picking one or two of your favourite ones and specialising in those. This allows you to develop deeper skills and abilities related to those runes, potentially unlocking some of the more interesting uses outlined in the descriptions given later in 'The Runes' section.

Additionally, you will always – and I truly mean always – start with using the positive aspects of runic forces. It is only after one has gained full mastery of the positive in all the above scenarios (self, others, larger scales) that one can safely descend into the negative or darker ones. Once those are mastered, one completes the runic mastery by re-ascending to the positive one final time, where the full breadth of runic forces, both positive and negative, are combined and a third polarity is formed. This third polarity is then what you take forwards in your development, and by it reach full mastery. Patience and persistence are the two most important keys here. One final thing to note, regarding learning the runes through practice in both Galðr and Seiðr: you start from the physical and work into ever more subtle parts of the Self and reality. This might surprise the modern practitioners who are used to working along other traditions, as most begin in the more subtle and move to what is generally considered a less subtle (denser) reality. From the Norse point of view, the physical body (Lik) is a part of the energy body trinity; it is the manifestation of the centrality of the Self just as Midgard (Earth) is the central point of the cosmology. For this reason, the starting point is the physical body. In practical terms, additional reasons should be mentioned: in some of the older traditions, the physical body was considered to be a type of 'star gateway' that allowed energies to be transferred in-between realities (as you will see in the practical section, the rune forces use the physical in such a manner). It is also where consciousness in human beings arises from; any work aiming to influence consciousness needs to include the physical body, just as any working attempting to manipulate awareness needs to be done in and through the energy body (for that is where awareness is born and rooted).

Effects of the Runes (Be Prepared)

When starting to actively work with the runes beyond the simple chanting of their names, you need to be prepared and observant of their effects on you, on your immediate environment, on your mental state, your physical, your Ørlǫg and the rest of your family or clan (Ætt).

Some might wonder: what on Earth this warning is all about? Let us look a little deeper into this. Unlike the typical use of runes these days, what you are about to learn is actual proper Galðr. Even when only practicing and training in Galðr, you will very rapidly notice that the rune(s) you work with have actual observable effects on both you and your life, as well as those around you (be they physical or not). You might wonder: don't they always? The simple answer is no; what is taught as Galðr in the mainstream is very limited in scope and it can either take years for even the smallest effects to manifest or it simply is nothing more than a mental exercise with fanciful name chanting. Here you will learn the keys to actual Galðr, which is termed High

Galdr in order to distinguish it from the mainstream version. In this type of practice, you will be unleashing the fundamental properties or characteristics of each rune's universal forces, and then you will be adding to it the actual power of that runic energy, merging the two and unleashing it on either the physical, energetic, mental or spiritual (or a combination thereof), first within your Self, and then in the reality outside of yourself.

As you can imagine, even the first initial unleashing of runic energy will have an effect. This tends to be subtle: a shift in perception, dealing with a mental block, bringing forth a long forgotten memory and so forth. Once you add the power aspect of that rune, you will be dealing with a whole new level of shifts in your life and outside of it. Depending on whether you are in harmony with that type of runic energy or are in opposition to it, the effect can be either positive or negative. It is a matter of working through them, no matter what they are, until things balance out. For instance, let us assume you get on with the rune ᚠ Fehu. You practice with it, things go really well, you run into a series of pure luck-fuelled events, you feel the fires of the rune activating your mind and opening up your awareness, you feel the rush of energy from it. You enjoy it all. That, ladies and gents, is a positive resistance.

In our modern era, everyone works on the basis that if something is good, feels good, and seems good, it should be encouraged or pursued. Little do people realise that all the things which are good are also inhibitors. They become exciting, you want more of what you perceive as good, you welcome them and enjoy them and in so doing, they distract you from the end goal: Mastery. The same is true for things which are perceived as bad or negative. Turning the tables around, let us assume that ᛋ Sowilo is a rune you absolutely avoid at all costs and don't get any results with. Here we have a situation of direct resistance. As you work with it, you eventually become able to unleash its powers and bam, things start going wrong: life throws hurdles at you which strike at your very Self, you lose confidence, lose energy, your 'inner light' (borrowing from the new age terminology) dims, you lose sight of your Self, you start to lose focus and purpose and eventually find yourself at the doorstep of depression. These would all be manifestations of the powers of ᛋ Sowilo. But why? Aha, we all have natural resistances to certain runic currents. In this case, as with any other types of resistance, they manifest along the lines of the properties inherent within the used Rune's energy. This is something we all have to work through. Most who are unfamiliar with energetic evolution would simply label it as 'evil' and keep away from it. The wise do the contrary. Simply work through the manifestations which are driving these things; each time the runic power strikes at your Self via an event or other in life work through those effects, work through the problems and reaffirm your Self (in the case of ᛋ Sowilo). What this does is actually fascinating. It will automatically synchronise you with the rune's energies and their vibrations. With each resistance you encounter and resolve, you become more and more able to control that rune's powers and its various forms of expression. Eventually, you will work through them to the point where, as you call forth that rune's energy, it will no longer throw obstacles in your path but will respond to your mind without any effects and then gradually with positives. When those are worked through it eventually manifests as pure power and essence along with its full spectrum of characteristics. This takes place at each level of our Self and for each rune.

It is important to keep in mind that it is not only sufficient to be able to use a rune and then rush to the next. You need to embody the energies, powers and characteristics of each rune before moving onto the next. On average, it will take between six months and one year to gain initial proficiency with each rune. Even those who are exceptionally skilled in energy and rune manipulation will spend at least several months on each. If you are moving too fast, then you will not be integrating things properly. Why so long? It has to do with the laws of manifestation of energy. This is where most of the time is invested and it is also where you will encounter most of the resistance from the runic forces themselves. Once the runic energies start to manifest in you or in your life, you need to slow things down, each and every time you repeat the runes. This is where the real challenges surface. Each rune's energy will interact with you in a given manner:

- Rejection: gives rise to life events that are confrontational to this energy. In other words, you will face negative events that are caused by this rune's powers in your daily life.
- Resistance: will manifest in life events where situations will arise that challenge you to act in accordance with this rune's energies.
- Neutral: nothing will happen; you will feel as if you have no response or are not making any progress with this rune's energy.
- Acceptance: you will experience odd positive events falling within the scope of this rune's domain.

– Harmonisation: you will experience boosts or run of 'lucky' events in the domain of this rune's power.

– Proficiency: you will be able to control the rune's powers and energies directing its manifestations according to your intended goals. The outcomes need to always be objectively verifiable until it becomes a matter of course.

These can be quite problematic in some circumstances, especially with specific runes. For instance, with the ᚦ Thurs rune, if you experience resistance, you will be presented with life challenges that can only be resolved with controlled aggression or confrontation. If rejection is experienced, you will be subjected to violent events in life. The only way to work through such things is to push for harmonisation with the rune itself; sometimes you need to take a break in your rune work and try again later when things have cleared up. Remember, not every rune will be manifesting in this manner but some can definitely be challenging. With each rune, you move from an initial reaction to a better and better one; it is only once you reach a certain degree of proficiency that you can move onto the next one. It takes time for the energies and effects of a rune to manifest during the learning stages, and the last thing you want to do is have the incoming effects of a resistant rune's energy pile up with those of the next rune you have moved to in a rush, and end up having to deal with multiple effects compounded, making your life a mess. This often happens to those who just pick up the runes and start regularly practicing without knowing these fundamental principles. Take it slowly, give it time, and proceed with caution. If you are unsure make sure you leave at least a solid three to six months between each rune you work with. This is a lifetime's work – no, multiple lifetimes work, so there is no need to rush and cause harm. Reading each rune, you will see what types of challenges you might have to face. This is why it is STRONGLY recommended to take things slowly. The less energy you pull into manifestation at a time, the weaker the effects are. If you overdo it and you have a challenging rune to deal with, you will get hit too hard and might run into real trouble which could lead to very bad situations. If you only make a little energy available, the events will manifest in a weaker manner and be more 'spread out' and be more manageable. It is unfortunately not possible to avoid these effects; you have to adopt the way of the warrior and battle through them until you have slain the beast! You have been warned: remember, the responsibility of what you do belongs to you. Not all these challenges are physical confrontation with some runes such as ᚠ Ansuz and ᛞ Dagaz; they are mental ones, which if you overload and are in rejection mode, can lead to mental health problems. Here, again, the best way to deal with it is to take it easy and slowly.

    I typically worked for one to three months on difficult runes until I moved into the Acceptance phase and then continued for a further three. It made things manageable during the challenging times and then even gave me a boost once those initial challenges were overcome. You will need to move through them in this order: Rejection->Resistance->Neutral->Acceptance->Harmonisation->Proficiency. Naturally, with some you will start further down these modes of functioning, and more towards the start with other runes. This is entirely dependent on the individual, their natural tendencies and life experiences.

If you have experienced the challenges of a given rune's influence already and have overcome them, that rune will no longer present any challenge to you, and it will have no resistance. However, if you assume you have experienced these already but have not, or if you have further challenges within its scope of influence, then you will still have to face those. Each rune will present all it can and in that way force you to grow.

This is why it is impossible to just do a course and end up a runemaster, no matter whether it is an online nine-week course or a nine-year one. You need to WORK through the runes and ALL of their manifestations first within the Self and then without the Self. Then, when you have finished that, you need to repeat the process in each of the Nine Worlds. Once this is done with every single rune can you truly call yourself a runemaster. Yes, the task is mind-blowingly daunting, but then so is evolution, and THIS IS evolution: direct, willed and guided. Do not worry; you will see that as you make progress along the way, you will develop and grow both in power and ability, beyond anything anyone who has not already done so can imagine. It is not the end point that is important here but rather walking the walk; it is during the practicing that you align all parts of your Self within and then with Creation itself. Perceptual unfolding, expansion of awareness, growth in wisdom and ability are but a few of the side-effects to be expected, and as those manifest, so do new realities unfold. If you are lucky enough to be working with someone who has already made progress in this way, they will know how to enhance the speed at which you can progress, if not be persistent and always remember the runes are within your very blood, your energy and your innermost Self. By mastering the Self, you master them, and vice versa.

Why Use the Elder Futhark?

Kylver stone was found during excavations of cemetery near a Kylver farm in Goland in 1903, the stone itself was dated according to archaeological methods to be from 400 CE and is one of the oldest historical evidences of the Elder Futhark. Looking at the stone, any careful observer will run into a few surprises:[9]

Kylver Stone found on Goland farm, dated: 1903

There are a few very important things to pay close attention to in this Futhark:

1. The positioning of the runes does NOT match that which is 'normally' accepted: in other terms, the ᛈ Pertho and the ᛇ Eihwaz are swapped in order, making the ᛈ Pertho the 13th rune of the Futhark instead of the 14th. We will look at the critical significance of this inversion below. Interestingly, if you refer to the rune song poem(see p.339) in the *Hávamál*, the descriptions given match when ᛈ Pertho is the 13th rune and ᛇ Eihwaz is the 14th. When they are not, the rune poem stops making sense.

2. Other things to note are that the ᚠ Ansuz, ᛋ Sowilo and ᛒ Berkano are mirrored to what is typically shown, along with ᛉ Elhaz, which is upside down. All these swapping of runes and mirroring are very significant disturbing the flow of runic energy, and in the case of the ᛈ Pertho-ᛇ Eihwaz causing a breakdown in the underlying numerology and phonetics of the Elder Futhark.

To those familiar with runes left on tombstones, carved in various objects and jewellery, they will be aware that often such depictions deliberately introduced errors to ward off any attempts to 'steal' their secrets. In other cases, the runes are used to fashion some type of talisman, in order to bring about specific effects. However, the Kylver stone is accepted as having been a teaching stone. Leaving the inversions and mirroring issue to the side for now, what is very important to us is the ordering of the runes, as we shall see below.

The most frequent question seems to be: why use the Elder Futhark rather than the Younger, or one of the manifold other derivatives? The reason for this is very simple from a practical perspective. The Elder Futhark is not only the oldest one we have access to, but its runes and their energies match the universal forces with such incredible accuracy that it is downright surprising. Additionally, the other Futharks are derived from the Elder one, making it the source. When you take a derived one such as the Younger, what you are getting is a derivative adapted by a group of people for their own purposes. In such cases, the energies represented by that Futhark are no longer universal; instead, those runes connect to large reservoirs of energy fuelled by those people (and subsequent users) and are fashioned for a very specific set of (human or social) needs. This is the main reason why each of those has a rune poem of its own. What this means for the rune mystic is that such runes are no longer linked to the universal forces, nor will they function in any of the other worlds. Yes, they will work very well – actually very rapidly, when it comes to dealing with affairs of the world and social needs – but once you try to push beyond that, their effectiveness wanes very rapidly. When you reach the energetic, some might still function according to the doctrines specific for those runes, and yes they might even function on the mental. However, as soon as you reach the spiritual you are at a loss, and finally on the archetypal, they are non-existent.

As you will see in the rune descriptions in this book, a lot of importance is placed on using the runes to enhance various parts of the Self, working with the energy body, the shadow, the Minni, the Hugr, the Óðr and with things in existence in their realities. This wide scope of potential possibility is brought into play because the Elder Futhark runes are representations of the universal forces that act on all those things. Think of the runes as access keys to those primordial powers: if you change the key, it will no longer fit the lock. If you have 5-7 keys, instead of 24 for example, you will be cutting yourself short of 19-17 doors and so on. Another problem with using human adapted runes (or any symbols for that matter) is that once you have fewer and fewer people pooling energy into them, their effectiveness fades, and the fewer people using them, the less powerful they become until their effects fade completely. Working with such Futharks using actual Galðr and Seiðr techniques would embody them into our very selves and permanently link us to them, resulting in those who use them having a direct pathway to influence each and every part of our beings. Not a wise move to say the least. With the Elder, those very universal forces are already within us; they already influence and shape our very beings and most importantly, no other person has a say over them (they are universal, hence not personal or clan forces). This once again is because the Younger and derivatives are not representations of a universal force. So from a practical point of view, the best solution is to use the original Elder Futhark.

Numerological and Phonetic Significance of the Ættir

Dividing the Elder Futhark into the respective Ættir reveals a lot of key essential numerological properties. Do note that this is assuming the 'correct' order (with ᛈ Pertho as the 13th rune and ᛟ Othala as the final one) as found in this inscription. Setting out the runes in their respective order along each Ætt gives us the following:

> Ætt 1: Fehu-Uruz-Thurisaz-Ansuz-Raidho-Kenaz-Gebo-Wunjo
> Primal Forces: (expansion, cohesion, conflict, harmonisation, proper course, transformation of journey/through experiences, exchange of forces/memories, synergisation)
> Ætt 2: Hagalaz-Nautiz-Isa-Jera-Pertho-Eihwaz-Elhaz-Sowilo
> Primal Forces: (seeding/destruction, reawakening, foundations, developmental, mysteries, universals, divine/spiritualisation, self – power)
> Ætt 3: Tiwaz-Berkano-Ehwaz-Mannaz-Laguz-Ingwaz-Dagaz-Othala
> Primal Forces: (victory/righteousness, seeding, awakening, unification, transference, solidifying, enlightening, becoming)

Ætt 1: F,U,Th,A,R,K,G,W
Ætt 2: H,N,I,J,P,Ae,Z,S
Ætt 3: T,B,E,M,L,Ng,D,O

Let us look at some of the underlying fundamentals in this distribution (or ordering) of the runes. As you will see, there is much to be learnt just for the placement of the runes. Some of these mysteries will be hinted at here, while others will be discussed later on, in order to avoid going too far off course.

1. Each rune's numerology when added up by column and reduced to a single digit gives us the following: 9-3-6-9-3-6-9-3 totalling: 48 (24x2)->12->3
2. This pattern of 3s, 6s and 9s is one of the most

mysterious and significant there can be. Additionally, the end sum of 48, which represents the full rune count twice (once for the negative and once for the positive), is extremely significant. The final 12 and back to 3 yet again holds very deep meaning (which will be covered later on).

3. Each Ætt has two vowels within it, and this has a deep-seated numerological and phonological validity: looking at the upper surface of these mysteries simply having two vowels in each Ætt shows a clear illustration of polarity. In the first Ætt this is the ᚢ Uruz - ᚨ Ansuz polarity, the earthy and airy elements acting as pole and ante-pole of each other. In the second Ætt, this is the ᛁ Isa - ᛇ Eihwaz, or the stasis and ever expansion polarity (ᛇ Eihwaz), and finally the ᛗ Ehwaz - ᛟ Othala polarity is one of the subjective (inner) vs objective (outer) Self (ᛗ Ehwaz as the various psycho-spiritual constructs of the Self, and ᛟ Othala as the harmonic foundation-home on which the Self stands).

4. This two vowel per Ætt gives us a total of six vowels representing the primordial sounds acting as the basis for universal phonetics.

5. We see the number 9 playing another role when we look at the final vowels in each Ætt. There are nine runes after each, and you have ᚨ Ansuz followed by nine runes to take you to ᛇ Eihwaz, then nine more runes followed by ᛟ Othala. This also yields three cardinal vowels: A, Æ and O, linked to the air element, all elements and earth, once again providing a balance between mind (spirit) and matter (earth) and a pole+anti-pole.

6. Another interesting thing to note is that you have 8 runes in the first Ætt, then the rune count goes to 16 (which reduces to: 1+6=7) and finishes off with 24 (2+4=6). If you look at the runes, this indicates the 8th in the first Ætt is Wunjo, then the 7th in the second Ætt is Elhaz and finally the 6th in the final Ætt is Ingwaz. When looking at these, you get ᚹ Wunjo harmonisation of one's environment and learning from it, followed by ᛉ Elhaz with a rising and a spiritualisation, to finally arrive at the ᛜ Ingwaz which indicates a new self-solidifying. Looking at it from a slightly different point of view, the 6th, 7th and 8th runes are ᚲ Kenaz, ᚷ Gebo and ᚹ Wunjo, giving you a harmonising, balancing and perfecting pattern (8, 7 and finally 6).
7. You also get an interesting phonetic pattern when looking at consonant distributions (including the fact that there are 6 of them in each) within each Ætt.

Many more insights can be found both in numerological patterns, phonetic ones and the distribution of the individual runes with each Ætt. For now, these will have to do; feel free to investigate and identify additional ones. For our purposes, these will suffice, as we can clearly see that moving a single rune out of its place would break one or more of these underlying rules and disrupt the effects of those positionings.

This is the reason why the correct rune order places ᛈ Pertho as the 13th rune and ᛟ Othala as the final rune.

Rune Energy, Power and Force

It is important to understand some of the subtle but vitally important differences in terminology when discussing the runes.

Energy: is just that – energy. It is usually without purpose but has a given set of characteristics and properties. For instance, Ice energy is intensely cold to the point where it pulls you into itself. We can use the characteristics and properties interchangeably (people do tend to confuse the two most often) to simplify things because the distinction between them has no practical purpose(s). These energetic characteristic and properties dictate the type of energy it is (in the above case, Ice is the type) and it is elemental which is a categorisation of its type. The only time we will not be using the energy characteristics and its properties interchangeably is when we look at energy transmutation (otherwise referred to by some as the alchemy of energy, where one energy type is transformed into another).

Power: a power is something a little different. When you have an energy that starts to condense, you gain a power. Here we are not talking about having more of a particular energy, but a more concentrated version of it. You can think of it as a type of materialisation of energy. Accumulation is a slightly – but importantly – different process where you gain more of it rather than changing its density. Think of it this way: you can have one unit of a rune's energy, and that unit can be either just a standard runic energy or you can cause a larger volume of energy to condense into the equivalent of one unit. You will still have one unit but it will be much denser (more compressed). So if I fill my glass with ᚠ Fehu energy, I have one glass of it. If, on the other hand, I condense an entire room's worth of ᚠ Fehu energy into the same glass, I still only have one glass of Fehu energy but the latter is very different from the former. The first glass will be filled with ᚠ Fehu energy, whereas the second time, I do it with condensed energy, which is ᚠ Fehu power. It is vitally important to understand this distinction because when we talk about a rune's power, this is what is what is meant.

Force: a force is yet again a completely different thing. Simply put, a force is an energy or power that has been imbued with purpose (or action) by a mind, an intelligence or by intent. So you can have either your ᚠ Fehu energy or your ᚠ Fehu power in your glass. That is then what it is, and when you want to use it to do something, you imbue it with whatever purpose you want it to have or whatever intent you want. Let us say you fill it with the intent to increase your wealth. Now it has purpose and scope of action, and in our example, both of these fall within the scope of the ᚠ Fehu rune and so it becomes a force whose characteristics are perfectly in tune with the purpose. It is universally legal and as soon as you send it on its way, it will go about its given task. In case you are wondering, a universally illegal example would be to intend it to freeze something. Here you have a mismatch of the energy type and the purpose. When this happens, those of you who can see energy will see it fold in on itself and collapse into nothing. It looks a little like an implosion or folding into its core before it disappears. This is why we need good and solid knowledge of the runes before we can use them. It becomes very complex once you start combining runes.

A force can also be universal; it is very similar to a runic force and is often used interchangeably. The only difference being that the universal version of it has its intent or purpose set universally. This will often be to do what the rune's force is meant to do, on the grand scale of things. It is not what you set it to but rather what the initial burst of creation set it to be instead. It is still a runic force.

It is worth spending a little time making sure you understand the key distinctions between a simple energy, a power and force. This is central to successfully unleashing the powers of the runes. If you take anything away from this entire book, this is what it should be. As a side note, these concepts also apply to Seiðr work, except there it is even more important since we are dealing with not only runic powers but also those of other worlds.

# Instructions Within the Hávamál

Know how to carve them,
Know how to interpret them,
Know how to tint (colour) them,
Know how to prove (understand) them,
Know how to ask them,
Know how to 'sacrifice' them,[10]
Know how to send them,
Know how to discard them.[11]

The *Hávamál* is one of the main written sources of instruction for Galðr. Before we delve into its depths, it is important to keep in mind that it is incomplete. This is a known problem: a lot of the source material has been lost and we need to work from often incomplete manuscripts or ones which are out of chronological order. This is one of the main reasons why the *Hávamál* itself gives poems for 18 runes rather than 24 (the final 6 are missing). Many use this as an argument to justify using one of the adaptations of the Elder Futhark, namely smaller rune sets such as the Younger Futhark. However, as we have seen in the chapter 'Why Use the Elder Futhark?', the 24 rune structures is critically important and has links into many aspects of Creation itself, which these derivative runic systems do not. By excluding six runes from the totality of the runic flow, links into vital cosmic energy fields, and phonetic and numerological laws are lost. This results in disconnecting the runes and our work with them from the primal universal forces which power them.

In the *Hávamál*, you will find eight instruction sets given with respect to carving, reading, colouring, understanding, evoking, scoring, sending and discarding the runes which are cornerstone instructions for Galðr. Each of these refers to a complete set of practices in their own right and when combined in a sequence allows you to unleash actual Galðr (which has been termed High Galdr). Most of the required skills will have been developed, if not fully mastered, in your work throughout the previous books: *The Breath of Oðin Awakens, The Spirit of Húnir Awakens (Parts 1 & 2)* and *The Blood of Lóðurr Awakens* (or *Roadmap to High Galdr Rune Work*). The final few are to be dealt with in these pages.

Know How to Carve (Cut) Them

This one is fairly simple and straightforward. It involves learning the shapes of the runes themselves. There are many 'alternative' shapes for them found throughout history. As far as High Galdr is concerned, using the original Elder Futhark ones is key (see rune illustrations in 'The Runes' section below). Each force adopts a form that matches its intrinsic characteristics symbolically, and this is the reason why each rune adopts the form it has. It is impossible for a force to be enlivened in a form that does not match those characteristics. What does this reference to symbols mean? Simply that they have to represent the force in a matching form (or shape) when making it manifest in creation. For instance, the Hamingja is usually symbolised by the sword... why? The sword is a representation of will, more specifically willpower. For willpower to strike or have effect, it needs to be projected, used and aimed towards a specific goal, and it needs to be sharp and strike with utmost precision. That is what we do when using megin, the power generated in the Hamingja (see *The Breath of Oðin Awakens*). Should any of those characteristics be lacking, your sword (will) either fails to hit the mark or it strikes with insufficient force, or worse still, you can end up striking yourself. This is all true of will when used consciously in a practical manner. A surgeon's scalpel is also a good symbolic representation of a mastered will – is that not a small super-sharp sword? Back to our analogy: the Hamingja is represented by the sword because they both cut sharp, channel (and generate) the power used by the will and are used to strike with precision. In view of this, the shape of a sword, knife, dagger or any other form of blade is an appropriate form to be used in cases where you wish to embody the force of will into it. This same symbolic embodiment rule applies to all of creation and all shapes within it. Another example would be the rock as an excellent store for the elemental forces of the earth itself and so forth.

    Avoid at all costs the tendency of confusing symbolic representation within form and shape with a slightly different process, that of empowering something with a runic power. Here, the power of any rune is imbued into any object or form in order to add that power into it and have it functioning/radiating from within it. It is a very different practice and produces a very different end result to that obtained from embodying a runic force into a form. When empowering, you are allowing the power (or energy) to be contained or flow through something, when embodying, you are pouring the very essence of the rune (its force – see 'Rune Energy, Power and Force p.34) into that form, it becomes alive within it rather than just flowing through it or being stored within. The actual practices for both are very, very similar, which could be why there is confusion over the two. With the empowering, you are also only working with a specific part of the total capabilities of a rune, while with embodying you are working with them ALL, even the ones you might not be aware of.

With the runes, we are very fortunate as we have the shapes of the runes that represent underlying forces and can work with these. By using those shapes, we can effectively embody the full essence of a given rune. If space permits, we will look at how embodiment of rune essences works and how to do them yourself. If it does not, I will include them in the next manuscript or an additional one. Before leaving this topic, those of you who have worked through the *The Blood of Lóðurr Awakens* will be aware that the rune can be embodied in our bodies in a special way: through our DNA. This is mainly because the forms of the runes exist in a symbolic way in our chromosomes. Men have all 24 runes encoded in their genetics (due the ᛟ Othala rune being embodied in the Y-chromosome) and women have a dual ᛞ Dagaz (found in the X-chromosome, do note the scientifically minded will be aware that only one of the two X-chromosomes is active) instead. The reasons for this are complex and I do not have the time or the space to go into them here; we will look at the advantages and reasoning of both setups when dealing with the polarities of the runes. For the time being, keep in mind that representation and anchoring for the runes exists in the very structure of our genetics and for this reason, they are fully accessible by our biology as well as our minds.

You will need to have memorised the shapes of the runes perfectly. Recalling them, visualising them and projecting their forms right in front of you with eyes open and closed needs to be mastered to the point where you can do so effortlessly in both a flat manner (two-dimensionally as if you were drawing them on paper) and three-dimensionally (as if it was a construction with depth in the shape of the rune). For the adventurous few, you can push this into a four-dimensional manner as well, by transferring your awareness into the central point of the form of the rune and looking at how it expands through space from there. This can be very difficult for those who are not used to working with this additional dimensionality. Should you struggle with it, do not worry, just skip it for the time being. It is not used at this point in your rune learning. It will become important when working on the archetypal part of the Self (from within the Spark of Self), but there is a lot of work to be done prior to that. When doing this with eyes closed, you visualise it as a shape in the blackness straight ahead. Having mastered this, you can optionally proceed to practicing the shifting the spirit into the runes *The Spirit of Húnir Awakens (Part 1) p.41.*

These few practices will ensure that you are able to shape (carve) the runes energetically without having to spend too much energy concentrating on getting the shape right. It should become so easy that it is almost an automatic reflex. Doing these practices also enables your biological awareness, shadow and energy body to start being exposed to the flow of runic energy within them. Those parts of you then (depending on how familiar they are with it) replicate this flow of runic energy as you draw them out in their own levels of reality. Eventually, you get to the point where tracing a rune with your physical hand causes the energy body, shadow and mind to trace it simultaneously with you if you intend them to. This in turn results in a rune being traced on the physical, and in the energy realms (loosely termed by the new age community as the 'astral'), shadow realms and mental. Then by focussing on the rune, it replicates on the spiritual and intending it to be, after much practice, spills it over to the archetypal level. This produces a six-fold embodiment of the rune for you to work with. It is this type of multileveled shaping, vocalising and sensing which allows the runic energy, power and force to manifest and make the your High Galdr work.

Know How to Interpret Them

Knowing how to interpret (or read) the runes is a somewhat more complicated matter than knowing how to carve them. What this is referring to is not only a matter of recognising the runes on paper (or in carvings) but also reading the runes off their energetic patterns. Those of you who have worked through *The*

Spirit of Húnir Awakens (Parts 1 & 2) will understand this to refer to sensing. Where you feel (or sense) energy and are able to pull information from that energy.

Because this is somewhat tricky to achieve and it takes time to develop the spirit to the point where it is able to use the energy body to read energies, you will find detailed information on each rune's scope, characteristics, effects and uses detailed in the chapters providing each rune outlines. All you need to do is to familiarise yourself with them and then imbue their energies with those characteristics or effects. We will look into this in a lot more depth when discussing each individual rune and it will become easier as you practice, until eventually it is almost automatic and effortless. This is once again one of those situations where the more you practice, the easier things become until they are so familiar that they are effortless.

Reading about each rune's effects and powers is only a quick shortcut, allowing you to proceed with your practical efforts in mastering the runes. It is well worth learning how to properly interpret them through reading the information from the rune's energies. The full explanation and practices are given in 'Runic Energy Learning'.

Know How to Tint (Colour) Them

Here we come to the one of the essential components of runic work: energy types via colour. This is where you take the first step in synchronising your runic work with the giant cosmic energy fields (there are 48 of those, two for each rune; now you can start to see why 24 runes are so essential).

When looking at colours in respect of the runes, you will often find conflicting information in various published materials. Traditionally, the runes we etched or carved into wood, leather or most commonly stones and metals, and then bled. In other words, the rune mystic would fill his blood with a given rune's power and by bleeding into the rune's carving would embody the rune's essence into the form of the rune. This process was repeated until all the runes were embodied. This is why a lot of runes these days are depicted in red (as a replacement for blood) on the basis that the red colour corresponds to the red in the blood and it would have a similar effect. Quite to the contrary, actually, but that is another matter altogether (see the chapter 'Dangers of Correspondences' p.67). This technique can, however, be used in terms of traditional colours for all the runes. The reds are symbolic of power, the greens of transition from one reality into another, the blues (specially dark blues) to trances and ecstasies of the mind, the golden hues to divinity, the violets to universal forces, whites to purity and light, and the blacks to quintessence and darkness (dull ones). Such uses, however, fall into the remit of Seiðr work rather than Galðr per se.

When dealing with Galðr, we have a simple set of rules for the colours to be used with the runes: each rune's energy has a specific universal colour unique to itself. Those are the ones we use when working with High Galdr, as our goal is to tap into those universal forces. There is a specific colour for archetypal use, which we will look at a later point in time. The other colours uses apply when unleashing Galðr in the other eight worlds. Each world has its own manifestation of the runic currents – for instance, here in Midgard ᚠ Fehu appears as a bright red, in Muspelheim it is a blinding white and in Niflheim it is a dark dull wine red, whereas in Vanaheim it appears as a blazing green colour. In this title, we are dealing with the universal colours as those are the ones that apply not only to Midgard (Earth) but also to ourselves (we are children of Midgard) and to the general outpouring of the rune's universal forces. Just changing the colour to that of one of the other worlds will simply result in a failure to synchronise with the rune's actual forces. If you wish to use the runes as they manifest in some of the other worlds, you will need to embody yourself there and cast the rune from within that world. More on this in Seiðr work, but before we can run we need to learn the basics!

As you progress in your rune work and perfect your Self, do not be surprised if the rune colours you work with change ever so slightly; the hue will change as your perceptions change. It is nothing to be concerned about and most certainly does not mean something went wrong – quite the contrary. I am including this little warning here because it happens more often than you would think.

The universal colours for each rune is given in its listing in 'The Runes' section.

Know How to Prove Them

Proving the runes is very much misunderstood. Most will struggle to logic out how one goes about proving a rune and instead rely on alternate translations of the term 'freista', or other terms such as understanding, testing and so forth get relied upon instead. 'Prove' is actually the closest and oddly enough most appropriate term when referring to the actual practices in relation to rune working.

So what is meant by proving a rune? How can one do so? The answer is actually very simple. We talked above how when we work with a given rune, the form is important, as is the colour used, and the characteristics and power need to be brought in line with the universal manifestations of that rune. The synchronisation mentioned is key and this is how you prove a rune, if done correctly, and you are able to synchronise to the universal, you will have proven it to be true. If you fail in any of those respects, you will have failed to prove it. It is only by proving a rune in this manner that you can call out to the universal runic force and proceed to ask it (see the next section) whatever it is you want to ask of the rune(s).

One important part of proving a rune involves picking the correct rune for the job at hand. You can think of this as knowing which rune to use, when to use it, and by doing so correctly, the purpose for which you are using your rune(s) and how the rune's scope of possible effects will align perfectly. This is often termed as having proven the rune in accordance with your purpose. It is very simple to understand, let us take a quick example, say you are cold and need some heat. Using the ᛁ Isa rune, which is an Ice rune, would be totally wrong as a choice; even if you are trying to banish the cold in order to use the ᛁ Isa rune, you need to connect with and synchronise with the root of all cold in existence, and that in itself would increase the level of cold you are exposed to. A fire rune would be the answer here: a fast heat ᚠ Fehu, a gradual warming up ᚲ Kenaz, ᚾ Nauthiz to twist events in order for them to lead you to a warm place, or ᚦ Thurisaz to increase your blood pressure and internal metabolic activity. Which you pick depends on your circumstance and needs. Picking the right rune for the job proves its use and your mastery in that that respect. You are in both of these cases causing a perfect harmonic synchronisation with your intent and the underlying universal intent of the runic force.

Merging all eight of these instructions and following them correctly to the point in a single rune vocalisation will result in a call out to the actual universal rune force selected. When it responds, you will have successfully proven the rune. It is this 'like attracts like' flowing from your rune work to its universal force and it responding back to your will that is the proving of your rune. This causes an energetic trinity to be born.

It is worth noting that the way we prove (and ask – see below) the runes in Galðr and Seiðr differs. These are the only two parts that change across the practices. Here we will focus on the Galðr methods.

Know How to Ask Them

This stage of the process takes pulling the runic energies into manifestation one step further. Like the previous stage, it requires a little insight into what is being asked of you.

This part of the instructions involves understanding the impact of sound. When asking for something, you typically voice your request: you express your desires, wants and needs by means of actualising the thoughts you have concerning them, by means of your voicing them. Basically, you tell someone or something what it is you want by making your thoughts into words which you speak out loud.

Sound plays a fascinating role in creation and to understand it, you need to know one fundamental energetic reality: energy imbued with sound gives it life.

It enlivens things, it makes them vibrate, and vibrations dance and interact with each other, producing more in turn which amplifies the original sounds (that is why many traditions refer to dance as an act of creation: in the Norse we have the reference to Oðinn being the 'king of singers' – in other words, the master of sound). Taking these concepts into more depth, you can see the flow of events in creation: sound vibrates, it is a facet of air, as is speech, which is interlined with intellect, which in turn gives rise to knowledge and converts it into understanding, which is then used to prove the validity and reality (life) of the rune itself. It is worth spending a little time reflecting on this in order to develop your own understanding of things.

One other fascinating key here is that the traditional air is, in our scientific age, called the electromagnetic force. That too is the root of life, for everything alive gives off some form of electric and magnetic vibration or energy. However, in Seiðr, sound is more often seen as a manifestation of elemental water than air. You can feel sound; when a strong boom or bass echoes outwards, you feel the vibrations on your skin as it touches it. Sound travels through water, and it always causes an emotional response, whether it is the blaring music at the nightclub sending you high, or a booming sound sending you into a state of fear, or even the sound of those creepy creaking floorboards, which terrify you in the middle of the night. All sound waves vibrate at given frequencies and all have a temporal frequency. The best way to think of this apparent opposition of elemental influences is simple: water in Norse terms is both fire and ice; it is a product of them both and hence has both electric and magnetic characteristics just as does its airy twin. Water and air are very much two sides of the same coin – if you think about it, both contain each other (air can be moist, water carries oxygen within), both are carriers, and both are essential to life, and breathing balances out the pH and acidity of the water in parts of our biology), both water and air can produce weightlessness – their similarities are most striking. We will look at the elemental forces in creation in Seiðr work in far more detail. For the time being, suffice it to say that sound uses these two as a means to propel itself into creation and by doing so, gains two key characteristics: life and balance.

As far as practice is concerned, we will see how each rune's name has a key sound within it which is what you vocalise (or sing, if you prefer) to enliven the energies of that rune and link it with the rune streams and rune fields in creation. This allows us to not only use the rune name but also, if need be, to unleash the full potency of that rune only by using the sound of the runic energy's vibration itself. This is one of the main reasons why I do not make much of a distinction between the various rune names when people ask if they should use the Germanic or the Iceland ones. The differences are very subtle and not worth insisting upon. Both versions contain the key sounds for the runes (although three runes have a slight variation, for reasons we will discuss later). When combined with its shape (form) and colour, it forces the influences of that rune into duality (down into manifestation). Please refer to 'Fundamentals of Runic Vocalisations' see p.71 for the practice technique(s).

This is how you ask the runes; what all this vocalisation does on the universal side of things is to use your generated sound waves to grab the attention of the intelligence of the rune's energy. It calls out to it (when done correctly). You will see, when we look at the complete practice, that so far you will have gained proficiency with these basic rune skills: to shape, establish likeness, colour and now vocalise. You will have brought your runes into a state where they have similarity in terms of colour, of likeness (in terms of characteristics and expression), of their fundamental essence (in terms established form) and now you have added vibration. This has, in effect, started to enliven them. Remember, the universal energy is not only alive but also intelligent; we need to get to the point where the rune work produces something alike to all those aspects of the universal runic forces. Two final components are needed – fortunately, those two are found in the next two set of instructions.

Know How to Sacrifice Them

This one tends to confuse everyone no end and results in all sorts of hilarious interpretations and practices. It is important to understand that the English word sacrifice is not, technically speaking, the correct one to use in translation. The old Norse term used here, 'blóta', does not really fit well with the English word sacrifice. To understand this better it is worth looking at what the actual 'blót' is referencing: a sacramental feast or meal would be the correct way to contextualise this. It is commonly used to also mean 'blood sacrifice'. The difficulty most readers have is how to contextualise this in terms of the runes. As usual, the traditional teachings are hinted at here but never fully explained, and once you look at those, it will make perfect sense. The *Hávamál* is just that: pointers to knowledge taught individually, rather than being put into written format.

There are a few important energetic components to a 'sacrificial' meal, which unsurprisingly also occur in cases of ritually sacrificed meats you regularly consume these days. Certain mainstream religions require meats to be obtained from animals killed in specific religious manner and ceremony. Such acts produce the same end results as a sacrificial meal blót, but with energies that are alien to those who are not part of those religions. As a side-note, it would be best not to consume such meats, or if no alternative is available to you, use the rune ᚺ Hagalaz to purge those energies from them before consumption.

What happens during such ceremonies is fascinating: the life force of the animal is slowly and typically painfully drained out. It is then sent to or consumed by the deity to whom the ceremony is dedicated. As a return flow for this life essence, energy from that deity is sent back and absorbed by the meat of the animal. The more pain and suffering generated, the greater the spill and activation of the life force – remember, emotion generates release and loss of power (megin). Just imagine how terrifying it can be to knowingly have the life siphoned out of you as you bleed slowly in agony until death takes you. A most unpleasant experience to say the least, but one which produces maximum outpouring of essence. The universal laws of ᛈ Gebo require an equivalent return for the exchange and what you get is the energy of whomever you sacrificed the life of the animal to.

With a sacrificial feast, the same rules apply except the outpouring of life is much more limited: because it is done during the course of a celebration, the life force of the participants is carried along with the sacrificed foods. This can, depending on the emotional state of those participants, generate even greater outpouring of energy in the form of pure megin. When the gods or goddesses receive all this energy and life, a return flow occurs. This will typically be energy from their domain or type that matches it. For instance, if you sacrifice a jug of mead to say, Thor, you will get a combative, invigorating strong masculine energy back, if you do so to Oðinn, the return energy is one which can bolster your mind and send you into ecstatic trances of the consciousness. Freya's can increase the love frequency, bolster Seiðr powers and even increase fortitude and wealth in your life and so forth. Meats absorb energy extremely well; it is pretty much automatic, with pork and beef being the two most efficient in this respect. All other foods will need to have the return flow imbued into them. In the old days, this was done by the priest or priestess of sacrifices.

Whoever consumes such foods or meats will take into themselves the energies which were returned as part of the sacrificial exchange. This is why one needs to be very careful about eating these types of foods – taking in an energy which is harmful or adverse to one's inherited energy system can cause a lot of harm. Foods can also passively absorb energy. Most of what we buy in supermarkets has had its natural energies purged to such an extent that it will simply pick up anything from anyone. A person who is negative, or someone angry or worried can easily pass by and the food will siphon off small amounts of that not-so-lovely energy. Why? You cannot have something with no energy in existence: destroy the energy of any living thing and it will siphon up energy from wherever it can get hold of any (ᚾ Nauthiz principles at play here). Now I will let you work out what happens when you consume that! The answer is simply either don't – get your food off local farms where farmers really care for their animals and love them (extremely positive energy there) – or if that is not possible, use High Galdr with the ᚺ Hagalaz rune to purify it before consuming it.

Back to our topic at hand: so how do we apply this to the runes? Two ways: first we need to complete the runic energy and then we need to sacrifice it to the rune itself and wait for the return flow. This forms part and parcel of the synchronisation with the universal rune forces we have touched upon in the previous sections.

Scoring a rune or sacrificing it is a very simple practice for a mystic who wields runic energy. If you think of all these instructions as stages in the process of unleashing runic power, you will see up to this point you will have gathered a lot of runic energy, enlivened it and forced it to manifest into the energetic levels of reality. You are, in a few words, wielding an aspect of life; it is something living by this stage (well, almost). When studying the life force, you will see that all life in existence starts in exactly this fashion (we will cover all this at a later point in time). What is implied by sacrificing is the sending off of this living energy in exchange for a like energy from its universal source.

Before you move onto sending it off to do something (which is, interestingly, the next part of the *Hávamál* instructions), you have got one final component to add to the rune energy: a sensation. Sensing, or what one can term a non-physical touch type of feeling, is an essential component of life. It is so important that this sense is one of the fundament parts of our Self at the highest level of our identity: the Óðr. All things that exist are felt (sensed). Some of you might know that when one dies, one gradually loses the ability to feel.

What this part of the traditional knowledge tells us is that a lot of spirits opt to incarnate into flesh in order to regain this ability. What they do not tell us – well, not those known to the mainstream in any case – is that while here in flesh and on Midgard a spirit (Óðr) can be trained to sharpen this skill to such a point that it becomes limitless, thereby making it a permanent feature of its very being. This type of enhanced sensing reveals everything; people find it very disturbing when they come into contact with individuals who are in possession of this type of sense because they can know everything about everyone – well, whatever they focus on. You see, there is no such thing as privacy; everything is energy and all energy can be sensed, provided you know where you focus your attention. It takes herculean effort and complex rune work to hide anything in the grander scheme of things, which is possible but so rare and complex that it is a waste of time except for a few circumstances. Our time is best used for evolutionary practices than it is to hide in this manner. Back to the runes: each rune has a specific life essence, and they all express some part or other of the totality of the life streams in creation. Because of this, we are able to gain specific sensations from each of the runic energies and corresponding forces.

Those sensations are used when working with the rune energies. By imbuing exactly the same sensations to our rune as its universal counterpart, we achieve perfect harmonisation with it, as you will have seen in *The Blood of Lóðurr Awakens* when you were working on sensing your own energy body (Hamr) sensations, and the very act of experiencing how something feels leads to an establishing of contact. In this case, connecting you with the universal rune energy. Its enlivening process, up to this point, is then set alight with the final spark and in such a manner as to bring it into perfect harmonious vibration with the universal one. It is only then that we can send it, for then you are truly working with like attracting like.

On the practical side of things, because you need to imbue the energy with the correct sensation (or feeling), there will be two main parts. The first is to do this and complete the enlivening of your rune energy, the second will involve the sacrificing part and obtaining the return flow (from the universal rune's energy). Fortunately, the actual practical side of things is quite simple (in terms of Galðr, but not so for Seiðr work).

For our purposes now, you will have to imbue the vibrations of your runic energy with certain feelings. These are traditionally linked to the elemental influences: fire, air, water, earth and ice. In modern terms, we link them to the scientific ones: strong nuclear force (electric), electromagnetic force (neutral-balanced), weak nuclear force (magnetism), gravitational and stasis. Please refer to the chapter 'Runic Energy Sensations' p.77 for the actual practice. Additionally, for those of you who want to play with the polarity of runes, this is where you can tap into the individual polarities via sensing those characteristics (polarities will be discussed in the advanced topics, but you will need to master the basics first).

Know How to Send Them

This one is simple yet so many make a total mess out of this instruction. Believe it or not, I have even had someone tell me that they put their rune work on paper and actually send it off by mail to their target!

Let us be clear from the outset: that is NOT the type of sending referred to.

Here you have a few alternatives for how to execute this instruction. For ordinary Galðr and Seiðr work, you would typically send off the energy by thought or directing it via spell-weaving (this is what the stories of old used by the Völva were for). In terms of High Galdr, since we will be using it for influencing our lives, and those of our friends and family, as well as working on the cosmic and archetypal levels, we use Intent to send off the living runic energy. Imbuing things with intent is a universal way of directing energy towards specific goals. The advantage you have is that with Intent, you can use it in all levels and dimensions of reality. Intent is an important key in all higher practices; it is a universal force which human beings can partake of. Much about how to access true intent has been covered in my previous publications, so there is no need to add dozens of pages to repeat the same here. A good summary of all the Intent material can be found in *Roadmap to High Galdr Rune Work* (p.145) 'The Great Mystery of Intent' or spread across *The Spirit of Húnir Awakens (Parts 1 & 2)* and *The Blood of Lóðurr Awakens* titles.

What we do need to do next is look at is how and when Intent is introduced into our High Galdr. For this, you will need to decide not only what rune you want to work with but also what do with it, or what goal you want to set it to achieve. This should match the scope of the rune's influence and whatever your aimed usage is. It ties back into knowing how to interpret and ask them.

One final component needed is that of time – well only in certain cases. From a practical point of view, when you imbue your living runic energy with time, you are letting it go. It separates it from your scope of influence, very much like branching out. The seed drops from the tree under the influence of its own time/fate. When working with runic forces, you will have to set when their effects start and for how long they last, or you can set a starting point and end point (when the effects should stop). Providing your gravity (or condensation) is sufficient, those energies will exercise strong effects until their time is over. The formula for time to goal achievement or amount of influence exercised by your rune work is simple: *amount of energetic gravity + time = strength of influence exercised over each point in time* (in human terms: each second). If you are seeking to reach a goal, it becomes *strength of energetic gravity + time = speed to goal*. The stronger your gravity, the less time it needs to reach the desired outcome. The weaker the gravity, the less effect over time you get. To increase the effects, either increase the energetic gravity or decrease the amount of time it exercises its influences.

    This takes a little thinking to grasp but it is well worth getting to grips with – or at least the underlying concepts. If you want a big bang effect, you need to produce a massive energetic gravity over a very short period of time. If you want a strong protective shield, you want strong gravity over a longer period of time. If you want a healing effect, you want a weaker gravity over a short period of time OR a stronger gravity over a longer period of time. Both of these will provide a gentle healing energy outflow without overloading the body or burning it out! These few examples should prove to be a good starting point in your reflections on this matter.

Final notes on time: if you want to exercise your runic influence on purely energetic things (such as the energy body), spirit or the archetypal level of reality time is excluded, the dimensionality of time manifests AFTER those levels and hence time has no effects there. Those are entirely timeless realms in reality. It is only a matter of energetic gravity in those cases, as you are working in a timeless dimensionality. You will also need to intend the runic forces to spill over or condense into wherever you want the effects to happen: into the energy body for energetic effects, the spirit for spiritual effects, the mind for mental effects and the Fylgja or the Önd (breath) for archetypal effects. Providing you have worked with those parts of the Self, they should automatically be responding by now. This can finally allow you to grasp why it was so important to get a basic familiarity and use of the various parts of your Self before embarking on High Galdr itself. Without that, doing these practices would have proven most difficult, if not impossible, causing all sorts of a mis-match of results at best or proving to be completely ineffective at worst.

Know How to Discard (Send) Them

Discarding a rune is simple – actually at first, it might appear extremely simple. The underlying concept is a discarding of all the rune energy, power or force, letting them go on their way to do whatever it is you needed them to do. This is why sometimes the alternative interpretation of 'send' also fits here. Energetically, what we are doing is actually discarding the rune from our awareness by sending it off to do its job. As far as the rune worker is considered, all the rune force is in fact discarded from him or her (unless the goal of the rune work was to cause a change within, and even then, some discarding takes place). When the discarding is done, even thoughts of the rune work are discarded and not returned to. Thinking about what you did would only cause interference and distortion as to what happens. Why? Because the rune forces don't always take the path into manifestation you would expect. We never ever ever direct how it manifests, just what the end result is going to be. In this way, things can take their course towards the goal you have set by using the path of least resistance or the most appropriate way to manifest. It can produce some rather interesting surprises, to say the least.

There are a number of different ways to perform a proper discarding of the rune forces. Here it will depend entirely on how you want to proceed and more just as importantly on what you are trying to achieve. Let us go through a number of example scenarios.

Assuming you are trying to make something happen in life, whether it is increasing wealth, winning a court case, gaining a new job, finding a love, seeking out some sort of opportunity or removing something from your life, all these are ultimately speaking the same, as far as discarding is concerned. As you will see, the scope of action is an event or situation in your life which is sought or to be changed, but one which is outside of the Self. Discarding in these situations simply involves sending out the forces into the world. This is done in a straightforward manner by visualising the shape of the rune you are working with, then willing all the runic force within you to pour out into that shape. Once you no longer feel anything of the rune within and you have a pulsating rune outside of your Self, you can will it off into the world. As you see it fly away (or sink into the ground) or shoot off, you let go of everything you have done and go about doing something other than rune work, to make a clear break in any of the connection your mind has left over.

In situations where you need to cause an influence emanating from you into your immediate environment, such as making yourself more attractive, boosting your confidence, or augmenting some part of yourself when interacting with people, instead of pouring that rune force into the shape of the rune and sending it away, you would make all the force flow into your aura, willing it to radiate from there and affect everything (or everyone) you come into contact with. A healer using this method along with the ᚢ Uruz rune force can work wonders just by willing it to radiate about him or her and walking into a hospital ward, setting the rune to alleviate ills or boost healing speed of anyone you come into contact with (for goodness' sake, avoid getting creative and walking into an infectious area!). Another such application would be to use the ᚺ Hagalaz rune and set it to radiate about you, clearing the space of all external spiritual and energetic influences. This is a solid reset button on all the energies you come into contact with, purifying them and purging any external influences (be careful not to purge a space in which you store charged items, or you might forget to exclude them and purge everything!). You can even expand the radius of radiation of the rune force to instantly wipe clean an entire room or building!

Other useful tricks involve infusion the rune force into your physical body. For instance, using a ᚦ Thurisaz rune force to enhance aggression with ᚢ Uruaz to boost strength and setting it up to run until after a gym session will increase your physical strength in the gym! <Kenaz can be use the same way to force a fat burning response. Just take it slow when affecting your body or any other part of the Self; it does place a strain on the nervous system and on the energy systems. It also takes our biology some practice to get used to and understand what effect is happening to it. Overdoing it or trying to rush things too fast can cause you health problems and all sorts of other energetic issues. Slow and steady is the key! When you have infused your body with the said energy, you simply move onto thinking and doing something else. Distract yourself from the runes, from what you have done and what you might or might not expect to happen. Only after the time you have set has run out should you look back and observe just how effective it was. Personally, I would recommend a good hour or two after the effect should have ended. In the example of the gym, when you get back home, have food and rest up, then think back and compare how you did, whether there were any noticeable effects and so on. In case of the rune force flowing about you and affecting the environment, the same rule applies. Wait for a good while before thinking about how it went but never fail to perform an objective analysis of the effects: when it fails, acknowledge it, and when it works do the same. It is only by being brutally honest with yourself and discarding all other possibilities that you can genuinely determine whether your rune work has indeed caused changes within you or within the world.

  You will notice over time that with repetition, results not only manifest but it becomes easier to do the entire practice. That is what we want. You should also notice that the effects are far more powerful the more you work at it. Your entire Self will naturally progress and synchronise with the runes, allowing more of the rune force to be generated and manipulated according to your intent. It takes assuming the best possible skills and circumstances about 6 months to get a good solid grasp of a single rune. For ones you struggle with, it can take from 9 to 12 months. It might appear to be a long time, but in the grand scheme of things, it is not because during the entire time, you are building up small results, which are cumulative. It is not a matter of fail or succeed. It is a matter of scaling up the level of success where you start at 0% and fail, then move up towards your first 10% success, which might appear tiny, to the point where you question whether there even was a response, then 20-30%, where you could just swear you noticed something but are not quite sure you did. Once you hit the 40%+ success level, it becomes noticeable and doubt no longer comes to mind. Eventually at 70%+, you no longer even bother questioning things and automatically recognise the effects without even looking for them. Keep at it; things start hard but they do eventually become easier. Build on the small successes, and you will eventually get to the bigger ones. This is why it is often recommended to start with smaller goals; they are easier to achieve and prove to have less resistance to manifesting. Such small goals are ideal for when you are building up your skills with a new rune, simply because you can move from the 0% success to the 100% so much faster and with less effort than you would be able to for a larger one. Your goal at this stage is not to make any grandiose thing occur; instead, it is to build familiarity with the rune's energies, its forces and the practices.

There you have it: the rune method from within the *Hávamál* has now been revealed to you fully. This will form the basis of all your work in High Galdr. We will look at additional workings, practices and theories which you can put to use to augment your powers and skills just after taking a quick look at the full technique itself – see 'Using High Galdr – Technique' p.79.

    This, ladies and gents, is how actual Galðr is done. A lack of understanding of these intricate processes and insights into the teachings that compliment these instructions results in ineffective or weak outcomes of runic work. Let us now turn to the detailed and complete techniques that bring all these elements together.

Runic Energy Learning

When trying to learn directly from runic forces, it is important to understand how this works. It is a very different form of learning, and one can be forgiven for labelling a direct transference of knowing rather than learning as a process. It differs greatly from what we are used to in several ways. The more noticeable is that when learning from energy, you gain knowing without learning per se, and this knowing is then transferred back to the conscious levels by ways of perfectly clear and precise insights, direct information or memories from somewhere other than your usual recall. You can think of it as a set of rapid 'aha' moments which your conscious mind then uses as a springboard to further understanding, allowing it to reach deeper into whatever subject matter you are 'learning' from.

When your consciousness is being assaulted by these 'aha' moments, you need to stop whatever you might be doing or thinking of and actually get involved in the thinking about these insights. Most people will gain a realisation in this manner but either be preoccupied by something else or try to remember it for processing later on. This critical mistake is what robs them of all the benefits of such insights or spontaneous knowing. Why? Simply due to our physiology and how it functions. This type of insight is a higher form of knowledge, which imposes itself in a flash on our brains. It activates entire neural networks inside your brain, which either were never connected previously or did not even exist (it forms temporary loose new connections). Because this is so incredibly new, these new activations of neurons in the brain are very fragile and temporary. If you actively engage in thinking and working out whatever insights you may have gained, you will strengthen these connections rapidly to the point where they are accessible later on. Each time you do so, the stronger they get, the easier it becomes to remember, and the more energy you ground in your brain's new physical structure. Done properly, you are basically seizing the moment and hardwiring it into yourself to use as and when you need or want to. If you ignore it or put it off for later, then whatever you think of next will simply overwrite new connections and the neural networks of your brain will re-configure to purge out these new ones, because your conscious mind has deemed them unnecessary. The more often you do this, the quicker and more adept your brain becomes to processing knowledge in this manner, and the easier it will be. This wiring of neural structures is how we learn as infants and throughout our lives. As your brain matures, it gets better and more efficient, but it also becomes more hard-wired. It is, when thought about, very simple and logical.

 Back to the runes and learning from them. When accessing a rune's energy to gain knowledge from it, its energy is like a laser beam of information and awareness, or rather intelligence, but essentially a different and unknown form of intellect to our understanding. Because we are also beings of energy and our energy is both intelligent and aware, we can communicate with such universal information directly. The moment this beam of runic energy hits our energy sphere (aura), it synchronises with the internal awareness, which is like countless threads of light within our energy body. Should you successfully synchronise, the external universal (intelligent) runic energy beam spills into the corresponding energy thread inside you. Energy flows from the external into the internal and pools on the inside of our auric field (which is actually your energy body, not just a pulsing of energy from within, as commonly believed). This causes a reflection, which our own internal perceptions receive in the form of those flashes of knowing and new insights. They can be interpreted by our minds as events, information, objects, new connections between theories, new ways of looking at a given problem and so forth. Do not automatically assume that all these insights are true in terms of what you know. When our minds interpret them, they often get muddled with wishful thinking, imagined things and illusions. This is why we develop a sharp silent mind to cut through all that nonsense. The way we interpret these universal truths is based on our own understanding and knowing. Yes, it stretches it out and pushes them into new territory, but by the very fact that when learning to do this requires this interpretation, it can lead to misconceptions, self-delusions and misinterpretations, most of which are due to the conscious mind and how it tries to ascertain this new information. The conscious mind has an annoying tendency of muddling things up in sometimes the most spectacular ways. The only firm way to avoid falling into this pitfall is to validate everything, test things out, try things out, ask other people to try things out, and ask if logic can interpret things. Ask if you use this or that, what effects it will produce. And most importantly, ask if it is anything that makes you feel great or important, as that is a major red flag, and an ego-boosting set of interpretations is practically always incorrect. Our minds are extraordinary receptors to things floating about in the mental level of reality, which unfortunately makes us very prone to manipulations and illusions. Be firm, and discipline your mind with an iron fist! Always. In time you will learn to recognise these things and automatically push them to the side when they try to interfere (for more information on mind and spirit, please refer to *The Spirit of Húnir Awakens - Parts 1 & 2*).

Back to the issue of information reading from energy. This mechanism of 'interpreting' reality is one of the reasons why saying that the world is not real or is an illusion has gained so much popularity, as it is in effect a reflection which is entirely dependent on our own level of perception and awareness. Each person will have a different perception of what 'reality' is and will have different 'strands' of intelligent energy they can perceive (this is dependent on their 'auric' field, hvels and their capabilities).

When we look at each individual rune, its scope of action, its powers and the functions of its energy, always remember in those energies is also the information and the knowledge of how to apply these effects and what they are. For instance, when looking at the ᚾ Uruz rune, you will often see that it is strongly associated with healing in all its shapes and forms. It is the ultimate healer's rune (along with ᚹ Wunjo and ᚲ Pertho). But this does not only refer to the power to heal; it also refers to the knowledge on how to apply this rune's powers to perform whatever healing is necessary. Understanding and mastering how to gain that know-how from the rune's energy is an invaluable skill to develop and is referred to in the *Hávamál* as knowing to interpret (or read) the rune. It is wise to keep in mind that you can only build knowing gradually and this, in the case of human beings, is typically firmly rooted in our interests, experiences and abilities, although there are exceptions. To put this in context, someone who has been practicing healing or even medicine for many years will be able to gain far greater knowing from ᚢUruz energy than someone who has just started yesterday. The runic energy builds upon what you already know; it expands current knowing and capabilities and awakens potential capabilities. In the case of our medic or healer, this will be vastly superior to the newcomer. Both will benefit but at a different level of expertise and ability. Someone who has no healing or medical knowledge, has no interest in the field, no ancestral capacity and has just decided to embark on healing will have the least benefit. He or she will have to start from the first step and might even struggle to synchronise with the energy to establish that connection needed for knowing to flow. Should they give up? Definitely not; that would be defeat before even trying, but it is worth knowing that it will require more effort, time and practice than for someone else. We all move at our own speed and in our own direction; remember, creation favours that which is unique, hence we are all diverse and different from each other. That is how it is meant to be. So struggle with the runes and fields of expertise which are not a given to you; doing so will help you build perseverance and a powerful will. Never give up on your dreams... conquer them!

If you have absolutely no interest or desire to get involved in healing, don't, and if like myself you have strong ability but don't like using it, don't. Everything happens in its own time here on Midgard (Earth). ᚢ Uruz has many other wonderful secrets to share besides healing.

Energy to Information: Using the Rune Energy for Information

Start off by going through the section 'High Galdr – The Technique' see p. 79. Having run through those 15 steps, you will be at a point where the energy of the rune is pulsing in and about you. Sit quietly in the rune's energy, bathe in it, feel it and sense it. Allow that energy to 'speak' to you and imbue you with the knowledge it contains. Still your mind and allow thoughts to flood it from the rune's influence. Observe and take note but do not analyse yet, let the rune's energy steer your thinking along its force's flow. Once you are done with these observations, simply dissipate the rune's energy and then proceed to ponder upon whatever information you have gleamed from it. Analyse it all; does it make sense to you? Is it in conflict with the rune's underlying characteristics? If it is discard it and restart. How does it relate to what you already know? What hints at future knowledge does it provide? What do you not yet understand? Take note of all these questions and learn from them. Remember to focus on your sensing; do not limit yourself to thoughts, sounds, feelings, or images. The trick here is to avoid limiting your perceptions to their usual scope of functioning, and instead open them up more and more each time you practice this and gather additional information and insight. This is the only way you will be able to eventually read the rune fully. Once done, simply let it dissolve and fade away until none is left. Take a few moments to run through whatever you may have read of the rune. If need be, take notes.

When decoding the knowledge you have received always keep in mind runes are universal forces. Should any of the information be related to you personally, or impact your life directly be very cautious. It is most likely not genuine, these forces do no care for any single being, they are impersonal and universal. They only ever provide knowledge relating the universal/general applications of rune energy, forces and powers. They never speak about you specifically or anyone in your life, when this happens it is not coming from the runic forces.

High Galdr: Runes & Rune Secrets

Dangers of Correspondences

This is a very popular modern-day concept when it comes to many traditions and methodologies. It might come as a surprise to many to consider that it is inherently based on a flawed understanding of its fundamental conceptions. Let us look a little deeper into what is meant by this.

When considering what is typically understood as a correspondence, you can see very rapidly why it is flawed. A correspondence is usually understood in the following manner: one concept, object, thought, desire, energy or so forth is taken as being equivalent on another based on their 'likeness' or similarity. Let us look at this in terms of runes and the tarot cards, which are all too familiar territory to most. Take the rune ᛋ Sowilo, for instance, which is often said to correspond to the Sun tarot card. Why? Because they share certain fundamental similarities: they both express solar influences, generative powers, life giving principles and prosperity and both are typically (erroneously) deemed to be masculine. With all this in common, they are said to correspond to one another and hence are interchangeable in energetic terms. This is of course a highly simplified view of the matter, in terms of our example, but even at this level it falls foul of the underlying energetic realities. What it does illustrate all too well is how the entire concept of correspondences fails on one level, and that is simply this: the two things which correspond to each other share an energetic commonality but that does not fundamentally make them interchangeable or even like each other. They might have a frequency likeness, but that does not by any stretch of any definition make them alike. It is the same as saying that being in a relationship would make those two individuals interchangeable because of the initial likeness they shared (which is why they were pulled towards each other and ended up a couple). See how it is ultimately absurd? The same applies to energetic realities: 'as above so below, as below so above' comes to mind here, the cosmic principle of the Irminsul.

The same applies to the misunderstanding of how numerology works. Just because certain things express the same energetic principles (as indicated by them expressing the same laws in terms of numbers) does not mean they are one and the same, nor that they express those same laws at the same levels of reality or in the same ways! What the entire concept of correspondences is, nothing more than the attempts of limited awareness (and minds) to bridge into the abstract without having the experiential and perceptual development needed to separate the wheat from the chaff. That is why fundamentally it is incorrect to say that the Sun tarot card corresponds to the ᛋ Sowilo rune. Take the following into account with the following example: the life-giving formative characteristics expressed by the Sun card are found expressed by the ᚢUruz rune, the enlightenment finds expression in the ᛞDagaz rune, the prosperity characteristics are found in ᚠFehu and ᛟOthala and so forth, it is only the initial outpouring of Light and expansive power which is expressed by ᛋSowilo. Even the gender correspondences fall flat in reality because the Sun is feminine whereas the ᛋ Sowilo rune in the energetic realities is masculine.

The very concept of correspondences was used in terms of pulling as many 'things' with likeness together in order to enhance their common energetic frequency. This was most often used in 'rituals' of some sort or other, when the underlying goal was to bring together as many things as possible that represent the energetic current of that ritual. This would in turn cause a strong harmonic echo with that energy, enabling the practitioner to direct it along his or her desires. Naturally, we do not bother with those processes; when using High Galdr, there is no need for all that. All you do is elevate your awareness and utter the runes in the correct manner with intent to unleash effects which are far superior to what one person could ever achieve on their own otherwise. You will have trained your body, mind, and all other parts of the Self up to this point in order to make this a very simple process, and then connecting with the runic energy will provide the springboard needed. You could think of it as the former being the attempts of a newly emerging child's mind trying to reach up to his or her goal by taking baby steps, needing crutches and help to get from point 1 to 9, and the latter as the adult being at step 9 already and simply applying his or her knowledge, will and intent, not needing the baby steps – because moving from 1 to 9 has become such a natural thing to do, it is done almost reflexively. Actually, if we are going to be accurate, the adult in this scenario would have evolved to the point where their awareness sits at about 7 or 8 of this 1-to-9 scale rather than at the 1. The hard work in developing the Self will have not only elevated it to this point but also grounded it at that level. What we work with are actual energetic colours, the sounds with which they vibrate, the sensations which flow through them and the characteristics of the force of those runes; there is actually no need for any type of correspondence, as we work with actual forces of the runes and as such gain a degree of precision exceeding those of simple correspondences.

This and the fact that runes represent unique cosmic emanations is the reason why we will not work with correspondences. They are simply not only unnecessary but also introduce too many flaws into the process and outcomes you are striving towards. We leave those things for those who need them – we do not. In Seiðr work, you will encounter some of them because they are used to symbolise various parts of the Self and expressions of the Self in the external realities – in other words, they are symbolic vehicles for characteristics of the Self, but even then their uses are fairly limited.

Fundamentals of Rune Vocalisations

When it comes to rune vocalisations, a little lesson in sound and music is required here. Each rune's sound 'wave' matches exactly one of the frequencies found in the musical solfège. Most of us have at some point or other of our childhood schooling been taught these. Those of you unfamiliar with this might recall the Sound of Music movie or musical (by Rodgers and Hammerstein, 1959). There was a song in there teaching young viewers this very solfège. Rather than get lost in the entire song, let us look at the important part, namely the underlying solfège syllables, which go along the lines of:

Do (Doe), Re (Ray), Mi (Me), Fa (Far), Sol (Sew), La (La), Ti (Tea), Do (Doe)

The words in parenthesis are the English words that phonetically match the solfège syllables. The pitch in your voice for each of these increases upwards until you hit the 'Ti' which should be the top pitch. For the final 'Do', you bring back the pitch of your voice to the lowest and push it a bit lower than the initial one.

For those musically educated, you can also make use of the full octave along the basic scale: C-D-E-F-G-A-B-C.

Back to the runes; as you can see, these match the eight runes per Ætt perfectly and this is not by means of coincidence. These also match the eight universal sounds which, when sung in perfect harmony, gives rise to the ninth as they combine in perfect unison. For our current purposes, it gives us an exact guide to vocalising each rune along the correct scale. The vocal scale of each rune is listed alongside the other rune's characteristics in 'The Runes' section.

When you vocalise your ᚠ Fe, ᚺ Hagal, and ᛏ Tiwaz do it along the initial Do vocal range (they are deep-sounding vibrations). Progress upwards until you have practiced the right pitch for each rune. This part is probably the most important of all because it serves two key purposes: firstly it harmonises your rune vocalisation with its universal frequency of that rune, and most importantly, it enlivens it. It is the sound, via controlled breath, which gives a rune life. Only once you enliven it and it becomes living energy or force can you send it out (as instructed in the *Hávamál*).

The practice in this section requires you to go through each rune in sequential order and learn to chant its name. Pick either Germanic, Icelandic, or even just the sound letter itself or do them all! But do not switch mid-practice. If you start with Germanic, do all the runes using the Germanic and vice versa, in the correct scale as given in the table above. When you have learnt to do so, pick the runes at random (or in any order you prefer) and make sure you can still chant it at the correct frequency. You are not visualising or imagining anything here; this practice is purely based on phonetics.

The next stage of the practice is to do the same but only using the sound (you are imagining the sound only in your mind). If you need to, you can still pretend to chant it out but no physical sound should leave your lips. It is all mental.

The final stage involves whispering the rune names. This is done in two ways. The first is to simply replicate the same thing you did when chanting them out loud. A simple no-nonsense version of the name. The second part of this involves bringing the whisper from deeper within, thus slightly elongating the rune's name. For example, the first version is simply a 'Fehu', nice short and firm. The second would be a 'Fehhhhoooo' – you need to feel this emanating from deep inside of you, taking up all the breath in your lungs (without straining!).

Once you have mastered those, there is one final set of vocalisations you need to be able to do. They are not used in this title but for the sake of completeness are included (it also avoids you having to backtrack). Here you will split the vocalisation across two types. What this means is that you start your rune vocals in one mode and finish them in another. Let us take ᚠ Fehu as an example again: you would start with the 'Fe' part as a mental vocalisation (no sound spoken) and finish the 'hu' part as a full-voiced one (not whispered), then inverse this. Follow on by starting the 'Fe' as a mental and finish with the 'hu' in the whispered mode. When you have mastered this, you can proceed with inverting it. Finally, you would do the 'Fe' spoken and the 'hu' whispered. To finish things off, we have the 'Fe' whispered and the 'hu' spoken out loud.

In effect what you are doing can be summarised as being:

1. Spoken out loud.
2. Only mentally (nothing is spoken, just imagined).
3. Whispered (in a normal fashion, like when you speak the rune name).
4. Whispered (in a deeper elongated way)
5. First half of the rune name only mentally sounded and the second half spoken out loud.
6. First half of the rune name spoken out loud and the second half is mentally sounded only (this is the inverse to what you did in 6 above).
7. First half is mentally sounded and the second half whispered.
8. First half is then whispered and the second half is mentally sounded (the opposite of what you did in 7).
9. First half spoken loud and second half whispered.
10. First half whispered and second half spoken (the inverse of what you did in 9).

Do all these practices without visualising anything other than the actual form or shape of the rune (if you need to). Should you not need to visualise anything when practicing the vocalisation then even better.

What all these practices do is not only teach you how to vocalise each rune's name at the correct frequency but also enable you to start synchronising the sound waves you produce with the universal runic frequencies for each rune. The reason you use the different vocalisation types: no physical sound, whispered, deep whisper and out loud is simply because they produce different results and affect different parts of our Self and reality.

1. Mentally sounded only (not spoken out) will always affect the archetypal levels, the mental and spiritual levels ONLY.
2. Whispered runes will always effect the above AND energy body as well as the energy realities in a broader sense.
3. Whispered deeply runes effect all the parts in mentioned under 1 AND the shadow Self (Sal) and shadow realms. It will not affect the general energy body or the energy realities.
4. A rune spoken out loud will always affect all these levels including the physical body and physical reality.

This gives you a good set of tools to direct the flow of runic power with precision to the part of reality (or your Self) you wish to affect. Remember it well.

The practices where you start with the first half of a rune's name in one mode and switch to another for the second part takes this to an even more interesting level of precision. Here what you are doing is causing the runic power to flow from one part of reality (or the Self) into another. For instance, where you use ᚠ Fehu by whispering the first 'Fe' part and then speaking out loud the final 'hu', you will be using the ᚠ Fehu forces from the shadow or energy levels of reality and dragging their effects into the physical and so forth. As mentioned above, this does not really constitute part of the materials covered in this title but is a pretty essential practice for more advanced work and for Seiðr work. It is definitely worth investing the little extra time at this point in time, in order to gain this skill. Should you opt not to, it is your decision to make and you will definitely not be at a loss for any of the other practices covered in here, but you might have to return to all this and restart the whole training with those additional runic vocalisations if, at a later time, you opt to start some of the practices which require them. As always work at your own pace and time.

Runic Energy Sensations

What you want to do is take each rune in turn and as you visualise its shape and form, feel the associated sensation. Visualise the rune in front of you and see it radiating its universal colour. As this radiating energy makes contact with you, the elemental sensation for that rune will be felt. If you do not feel it automatically, it is permissible to image it. Eventually, as you gain proficiency, you will start to automatically feel it. Do this for every rune; you can find the runic sensation information in 'The Runes' section.

Let us take an example to illustrate this. When visualising the rune ᚠ Fehu, feel an outpouring expansive explosive heat radiating out of the rune as you see its vibrant red energy pulsate out towards you. Spend a few moments in mediation under the effects of this rune's energy, then let it fade away. Do this with all the runes one after the other until you have completed the entire set. Then, pick the runes at random (or in any order you choose) and repeat the practice with those specific rune.

You should get to the point where no matter which rune you think of, you can immediately, off the top of your head, just by visualising its form, feel the relevant sensations flowing out of it and see the colour of its energy pulsating. This needs to be almost automatic and totally effortless. Be persistent with your work.

Using High Galdr
The Technique

Time to start pulling what has been discussed so far into the beginning of a final practice. Here you are in effect working with the first part of the actual practice, which will be expanded below. It is important not to rush and to take this part slowly because here you will learn about the keys to getting all your Galðr to work. Practicing this technique, you will understand exactly what Oðinn meant when he instructed Loddfáfnir:

> [...] 'it would be good for you if you
> get them,
> useful if you take them in,
> needful if you absorb them.'[12]

First pick a rune, it can be any rune, your favourite one, one you feel the most excited about, one you are most curious about, one you feel a pull towards, or best of all, one you are most familiar with. Not to worry if you have more than one; whatever rune you choose at this point does not fix anything for any future practices, so feel free to change at any time (just not mid-practice!).

Start by sitting down, taking a few deep breaths and move your attention away from daily life. You can always deal with whatever needs to be dealt with later on. Now is rune time!

Start by visualising the shape of the rune. You can do all this work either with eyes closed or open. Should you decide to keep your eyes open, when you visualise the rune you need to see it floating mid-air right in front of you. It needs to be so real that it looks as real as any other object you might gaze upon. In your mind, there should be no distinction between the solidity of your rune and say the wall or tree or whatever is in front of you. In cases where you close your eyes for this, you need to visualise your rune in the blackness of the back of your eyelids straight in front of you (we are not using the out-of-focus sides trick at this point).

Once you have your rune there and are focussing in on it, you need to spend a few minutes reflecting on all the things about this rune you know of. Use 'The Runes' outlines to get the key characteristics from its scope of influence. Here is when you want to recall them all and feel them as if they were flowing out of the rune itself. Let us put this in context; rather than keep giving examples with ᚠ Fehu, let us look at the mother rune: ᛒ Berkano. With ᛒ Berkano, you would feel the feminine energy of nurturing, you would feel the material dark powers of the 'subconscious' pulsing out of the rune, you would feel the womb of creation's processes nurturing a future life form. You would feel the pain associated with birthing, you would feel renewed essence just waiting to rip out of its domain, and you would feel the seclusion from the world and existence.

The mysteries of the hidden and secret flow strong from this rune. Do not worry if you cannot pin all these down in the first attempt; all you need to do is get a glimpse of something which feels like it. Naturally, working with this rune is easiest for mothers, then women and is most difficult for the young. For men, it should be avoided. It is used here as an example; pick another should you want to. The trick is to use a rune you can connect with easiest, and leave the harder ones for later.

When you are happy with this part, keep the sensations of all those things flowing but now tint the rune's shape with the dark green colour (ᛒ Berkano's energy universal colour). Allow all those feelings of the influences of the rune to flow within the energy and its dark greens. Spend a little time willing the energy to increase in strength and imagine each time it makes contact with any part of your body that it sends a strong sense of all those sensations over you. On the skin, it feels like a mother's touch, and in that touch the very mystery of motherhood washes over you. For those who synchronise well with this rune, it is an utterly unmistakable sensation that can lead them to the universal mother (mother is key here – the energy of a woman and a mother does have an underlying sameness but the distinctions are so profound that often it can feel like a completely unique energy in its own right).

Seeing as we do not have a purpose for this rune other than practicing with it, you do not worry about selecting a specific rune for what you intend to achieve. Your intent here is to gain mastery of whatever rune you are working with. In other words, you are automatically synchronised with the right rune: no matter what rune it is, it is the right one. As you bathe in the sensations from the rune, accept them, feel them echoing inside of you, flowing inside of you. See your visualised rune moving into you. Here we are going to use a bit of a Seiðr trick to speed up your mastery. You need to feel the rune as the centre of this energy and all its sensations move into you; guide it into where you would usually have mid-chest your heart hvel (the Norse equivalent to chakra). Root it there. You will feel all those runic energies flowing out of the glowing rune in your heart hvel and radiating out of your Hamr (energy body) and Lik (physical). See the dark green (for ᛒ Berkano) pulsing outwards and flooding you. This is the true function of the heart hvel – which is nothing to do with love and all that nonsense – it is the connector between realities. The crossroads of our energy system and the universe at large. Do not overdo things here; just a nice gentle pulse of runic energy. Overactivating this hvel can turn things on too much and overwhelm you rapidly. Go gentle and slow. Should any discomfort happen, move the rune and all its energy back out of you and have it pulsating from just outside. You will still net the results of your practices, so there is nothing to worry about – things will just be a little less intense. Bathing in the energy, meditate on the fact that you are one with them. This triggers synchronisation, and the heart hvel is the hvel of synchronisation with universal forces.

As synchronisation happens, you will start to feel the elemental influence of the rune. In case of ᛒ Berkano, focus on the heavy, moist and somewhat denser feeling. Think wet earth in your garden into which you are about to plant your seeds. It is this moist earthly feeling which belongs to ᛒ Berkano. It flows out of all the dark green energy of the rune, along with all the feelings of its powers and scope of action (you have impressed upon it above). You need to blend them all together into the dark green energy.

Once you have managed that, the final stage so far is to speak the rune's name out loud and enliven it. Chant its name. You can select a few modes here, and I suggest the following: speak its full name as a whisper, then speak it out loud, then allow it to echo in your mind. This causes it to manifest in the energy body first (Hamr) which is why we used the heart hvel; through it, it is then pulled into the physical body (Lik) and finally it bleeds over into your higher bodies. Our physical bodies are connected to the higher ones and mind directly. What we are doing here is using the functions of the energy and physical bodies to help guide the rune's power where we would want it to go anyway. This boosts our end results.

At this point, the energy will get a type of vibration when the sound of the rune's name has merged with it. You should hear it echoing through the energy and it should be imagined strongest within the shape of the rune itself. Those of you most sensitive to energy will sense a type of life in the energy. It is impossible to describe what this feels like exactly because it is totally unique to each of us. Whatever you sense as life or being alive will be, to a lesser extent present, in the rune's energy now. It is also there as a tint or hue in the sensation of it. It might take a few attempts to get your awareness to zoom into this but you will eventually.

Once you do, let go of all the energy and the rune, and will it to be sacrificed to the universal rune force for ᛒ Berkano (or whatever rune you selected to work with). It is just a willing and thinking of where that is needed. This part can leave many confused because the typical thing to happen is either a sudden loss of all that energy or everything just goes blank as if there is nothing there, where the energy was a second ago. Do not allow this to unsettle you; it is exactly what is supposed to happen. Turn your mind on the infinite expanse of existence outside of you. Think of the span of all existence and creation, which is stretching out infinitely around you and your body. We humans are nothing more than a tiny speck of a glimmer of light in infinite existence. There, you will notice a response echo back – this echo of universal ᛒ Berkano energy will flood you. Allow it to: you need to maintain a silent state of mind here, and any distractions run the risk of interrupting this echo. Still its chatter and surrender to the incoming force. The better you are at this, the more of its energy will flood you. It will feel very much like the ᛒ Berkano energy you sent out but different: its amplitude is at a whole other level and its 'thickness' (for want of a better word) is very noticeable. With all these universal rune forces, there is a noticeable otherness present, a something else, but what that something else actually is, its nature always escapes us. Our human perceptions are just not capable enough to directly perceive what it is. But it matters not; we are not after detailed analysis. What we want is the universal force and that is exactly what we get. Allow as much of it to fill you as you can hold, and hold onto it for a while. Usually, you get a directly proportional return of what you originally sent out.

In Seiðr work, we have access to other more intricate practices that achieve the same thing but go about it in slightly different ways, which yields a greater inflow of energy. Those will be covered at a later point in time in the relevant literature. For Galðr work (including High Galdr), this is how we work. As your familiarity with the universal rune forces and your ability to synchronise with the rune increases, the return flow is automatically increased sometimes to astounding levels.

And here, ladies and gents, the sacrifice and its entire purpose completes. For now, enjoy the actual universal energy for your rune and then will it to fade out of you. Visualise its energy fading, getting dimmer and dimmer; hear its sound getting more and more distant and quiet, hard to hear, and the sensations and feelings begin to fade. When it has all faded to the point where you cannot feel, see, hear or sense any of the rune's energy and influences, you can end your practice. The reason we are ending it this way is that this runic energy is not quite complete yet at this point. We still have two more instructions of the *Hávamál* to cover before it can be put to practical use.

The intent of this practice is to develop you as a Self and your mastery of the runes. It goes as far as developing your skills in generating the runic energy, sacrificing it and then experiencing its return actual universal energy as part of the return flow. Doing this practice will cause it to spill into each and every part of your Self. This is a slow and deliberate introduction of these forces to your Self, which serves to both develop it and to develop its ability to not only recognise, but also make use of it at various levels of your being.

Congratulations: you are now mastering one of the key mysteries of rune work and High Galdr. Now you have truly started your journey and taken your first step. At this point, it is wise to take a break. Simply will all the energy to dissipate out of you and fade away completely. Repeat the above part of the practice a few times with your chosen rune in order to establish a solid feedback before moving forward with the next part.

Assuming you have worked through the previous part of the practice and gained a good solid feedback, you may proceed. What you will do is keep the energy active in yourself. Now you are at a point where you want to send it off to work rather than just experiencing and allowing it to dissolve. With the runic energy active inside of you, allow your intent to build until you have fully expanded it across your biological awareness and it too is intending. The intent should be solely iron clad on increasing whatever characteristic or purpose you have selected to use this runic energy for. Nothing else should enter your mind or disturb your concentration. As you do this, allow the runic energy inside you to spill over into the physical body and merge with the building intent. You should feel the influence of the rune in each and every cell of your body. Doing this allows it to merge with your intent; the force of the intent and the energy of the rune's return flow will blend into each other quite readily and without needing any special effort on our part. You will notice it has a slight change to the speed of activity, based on your body type (see: *The Blood of Lóðurr Awakens* p.77 chapter on discussions of body types and their impact on energy). This is how it completes the personalisation of the resulting force (it is no longer a power or an energy; with intent, it becomes a living force now).

There is one last thing to do: since we want this runic force to produce a physical end result, we need to apply the laws of physicality to it. These are simple: condensation of the force (in other words, its gravity) and the effects of time. Condensation basically requires you to compress as much intent-filled energy as it into a form as possible. For us this is easy to do, since our heart hvel is the bridge to the universal and our body is pulsing with the intent, and the resulting force we just stream the runic force within us for as long as possible, either leaving it in the physical or shifting it into the energetic, shadow, mind raven, memory raven or spirit. It is not infinite, but depending on your skill, you will be able to maintain it for quite a while. You can increase the amount and quality of a rune's streaming force with practice and mastery. The second component needed is time. All things physical have a beginning, and period of existence, which cycles from building up to peak, then decay and finally an end. Those are the laws of natural existence and are reflected in ◇ Jera itself.

You are now ready to unleash it. You can just allow it to leave on its own or you can actually discard it in a number of specific ways, depending on your end goal. For the purposes of sending, the moment the forces are imbued with purpose and time causes them to disconnect from you and completes the sending. Pick one of the following, depending, of course, on what is most appropriate for your end goal:

1. If you are just practicing developing mastery of the rune: let its energy fade and disperse out of you until there is none left.
2. If you want to influence yourself physical or emotionally: keep the energy or power inside your auric fields, which is a perfectly fine way to discard them. This often confuses people because in our modern day understanding, sending something is typically interpreted as it going away and no longer being in the remit of your being. We seldom think of sending something when forcing it to shift from our physical and into another level of our Self. Little do we realise just how far from our awareness

and physical the other parts of our Self actually are. To do this, just visualise it as a coating around your body, just touching your skin but not penetrating it. This type of sending is excellent when trying to do things such as increase your allure, social confidence, and all effects which make other people see you in a specific way, as per the rune force's effect. For instance, the ᛇ Wunjo rune used in this way will make you seem very friendly and people will be comfortable around you. The ᛁ Isa or ᚦ Thurisaz rune will do the opposite, and so forth.

3   When trying to do something which will have a wider effect on your life, such as finding love, increasing wealth, bringing success and so on, you want to make the rune energy and power emit a powerful single pulse out where it just all bursts out of you. This way, it is released and goes on its way to do whatever it is you wanted it to.

4   If you are working with a runic force that you are not in harmony with, sending it simply requires you to eject the energy outwards. You can will it to emit a powerful single pulse out where it just all bursts out of you, with the intent for it to dissipate back into creation. This is my personal preferred method; it guarantees that you return to your own balanced state free of all the rune's influence and that its energy and power.

5   If you want to affect any other part of your Self, just direct the energy into it through

your body. See *The Blood of Lóðurr Awakens* and *The Spirit of Húnir Awakens (Parts 1 & 2)* or *Roadmap to High Galdr Rune Work*.

This completes the practice; once you have discharged the energy and power from within yourself and sent it on its way, depending on your proficiency with the rune and how much power you were able to solidify, you should see some changes gradually take place. It is important not to expect miracles here, especially not at the outset. So many expect to unleash the rune's power and have something happen within the next few days. This might be true for a master who has specialised in a rune, but is very uncommon. Usually, the rune's power will have to work through the best possible route to producing your desired outcome. This can take time and can also require more energy than you have provided in your first attempt. This is why it is best to do your rune work, wait and observe, providing a good reasonable amount of time (in proportion to your goal) has passed then repeat it if needed. Start with small goals and build up. As you gain small successes, you will increase in power. This build-up happens gradually but it is so much easier to reach when working with smaller goals. Aiming too big too fast will risk failure, and a chain of failures can dent your confidence and power considerably. Always remember, there are runes you will struggle with more than others – that is only natural, and if that is your case, select another one and try again with a different goal. Eventually, we all reach a point where bigger and bigger goals become accessible.

Quick Steps:

1. Pick a rune, any rune. It can be your favourite,

or one you feel most excited about. For the initial runes, it is important to have a pull towards the selected rune.
2. Start by sitting down, take a few deep breaths and relax. The more relaxed the better.
3. Visualise the shape of the rune there in front of you. Eyes can be closed or open.
4. When the rune shape is firmly set in your mind, visualise the characteristics and effects brought about by that rune as flowing out of it, as if they were radiating from within the shape of the rune.
5. Once you get the feeling of the rune's characteristics and effects radiating out of it, add its colour (as given in the rune descriptions) to your visualisation. Now the energy colour, and its characteristics should be radiating out of the rune.
6. Spend a little time increasing the intensity of energy flowing out of the rune. As it radiates out and touches your skin, sense all the characteristics in its touch.
7. As you bathe in the feelings from the rune accept them, feel them echoing inside of you, flowing inside of you.
8. See the rune move inside of you. You need to feel the rune as the centre of this energy and all its sensations move into you and guide it into where you would usually have mid-chest your heart hvel.
9. Feel its energy and its properties radiating throughout you from the heart region. Will it to spill into your energy body and from there radiate out into your physical. Make sure it is a pleasant pulse of energy, not

too intense or too weak.

10. Bathing in the energy meditate on the fact that you are one with the rune's energy. This triggers synchronisation, and the heart hvel is the hvel of synchronisation, it has nothing to do with love.
11. As you synchronise you will start to feel the elemental influence of the rune flood its energy. Allow this new sensation to flood its energy along with all the characteristics you feel within it already.
12. Now it is time to speak its name. Remember the rules of runic vocalisation p.71.
13. Pay close attention to the runic energy pulsating within you. It should at some point start to vibrate as you vibrate its sound or the rune name. When that happens, let go of all the energy and wait.
14. The energy should fade away from within you as you 'sacrifice' it. Moments later, a strong return flow will flood your body with the universal rune's energy. It will feel exactly the same but more intense, with a higher level of concentration and vibration within it. Maintain a submissive, silent state of mind, and allow whatever happens to happen.
15. As the return flow pulses through you, enjoy it, reflect upon its characteristics, allow yourself to sink into all the sensations you experience. After a few minutes allow the energy to dissipate and flow out of you, then fade away completely until none of it is present (you can no longer feel even the slightest hint of it).

This completes part 1. Now for part 2:

1. After reaching point 15 as described above, hold onto the universal runic energy (do not let it dissipate and fade away).
2. Now you are at a point where you want to send it off to work rather than just experiencing.
3. With the runic energy active inside of you, allow your intent to build until you have fully expanded it across your biological awareness and it too is intending. The intent should be solely iron-clad on increasing whatever characteristic or purpose you have selected to use this runic energy for.
4. Allow the runic energy inside you spill over into the physical body and merge with the building intent.
5. Finally depending on your goal, release the built up energy/power in the appropriate way.

Using High Galdr – The (Non-Self) Technique

With some runes, it is best not to work through the Self when using their energies, powers or accessing their universal force. This is especially true of ᚦ Thurisaz, ᛏ Tiwaz and ᛒ Berkano. ᚦ Thurisaz should be avoided by women, as it is extremely masculinising across all the parts of the Self and highly disruptive. It should also be avoided by those men who have an easy tendency towards aggression or anger. In case of this rune, it is always best to be cautious rather than sorry. There is no guarantee it will trigger those types of reactions but just to be cautious, use the technique given here to avoid any potential trouble. ᛏ Tiwaz should be avoided by women as well; it too is very masculinising in its effects. Those two runes' energies powers and forces are simply like this; no matter what intent or goal one sets them to aim for, there will always be a type of side effect with this type of result.

The same is true of ᛒ Berkano. It is what one can think of as the ultimate feminine rune and as such has a very feminising effect on all parts of the Self. As such, it should not be used within the Self of a man.

There might be instances where you do not want some of the other runes' powers to flow through your entire being. This is very true for those runes you struggle with and those which run in opposition to your Self. This technique can be used to start harmonising with those underlying forces without them affecting you until you are in synchronicity with them and can work with them by allowing them to flow through you.

The technique is essentially the same as the one given above… except that when it comes to the point where you are visualising the rune pulsing with the characteristics and purpose, you do not bring it into you in the heart hvel. Instead, you leave it just outside in front of you. The golden rule is simple: if you do not allow its energy to enter into you, its effects cannot be realised within you. Just keep the rune pulsing outside and when you practice its vocalisation, the elemental sensations and intensification, simply feel it with your mind as radiating from within the glowing rune in front of you. At the end, you can will its energy to fade or to pulse outwards towards a goal (remember to direct the pulse away from you, not through you!).

If you want to use the rune's energy and power for a goal, you will need to infuse it with your intent and will it to go towards its goal. This is slightly more difficult as you need to give rise to your intent inside your body and then direct that intent into the rune in front of you. When done, set a time if you want a physical result or are affecting the daily world, and see it shooting off (away from you) on its way.

In this manner, it is possible to unleash the rune's effects and powers without them affecting you; by keeping them firmly outside of you and separate from you, you can avoid running into the problems you would have had the rune been within you. Yes, it will be less effective, but it will also be much safer to work with.

Quick Steps:

1. Follow the same steps as for the practice given above until step 6.
2. Spend some time observing the rune right in front of you radiating. Meditate on its power, reflect on all its characteristics and properties. The longer you do this for, the more you will notice the elemental sensation pulsating out of the rune. When you do, move onto the next step.
3. Now it is time to speak its name – remember the rules of runic vocalisation p.71.
4. Pay close attention to the runic energy pulsating around you. It should at some point start to vibrate as you vibrate its sound or the rune name. When that happens, let go of all the energy; just observe without focusing in on it and wait.

5. The energy should fade away from sight and feel as it is 'sacrificed'. Moments later, you will see it flare up in front of you once more. Its pulse will be firmer and all the sensation will be radiating out of it as you come face to face with the universal rune energy. It will feel exactly the same but more intense, with a higher level of concentration and vibration within it. Maintain a silent state of mind, and observe for as long as you wish.

6. After a few minutes, allow the energy to dissipate and flow away from you, then fade away completely until none of it is present (you can no longer feel even the slightest hint of it). Or infuse it with your intent and will it to go towards its goal. This is slightly more difficult as you need to give rise to your intent inside your body and then direct that intent into the rune in front of you. When done, set a time if you want a physical result or are affecting the daily world, and see it shooting off (away from you) on its way.

High Galdr
Breathing The Runes

This is a practice used almost exclusively in Seiðr practices. I am including it here because it is most helpful in not only mastering the runes but also in awakening the energy body, as well as driving the runic power into it. Put in new age terms, using this method awakens the 'soul' and can enable you to feel it!

Please note, if you have any difficulty with your breathing, any breath impairments or medical conditions affecting your breathing, do not attempt this. If you have a tendency of hyperventilating, avoid this practice as well. Breathing practices should only be undertaken if you are perfectly healthy and have the OK from a medical professional. Now that that's clear, let us look at this breathing practice.

You will have to start off by taking a few breaths to relax. Keep your body in a comfortable position where no tension takes hold of it in order to maintain posture. Follow the instructions given above for 'High Galdr – The (Non-Self) Technique' p.92. As you end up with the rune pulsing its power and energy in front of you, allow this pulse and energy to expand outwards until it fills all the space from your point of view. Everywhere your mind turns to, there should be only that rune's energy; it should expand everywhere with you at its centre. Having got to this point you are ready to proceed.

Take a deep breath in. As you do so, you are breathing in the rune's energy, feeling its elemental sensations, hearing its sound travel with your in-breath, sensing its characteristics flowing into you. When you reach maximum intake of air (without straining!), let the breath flow out slowly and steadily, but this time just focus on air leaving the lungs. You keep the runic energy inside of you, which you visualise as having no organs or anything else – just your body's boundaries which you are filling with runic energy.

Repeat this deep breath intake of runic charge air, and exhaling of just air. Do this a total of 28 times. On the 28th breath, as you exhale (gently!), hold your breath until you feel tension to take in another breath build up. When you feel this, take in another deep breath and repeat 28 times, holding your breath after the 28th exhalation. Then breathe normally again, allowing the runic energy within you to fade away.

The point of this practice is to do 28 deep breaths, which will oxygenise your body and flush out its acidity, but also draw in runic energy. When you hold your breath after the 28th breath is exhaled, you will find that you can effortlessly hold your breath for quite a while. It is VITALLY important not to hold longer than you can without the body experiencing any tension. DO NOT struggle for your breath or try to hold on longer than you can comfortably do so. The point of this exercise is not to choke! It is to take in the deep breaths without strain, and to exhale slowly, relaxing your body as much as possible. This very process transfers the runic energy through your breathing into the energy body. Do not be surprised if you feel tingling, vibration or even humming from somewhere inside of you. Just make sure you do not strain yourself at any point doing this, not only because it is risky and could make you lightheaded but also because strain inhibits the flow of energy into the energy body. Straining pretty much makes the entire practice pointless. Do not strain yourself when breathing in, by attempting to breathe in too much air, and do not strain yourself breathing out, by trying to force too much air out, and do not strain yourself by holding your breath at the end of the 28 in-breaths and out-breaths. It is not a race. Just to clarify, you only hold your breath after you exhale the 28th time. This gives us:

(in + out) x 28, then 1 holding, then back to *(in + out) x 28*, with 1 final hold and then back to normal breathing. Staying relaxed and with no straining at any point whatsoever. If you feel any, stop the practice and try the next day. If you end up straining too much, skip the practice.

Remember, be responsible with your body and your health. There is no point causing yourself harm. It will only slow down your progress and might even put a long-term stop to it. Not what you want. Be patient, take it slow. If in doubt, feel free to skip this practice; you will not lose out. Once again, check with a medical professional before you do this.

THE RUNES

The Rune Fehu – Fé

Sound: f
Vocal Scale: Do
Numerology: 1
Natural Polarity: M - M - M - F - F
Energetic Colour (Universal): Vibrant red
Primal Power: Expansion, fire, outpouring of creation
Sensation(s): Expansive explosive heat

Archetypal Level of Existence

The primordial fire, appearing as a blazing sun, radiating not light but fire and more importantly, heat. It is the outpouring of the spark of creation itself, which bloomed into existence and gave birth to all things. ᚠ Fehu on the archetypal is the fundamental expansion, the ever-expanding force that underlines all life force, the outwards flow responsible for all evolution. It is the total sum of all beginnings and all evolutions. ᚠ Fehu's force is responsible for the initial burst forth into creation from the Ginnungagap. It has a very unique and special effect on intent. It makes it not only more powerful and better at transmitting itself but also gives it a type of vibration or hum effect, which enables your intent to influence a wider range of scope.

This rune is the primordial fire, that very first flame which sprang into creation. Raw and uncontrolled, from it all activity and power is sourced. Using it, it is possible to activate anything and everything in creation, as well as increase any existing activity already in place. Do keep in mind that ᚠ Fehu is essentially raw fire, uncontrolled and uncontrollable, although it is not as devastating a force as ᚦ Thurisaz.

ᚠ Fehu's force is the primordial principle of expansion and heat combined (whereas runes such as ᚦ Thurisaz and ᛞ Dagaz are primarily expansive, ᚲ Kenaz is heat and light, ᚾ Nauthiz heat and ᛋ Sowilo expansion and light). As such, it is a vitally important rune, for its powers govern all expansive phenomena ranging from the radiation, light, heat and atomic activity, in scientific terms, down to the expansion of the mind and spirit. It is also an enlivening rune, for the universal red seas of life force are expansive. The life force itself always seeks; it is a constantly expanding force seeking to promote life in all forms and states it can, and if it cannot, it will force a manifestation into existence to enable it to do so. Because of this, the relationship of the ᚠ Fehu force (and powers) and life itself is very interconnected; they are indeed a reflection of each other or if you prefer, two sides of the same coin (well, almost – you have ᚠ Fehu on the one side and life and megin on the other). ᚠ Fehu's expansiveness is what pushed things out into manifestation and is one of the key driving forces behind evolution itself. It is also the root of power; it is the reason why we have a huge ball of fire (the sun) as the centre of our solar system. Its power is somewhat distinct from others; it is not just a burst of energy, but also embodies the concept of radiation, and wave upon wave of ongoing energy releasing in the form of expansive radial heat is the nature of this rune. It is not a force that is released in a burst then gone (like ᚦ Thurisaz). It is important to realise that ᚠ Fehu is what gives birth to ᛋ Sowilo; ᛋ Sowilo's forces are the net result of the expansiveness of ᚠ Fehu minus its heat. This principle is used in a practical manner when you need to generate light out of fire energy (as is often done in Seiðr work).

Spirit & Spiritual Reality

This rune not only empowers but also generates new power, most specifically the megin (see *The Breath of Oðin Awakens*). It is strongly related to the will aspect of all spirits, as well as the foundations of spiritual perception, for ᚠ Fehu is not only expansion but also a carrier. It is responsible for the vibrational aspect of all sound and energy and can be used on the spiritual levels of reality to increase both speed and strength of their vibrational characteristics. As the ᚠ Fehu force causes the energies of all things to expand, so does it also influence all the information transmission within those energies (including those of the Self). Spiritually, it embodies the purpose of enlightenment of creation, even if it means having to destroy creation for that to be achieved. This is actually what is prophesised to happen when Surt leaves Muspelheim at Ragnarök (the Twilight of the Gods).

ᚠ Fehu is the rune of spiritual becoming, the emergence of a ray of the Self as a functioning unit rather than just a spark on the archetypal level. The spirit is nothing more than a ray of light emanating from this Spark of Self, one facet of the Self pushed into manifestation until it fully expresses that portion of the Self, and then it returns as a new ray of the Self and shoots outwards into a new type of manifestation, forming another individual which spring from the root of your true Self. This is why it is practically impossible to know our true selves; we are all ultimately only a single outpouring of a tiny emanation of it. Each emanating ray of Self will result in a different unique individual which a different mind, energy bodies, and physical body. Each of these is directly manifested as an impulse from the ᚠ Fehu force. It is the trigger that causes each emanation to radiate out of the Self.

In terms of spirits in general, ᚠ Fehu can be used to activate or even hyper-activate them; it will quicken and enliven the spirit but more importantly, it will push it to seek expansion. Without the power of ᚠ Fehu, each spirit eventually pulls inwards and collapses into a single point; that is when it is reabsorbed into the Spark of Self and is taken out of existence. By knowing this, you can use ᚠ Fehu to increase this outflowing of your own and other spirits, strengthening their existence and amplifying their activity.

The willpower and intent are strongly influenced by ᚠ Fehu. Whenever you falter, use it; when things seem overwhelming, this indicates a lack or weakening of this fundamental force within you. ᚠ Fehu is an excellent power to use when the stasis of ᛁ Isa starts to affect the spirit (or any other part of the Self, for that matter!). By applying its power at these higher levels of the Self, it causes the lower parts to receive full benefits as well because eventually, all propagates and expands throughout the entire Self.

Finally, when dealing with situations where spiritual darkness is encountered, combining ᚠ Fehu with ᛋ Sowilo is a most mighty weapon. The two runes amplify each other and their effects combine, producing a powerful emanation of primordial light causing all darkness to flee. If combined with ᛞ Dagaz, the darkness of the mind can easily be banished and spiritually dark environments illuminated with such force that it takes all by surprise.

Mind & Mental Reality

All activity (and lack of) in the mind is a direct result of the influence (or lack) of ᚠ Fehu. This rune's force has an incredible impact on the base activation of all mental skills, including but not limited to the intellect, cognition, memory and perceptions. A bright intellect is often attributed to the shining and shimmering fires of ᚠ Fehu on the mental level, as is the overthinking and never-ceasing onslaught of thoughts. Any thought can be activated and empowered by the use of this rune; it is an excellent rune to work with when empowering thought forms. When combined with ᚫ Ansuz in Oðinic trance work, it leads to intellectual ecstasy, awakening higher forms of pure intellect and inspiration.

ᚠ Fehu, through its association with fire, is also strongly linked with vision, be it spiritual vision, energetic or physical. Using it, one is able to activate and enhance one's scope of spirit vision in the mental levels of reality. This is a direct perception of images, no matter where or when one focuses one's attention. It is a spontaneous image in the mind rather than something seen by our eyes and brains. The mind just sees directly.

Combining ᚠ Fehu with ᛞ Dagaz, ᛋ Sowilo, ᛇ Eihwaz and ᛃ Jera (not in this order) unlocks prophetic visions for those with Spa skills.

When used with the help of a flame of any type, it enables the mind to rise to higher levels of perceptions, promotes the induction of trance by candle flame, and allows for projection of the mind through the flame into higher realms of existence (this is very often used by Seiðr practitioners).

Generally, all mental activity is strengthened by this rune; when affecting the Hugr raven (mind), you can quicken its flight. New impressions, longer inspiration waves, deeper and longer trances, and maintenance of intellectual persistence – all fall within its remit and can be greatly enhanced when used on the Hugr. It also produces a certain degree of mental endurance, where the usual intellectual fatigue can be lessened or even completely eliminated by those who master this rune. On the memory side of things, long forgotten memories can be reawakened. When something proves to be difficult to recall or memories become difficult to access, providing there is no neurological impairment, this rune can be very helpful indeed. Combining it with ᛟ Othala enables ancestral memories to be activated, and combined with ᛜ Ingwaz, it solidifies memory encoding. Do be careful and avoid overusing this; your mind needs to rest as well as be active, or it will burn out.

Energy Body & Energy Reality

On this level of reality, the megin aspects of ᚠ Fehu become very dominant; luck is now the main focus of this runic power, as well as empowerment of energies (be they your own or something else's). It strengthens all powers, be they what are usually called psychic or magical, purely energetic or natural abilities such as healing or perceiving, ᚠ Fehu will greatly enhance them (careful to avoid pushing them out of control – your power can end up consuming you! That is the true lesson of the flame). ᚠ Fehu's energies are very effective when it comes to generating new megin, for it is born out of them (see: *The Breath of Oðin Awakens* for more information on this).

ᚠ Fehu will help you work with any non-physical being related to fire or expansion, it will enhance your abilities to see energy and due to its carrier influences, it enables you to both attract and channel powers, no matter from where they are sourced. Do keep in mind there is always a price to pay for power (this belongs to the influences of ᚷ Gebo, which come into play with such an exchange).

ᚠ Fehu can also be used strengthen your energy body and awaken it (and all its abilities) to greater activity. Providing it with additional energy is a requirement when wanting to work with it, and so you should use ᚠ Fehu to generate as much megin as you can and every so often, allow it to flow through each and every part of your energy system. ᚠ Fehu is also extremely helpful when it comes to burning out blockages in the energy body, as well as making it more fluidic and adaptable. Directing this rune's power into the hvels (the Norse equivalent to chakras) will quicken them and also enable their secondary function as energy gateways to awaken.

ᚠ Fehu and ᛚ Laguz are the two primary forces constantly functioning in the energy body and all its structures. ᚠ Fehu is one of the four cardinal forces flowing through the energy body that needs to be mastered to fully awaken and control it. These forces act as a destructive mechanism, which tears asunder our energy bodies upon physical death and is often referred to as the 'second death' – well, it is its triggering force. Additionally, when it does occur, ᚠ Fehu ignites the entire energy body, releasing its full potential in one key moment, which frees up all the experiences and awareness to return to their sources and burn out the energy body itself in the process. Mastering ᚠ Fehu is a critical component in the mystic's work, designed to ensure this body is preserved rather than consumed upon physical death, for it is the home of awareness and personality, and the receptacle for individuality.

This rune is also sometimes referred to as the sending rune (along with ᚫ Ansuz being the receiving rune). Fire always emanates outwards when no obstacles are present, for this reason any energy, thought, power can be sent by applying the ᚠ Fehu force to it. It is a naturally outbound transmitter; it will, by its very nature, amplify and carry whatever you bind to it. Yes, it is entirely possible to use it as a receiving force but it does get complicated, as this needs to be intended and engineered; it is far more effective to use ᚫ Ansuz's naturally receptive force for this. Alternating between ᚠ Fehu (for sending) and ᚫ Ansuz (for receiving) communications across entire energy systems is possible.

Physical Body & Physical Reality

Here we enter the domains of ᚠ Fehu most will be

familiar with. Wealth and finances, as in mobile cash-flow, fall within ᚠ Fehu's influences on the physical. All types of income and financial strength are subject to this rune, as is the resulting success and social status resulting from this. Physically, its polarity is feminine and so it expresses its influences in a nourishing and comforting way (when expressing the positive-feminine pole). Just imagine the warmth in the house, which brings relief after facing the bitter cold outside! Or the child running into their mother's arms for a comforting cuddle. Interestingly, people strong in this rune's power often love to give and receive hugs, and are strong empaths (especially if they are strong in ᛚ Lagur as well). These are all expressed through ᚠ Fehu's influences. Additionally, what we call luck flows from this rune, in terms of unexpected opportunities or strikes of good fortune. In all things relating to fulfilment, ᚠ Fehu plays a major role. This is why it is commonly associated with possessions (and cattle). It is a rune whose energies lead to prosperity. Although it is worth noting that in its feminine aspects, this rune will need something to burn, like the flame being made of matter will burn through its fuel, so will ᚠ Fehu's energies; in its masculine pole, it is self-regenerating but unfortunately does not have the same effects in terms of wealth, prosperity and so forth. Hence it is not possible to keep on generating luck and fortune endlessly and forever (at least not with ᚠ Fehu).

In terms of our bodies, ᚠ Fehu's dominion extends to all activity. The movement and motions of the physical body are governed by it, as are all chemical processes in some way shape or form. When ᚠ Fehu is lacking, stasis kicks in and the lack of 'doing' becomes problematic. This can often lead to health issues and all too many times, we try to 'burn fat' to avoid becoming obese, which is an indirect link back into attempting to re-activate the powers of ᚠ Fehu within our bodies. ᚠ Fehu is the best support any sportsperson might desire.

Scientifically, ᚠ Fehu controls the activity and polarisation, as well as laws of repulsion. It is also known scientifically as the strong nuclear force. ᚠ Fehu can be used to manifest and increase all forms of fire, heat, atomic, electrical effects and activity.

The Rune Uruz – Úr

Sound: ū
Vocal Scale: Re
Numerology: 2
Natural Polarity: M - M - F - M - M
Energetic Colour (Universal): Green, a lighter version of it
Primal Power: Cohesion and formation
Sensation(s): Comfortable solidity, slightly moist damp earth but warm

Archetypal Level of Existence

This rune's force on the archetypal level is the ruler of formation and organisation – not intellectual ordering, but something similar to that of a natural biological organisation type. The two are very different and ᚢ Uruz ordering might seem erratic and unstructured to our minds, but it stems from a different type of order, one that grows progressively and results from endured reconfigurations and remodelling during growth. Its structures often baffle the intellect completely and are not accessible to any form of logic or reason, but are very much accessible to spirit and subconscious understanding. ᚢ Uruz is the rune of patterning for the purposes of evolution, and herein lies untold wisdom. It is the same principle that governs the birth of new spirits from matter, rather than matter manifesting from the spirits. As such, this rune's forces are responsible for the optimal order of existence based on purely the principles of that very existence. They are set and fixed but are ever-evolving. Whoever understands this contradiction gains immense wisdom for the understanding of creation, by way of eternal perfected stasis unfolds with such understanding. The forces of ᚢ Uruz are the perfect embodiment of the evolution into the great unknown, as and when it edges onto the knowable. At this level, one witnesses the shaping of potential into power and pattern, and one sees how the two merge and express each other in perfect harmonic unity. Through pattern, the power gains the potential for expression of itself, and through power, the pattern gains meaning of its own true nature. Reflect deeply on this, for here are found the secrets of shape and form.

When looked at, one experiences an simple spherical form within which are billions of trillions of interconnections constantly shifting and re-ordering themselves for manifestation, only to find out that they were perfect from the outset and manifested in exactly the most perfect manner they were intended to. This is a most difficult rune force to observe and can be very overwhelming to the human mind, even it has gained the ability to function on the greater level of things. It is experienced as an assault of possibilities by the observer all brimming with power, seemingly ready for manifestation down into reality, only for one to see that it has already completed all possible manifestations, for it came into creation perfect. This force is patterned (organised) power, uncontrollable, unyielding and unchangeable because it is perfected at its core.

Likewise, the ᚢUruz force is what gave rise to the initial harmony, that inner state of being that is perfectly harmonised within and moving forward in a balanced state. It is only after all its challenges that the harmony is reinstated and produced under will by ᛞDagaz before the new Self roots itself in existence (ᛟOthala). For at this point, the original perfected harmony of ᚢUruz has been grasped by higher forms of consciousness, which are then able to re-establish it consciously. Using ᚢUruz, you can re-established the initial harmonic state of anything and using ᛞDagaz, you can re-harmonise anything with it. This type of harmonisation is somewhat different because it includes the environment's impact on the Self; it is a more inclusive and cohesive type of harmony across all of the Self's manifestations, whereas the ᚢUruz one is harmonisation of the core essential aspects of the Self. The distinction is subtle but important because once manifest, the Self starts to express itself by creating new permutations of its core essential meaning: it adopts forms, it gains energies, it transforms and transmutes, it grows through experience and so on. All those additional parts are subject to ᛞDagaz's forces, whereas all the core parts are subject to ᚢUruz's. Sometimes the one is more appropriate than the other – if you want to completely harmonise and balance combine the two.

Spirit & Spiritual Reality

This rune enables the spirit of its user to be fully realised. It awakens the potential within, only to show that all that potential was already in action. The easiest way to realise its effects on the spiritual is to acknowledge the simple fact that you are already aware of these levels of existence but are not conscious of them. ᚢUruz will re-link your consciousness with these higher functions of your own spirit and remind you they were always there and active.

Its main function on this level is to enable whatever 'structures' are needed in the spirit, to enable and promote higher thinking and expression of intent or will. It is here that realisation of causality is rooted and gained from ᚢUruz. At this level, we are still working in terms of untamed potential and ultimate freedom to realise, here the ᚢUruz force governs the independence of all beings and represent the uncontrollable iron will of its users. It will smash through all causes that seek to disrupt its laws (the laws of patterning of power and their underlying unchangeability). It is the rune of expression of will and unfettered independence.

On the broader scale of things, the ᚢUruz's forces are responsible for organisation and re-organisation of the very essence of spirit and its circumstances, in order to allow it to start manifesting throughout reality. ᚢUruz organises and patterns the light of the Spark of Self as the spirit pattern sets; it is the influence of this rune which determines what type of spirit you (or anyone else, for that matter) will have, what its scope of activity will be, its limitations, its specialisations, what it needs to learn, how far it can progress and what its fate will be. Mastering this rune can offer the mystic not only a clear sight and understanding of all spirits but also a whole range of subtle abilities that enable that mystic to adapt these configurations. It does not include things such as changing the essential nature of a spirit in a way that would require its destruction and re-creation – which can only be done by the Spark of Self – but it does permit a changing of how its essential nature is manifest and expressed, it enables you to expand and extend the scope of activity of the spirit. More advanced applications of this rune can allow the blending of spirit characteristics from one spirit to another (providing they are alike) and the increase of the sensing, intellect, memory, inspiration and even intuition. Very advanced uses of it enable a spirit to fracture a part of itself out and merge that part with another spirit's fragment in order to push into manifestation a completely new spirit of the two originator's types combined.

Mind & Mental Reality

It seeds change by not changing things, for it expresses the deep universal unconscious (from our perspective, as in actuality there is no such thing as the 'universal unconscious' because it is all aware) and links our minds directly into it.

Willpower is influenced by this rune; it not only guarantees freedom of will but is also used to solidify the will and give it endurance as it manifests in reality at large. Another linked influence of ᚢ Uruz to free will is the freedom to dive into the personal unconscious. Doing so is one of the most dangerous ventures any mind can undertake but one worth it. In order to unlock true power, you will have to dive deep into your own unconscious in order to unlock its powers. You can also use this rune to dig up things from deep within, but be careful what you do dig up. You might end up with more than you bargained for! Working in this manner allows you to eventually blend the unconscious with the conscious and produce something that is not only the sum of the two but something more.

ᚾUruz is primarily a healing rune. As such, it can be used to heal any problems on the mental side of things no matter how problematic they may be. In theory, with a certain degree of specialisation in this runic power, it should be possible to heal many of the common and less common mental illnesses. The mind can be energised to a greater extent by ᚾUruz. These effects are not only limited to the mind but apply as well to memory.

With the ᚾUruz force, the first manifestation of cohesion takes place. At this level of existence, it can be thought of as a type of mental gravitational force which pulls thoughts, concepts, ideas and so forth, which are alike together, according to the principle of like attracts like. The more alike, the stronger the pull. This force then establishes a pattern in how all these are held together and with such a pattern established, the first birth of thought-form takes place. This in turn also influences the birth of the ego-consciousness, which eventually fully manifests in our bodies (or those of other species, if they are the ones being considered). This is what gives rise to the roots of cognition. It is the primary reason why consciousness of one type of being and another type are different, and is supported by a different type of awareness with different types of perceptive mechanisms. Using ᚾUruz this knowledge can be gained, and understanding of it provides the mystic with a wide range of consciousness patterning possibilities. Here, again, the same applies to memories.

Energy Body & Energy Reality

When it comes to the energy body (Hamr), ᚢ Uruz's influences are powerful to the point of being almost overwhelming. Its fundamental shaping forces are what gave rise initially to the Hamr and because of this, ᚢ Uruz is extremely empowering when it comes to this part of our Self. More importantly than just energising the energy body is that this rune's forces bring it forth. The energy body usually grows distant from the physical – and hence the conscious. Both of these grow from the energy body, like the outer skin of an onion. The longer you live, the further it withdraws until the point where it is so distant you die. This rune inverses the process – not suddenly, but gradually. By repeated use, it is possible to eventually bring it as close to the conscious as it was at birth. ᚢ Uruz is also the key to healing any injuries sustained during the conscious use of this part of our Self.

In terms of the greater energy realms and that entire reality, ᚢ Uruz is used to form and shape energy. It is the principal formative power in operation there. From its influence space, shape and all forms are created, as well as their characteristics such as weight, size and directionality. You can use this rune's power to expand your consciousness in a way that allows you to perceive the internal structures of things. Perceptions of the structures within the energetic structures in particular can be developed. It does not end here for these perceptions will enable you to also understand how the spirit weaves itself into them, and eventually through them into physical matter, where it is anchored. Should you decide to specialise in this rune's practical applications, possibilities such as repairing broken or damaged hvels, energy channels, damaged energetic structures of physical organs all open up to you. The most fascinating mystery, however, is that of the threads which bind the non-physical and physical to one another, and is most certainly one you should look into, for by strengthening and mastering these, you will be able to loosen or strengthen this binding and free the energy body from the physical in its most complete way at will. ᚾUruz is also the force responsible for the maintenance and functioning of the mesh of energy threads around the energy body, which maintain awareness and which, when fractured or pulled in too strongly, causes physical organ illness. As such, those specialising in healing with this rune should focus on developing their abilities to sense this mesh and learn to manipulate it. Much can be achieved from this and many people can be helped, not only energetically, but also in terms of easing physical symptoms.

Seeing as all events flow from these realms down into the physical, using the ᚾUruz rune, you can force an end and initiate a new beginning. Just before anyone asks, it is not possible to just create an end with this rune – its underlying force will always induce a new beginning. Much more could be said about this rune's range of influences and what can be done with it at this level of reality and the Self, but this will have to do for now.

Physical Body & Physical Reality

ᚾUruz grants us increased physical strength. Not only does this refer to actual muscular strength but also the resistance against illness. The skilled rune user can even banish fatigue as soon as it sets in using this rune's power. This rune is the carrier of life force; by combining ᚠ Fehu's powers with itself, life force came to the physical realms. Typically, the energy released by the rune usually works within the bounds of the physical body – in other words, it will amplify and strengthen it to the maximum capability it can sustain. With increased practice and training, the body's resistance to the radiation of the rune's power will allow you to push beyond its limits. In any case, great energy and drive is the gift of this rune. Health is increased, and all the various biological systems and sub-systems are harmonised and empowered.

In terms of the world at large, it causes sudden unexpected events and changes to occur. These changes cause outcomes that will be beneficial, once faced. As always, there is work to do when you want to go through any type of change. By the same rules, ᚢ Uruz offers the ability to shape circumstances by learning to shape power into patterns and weave into existence not only the power of this rune but of all the runes. That is how the initial fires (powers) of ᚠ Fehu at the point of creation were shaped into matter by ᚢ Uruz, to give rise to the reality we know and these we do not.

The most important aspect of this rune is what it does to our physical evolution. It brings out the unconscious power dormant within us, the animalistic or childlike self of our biological awareness. It brings it to the forefront, bringing with it full independence and action of will. It brings forth the wild side free of human dogma, morals and judgment. Our biological awareness not only has no perception of those things, but would not understand them if it did. Being able to communicate and connect with this part of ourselves and direct it is key to using it constructively (see *The Blood of Lóðurr Awakens* for instructions). Additionally, applying this rune at this level of the Self can be used to surrender to the wild instinct, which is required for berserker trance work.

The Rune Þurisaz – Þurs

Sound: Th
Vocal Scale: Mi
Numerology: 3
Natural Polarity: M - M - M - F - F
Energetic Colour (Universal): Red, a mix of crimson and darker angry reds
Primal Power: Conflict, destruction and awakening
Sensation(s): Bursting power, overwhelming explosive energy, when concentrated, outbursts and waves of static.

Archetypal Level of Existence

This is the rune of power, the power that is the fuel for evolution. It drives things forward, breaks down boundaries, and opens otherwise locked paths forward. This rune is not only the link to the raw primordial powers which gave rise to existence, but also embodies them within itself. It is the fuel for R Raidho's movement forward and for F Ansuz's shifts of consciousness upwards into ecstatic states. It is the driving force of existence and the willpower that pushes one into action. This rune's force is extremely masculine. It is the absolute manifestation of all masculinity in both its positive and negative forms (once it manifests). It is the genius and the creativity of insanity demonstrated by the composers, writers, artists and legends of old. It is also the force behind the sword that strikes the enemy in battle.

This rune's energy is fiery but not fire itself; rather, it is the expansive pulsating power. It is the force that pushes outwards and expands. Concentrated, it explodes, snaps and destroys. That is the most noticeable characteristic of the rune's energy. The other only becomes obvious once you have made a solid strong connection with it: that is the electric static emanating throughout the expansive pulse. From this comes its traditional connection with lightning, and by Thor's expression of this rune's power, so does his. Remember, do not make the mistake of thinking that this rune expresses Thor's power; it is Thor who expresses the power of the rune. The rune came first and the god embodies some part of its scope of forces – not the other way around. This is why associating the rune with the god or goddess can lead to confusion.

With any power, any rune, any energy, ᚦ Thurisaz can enhance it and amplify its effectiveness. It leads to unexpected mutations of power, alterations and unforeseen change. Is it for the better or the worse? There is no way to know.

The unleashed power of ᚦ Thurisaz is unplanned, uncontrolled and more akin to a burst of pure raw overwhelming power (rage). It strikes without remorse, without constraint, without planning... it just strikes. It is primal and primordial and just is. Trying to restrict the scope of action of this power and its underlying force is impossible. What is possible is to direct it to a specific location (or goal) and just let it go. What it strikes and how much damage it will do is totally unpredictable, for it cannot be restrained. It is like a massive blanketing of destructive effectiveness. Thor uses this force and channels it through his hammer Mjölnir, which gets charged with the power of ᚦ Thurisaz and is used to channel it, in a burst from within, and then it strikes whatever Thor targets with it. This is the source of much confusion because many assume that the power of ᚦ Thurisaz is like a boomerang, returning back to the sender. This is not so – the power and force of the rune does not have such directionality it is Mjölnir which does. Mjölnir is not ᚦ Thurisaz, nor is ᚦ Thurisaz Mjölnir. Mjölnir is nothing more than a tool used to direct the location of the impact of the unleashed ᚦ Thurisaz force. The rune mystic achieves the same, using his own hardened consciousness to act as a gateway for the rune's power, and just like Thor, the mystic pulls back that consciousness as the runic force devastates what it has been released upon.

Spirit & Spiritual Reality

The ᚦ Thurisaz force spurs the spirit into expansion, looking outwards, reaching out for experiences that will force it to grow and evolve. Its remit is both the propulsion of existence forward and the fuel for it. It activates and enlivens. This rune amplifies willpower, its strength, its persistence and pushes it into action. However, in order to use it, you have to be able to let go when it is unleashed and allow it to flow through you without interference. If you try to use your will to direct and control it, the end result is that ᚦ Thurisaz's force will shatter and devastate your will as it smashes through it. This is not a force to be micro-managed. Just point it here or there, release it and remain passively submissive; let the underlying force do what it wills without interfering. Like many other runes, it is able to activate spirit sight and perceptions at a higher level of reality; unlike the others, using this one can cause these abilities to be rather unpredictable. It is the rune of wild uncontrolled perceptions, consciousness sent into overdrive and going berserk. It is the fury of enraged battle, the blinding rage of the warrior. This type of hyperdrive has its place in practice as well; some spirits are raw and wild. When facing such a devastating power, there is simply no other choice than taking a submissive stance in the matter, if you seek to remain whole after it has passed. It is best to use it when other runes are unable to push your skills any further but to avoid it in all other cases. Think of it as an absolute last resort when no other rune or force will do.

The spirit screams out its individuality through this rune's power into creation, identifying itself as a self-standing separate spark of creation. Its birth is marked by the wild erratic sound that tears through everything about it (think of the birth of Ymir and how it relates to this!). Once this initial outburst has been endured, a calming of its newly risen energies can take place.

The fundamental forces within ᚦ Thurisaz are very much linked to the Giants, the primordial powers which were forcefully shaped into creation, and will at some point break free of those restrictive shapes into which they are bound, un-making creation for it to be remade anew. ᚦ Thurisaz is part of this fundamental cycle flowing from the spiritual into the physical and back again. ᚦ Thurisaz is the manifestation of raw masculine spiritual power within the great expanse of creation (which is feminine in polarity).

Mind & Mental Reality

ᚦ Thurisaz awakens primordial power within the runes and forces, and it forces them into action, but more importantly, it awakens our ability to touch upon them, pushing the mind beyond its bounds and outside its comfort zone, and forces a glimpse into the greater view of things. For some, this can lead to insanity; for the prepared, it leads into a glimpse of the forbidden. It stirs the mind into expansive understanding, a wide broadening of its reach and capabilities in order to grasp new possibilities.

In masculine spirits, the intellect can be sent into a frenzy using this rune. When combined with ᚢ Uruz, you can drive yourself into creative trances where you natural abilities go into overdrive. It facilities the capability of seeing and opening new paths on the mental levels of reality.

The mind of any man can be sent into euphoric ecstatic trances using this rune's power, sending the intellect, creativity, intuition, and senses into a type of mind-blowing overdrive. It is most difficult to put into words. The best way to get a bit of a concept of what it is like would be to compare it to having your consciousness grabbed hold of by a higher power and flung with indescribable force into higher realities. The sheer mental kinetic force would force your consciousness into hyperdrive because it would still be active, yet totally incapable of keeping up with the processing of what was taking place. This is what the Oðinic Berserker trances were all about – the only difference between those warriors and the rune mystic is that the former focussed on the physical sending their entire physiologies into overdrive as a result, whereas the latter sends his spirit and mind into the overdrive. Because of the state of mind that it induces, it is extremely difficult if not entirely impossible to carry back memories, knowledge or any form of impressions from such types of trance. They tend to be more practical, where a goal is set firmly in the consciousness before attempting the trance work, and when the intent has become sufficiently prevalent, the trance is entered into with the hope that the underlying intent was strong enough to direct the effects of the trance, without any awareness of what is going on. You might wonder what the point of it all is, especially if you have no awareness of any of it. You get glimpses if you are skilled in this type of work, but the main goal is not the gathering of knowledge or inspiration (use ᚠ Ansuz for that); instead, it is the achievement of some goal or other. Typically, we use it to break bonds, or to pierce through the upper heavens above Ásgarð – which requires tremendous force. Upon your return, you will have returned touched with energy beyond the scope of time, and transfer it into your other mortal bodies (mainly the energy body).

 ᚦ Thurisaz should never be used in the Minni raven (memory); that is a feminine current of the mind and is highly damaged by any contact with this runic force – as is any other feminine energy, being, spirit and so on.

Energy Body & Energy Reality

The drive to be, to become something more, to achieve, is governed by this rune. The power behind all desires, be they positive or obsessive, stems from whether the passions, lust and raw emotion all boil out of ᚦ Thurisaz. The most powerful of these is the desire to live, to survive and to exist (at any cost).

ᚦ Thurisaz's power can be used for what is the most dangerous awakening to energetic realities there is. It forces the skills and blockages open, even in those who are not prepared or ready for it. Usually, this can lead to losing one's mind or burning out with power overload. It can be used to force open the doorways of perception and energy reality awareness if needed. The energy bodies are not suited to dealing with energy overloads of any type. It should only be used as a last resort and was typically used with men because our abilities and perceptions of the non-physical do not come naturally as they do in the case of women.

In energy realities, ᚦ Thurisaz is the rune of attack and defence. It is the thorn shield when its power is woven around one's self. The powers of lightning and explosive sound-wave manipulation can be unlocked with it. It is also used for attacking and cursing; it is especially useful when dealing with non-biological entities. Many other wonders are available to those using this rune, but due to the incredible dangers involved and to avoid temptation, they will be left for discussion elsewhere.

One interesting application is the awakening of the Jörmungandr within. It is very similar to the concept of the kundalini force dormant at the base of the spine location in the energy body from Eastern mysteries. For us in the West, it is not a dormant force; when looking at the life force, we see it as active and through megin, its power is manifest constantly in our lives. Jörmungandr, according to Seiðr, acts as a container of the power you gained from the Spark of Self when its ray poured out into existence and gave rise to your spirit, which then eventually enabled the energy bodies to be formed. This power then sits at one of the gateways connected to the energetic parts of the sexual organs (which for men is circulated in a manner which causes it to link the testicles and the prostate, referred to as the root or central triangle). Interestingly, this is the third gateway within the energy body. It is also deeply connected with the first of the three triangles in the Hrungnishjarta triple-interlaced triangles symbol (this is what mistakenly has been popularised as the Valknut symbol – in reality, the Valknut is something entirely different. The Hrungnishjarta is a special spirit-life-based symbol, whereas the Valknut is a death-related, binding-down-of-life symbol). In order to free the power from the containment of Jörmungandr, the power of ᚦ Thurisaz needs to be used just as Thor did when he defeated Hrungnir in battle. Using the rune's power sets those contained currents free in men. Women have a similar set of mysteries which they use, linking the womb's energetic system with the ᛒ Berkano rune's force to awaken their own equivalent power. It is a distinctly different force and set of powers, but they both achieve a similar outcome in the end goal, which is the full awakening of the energy body and setting it free from the physical.

Physical Body & Physical Reality

No matter how careful one is when using this rune, its energy masculinises and awakens masculine characteristics in the human body. It can, in men, boost testosterone production, drive to physical activity and amplify both the need and capacity for sex. This rune has a very quickly destabilising effect on all things, life forms and energies which are inherently feminine, as it shatters their inner harmony and masculinises. Be careful when you use it on the physical and energetic side of things; many forces and parts of creation are entirely feminine and rely on this state of being, such as the planet Earth, the Sun, the Universe and so forth. Know that there will always be a disruption of all feminine energies and effects. It is unfortunately the very nature of this runic power. There are no ways to counter this or work around it; this rune's forces simply devastate any attempt to do so. There are always alternate ways of achieving your goal using other runes.

Another excellent use of this rune is for defence, just as on the other levels of reality, ᚦ Thurisaz can be used very effectively to build up a thorny shielding on the physical-social side of things. It has a natural tendency of keeping away things that are harmful by force. Think of the thorns: if they are not sufficient as a disincentive to touch, they will cause you to bleed, and by doing so, weaken you. That is exactly how this rune works in its protective capacity. Using it for shielding is very advantageous and can be thought of as an aggressive shielding technique.

Like in the other levels of reality, this rune is all about activity. It pushes the physical body and matter in general into greater activity – it quickens it. The body's musculature can be not only enhanced but also strengthened by it. Be warned: anger is quick to rise under the influence of this rune's power. Other purposes for which it can be put to use involve quickening world events, clearing up obstacles and returning curses, spells and even rune work against those who would strike at you. In all forms of sports and competitions, it is a boon to have its aid.

Notes

No matter how it is used, its effects are overpowering, it shifts things into the masculine polarity and is highly activating to the point of being destructive. A little of this power goes a long way! Most often, it was associated with chaotic forces for this reason. However, there is actually no such thing as chaos, just the disruption of an existing harmony in order for it to reharmonize in a novel way. It throws things out of synchronicity for them to find a new state to synchronise with. These disruptions can seem to our minds as chaotic, because they are to the human consciousness incomprehensive at times.

This is the one power we all submit to. It is impossible to come into direct contact with it and not be destroyed, unless one just lets it take control and submits to the flow of its power.

The Rune Ansuz – Óss

Sound: a
Vocal Scale: Fa
Numerology: 4
Natural Polarity: N - M - F - N - F
Energetic Colour (Universal): Dark blue-indigo
Primal Power: Harmonisation and balancing, uplifting power and freeing
Sensation(s): Airy, free flowing, light, temperate (neither hot nor cold)

Archetypal Level of Existence

This is the rune of ecstasy and freedom. It is the great transmitter. Here the concept is not one of expansion but of the information carried forth within the flowing powers and forces. It is the rune that brings forth actualisation and at the same time controls the reception of such information. With this rune, one is able to perceive deeply, drinking from the founts of knowledge and meaning. On the archetypal level, all things that seek to manifest have an essential meaning; it is totally unique to each and every force seeking to manifest. With this rune, you will be able to grasp some of the original meaning behind whatever it is you shift your awareness to. Do keep in mind that this does not mean you will necessarily be able to understand or consciously process what you perceive. Those fall within the dominion of the intellect, which in turn is one aspect of the Self within manifestation. This original meaning or conceptualisation of the purpose of things and beings is beyond the grasp of the intellect; it falls within the remit of pure knowing and sensing. However, a consciousness elevated to functioning at this level can and will catch glimpses of these meanings, which it might be able to conceptualise partially, and is most certainly able to grasp them intuitively. It is very much like looking at a face covered by a mask, where you can see half of it and the other half is totally beyond your comprehension or capacity to grasp even the remotest glimpse of. Raising one's consciousness day after day, every day of your existence, will enable you to peer into this level of existence, where taking a single glimpse will result in such a vast expansion of the Self that it could be described as the equivalent of multiple simultaneous enlightenments.

This rune is, at its very root, the source and end point of all knowledge, wisdom and understanding. It is the point from where it all begun and where it all leads to. It is strongly associated with the well of Mimir; however, its remit is not only that of the past, it is of all-knowledge. It is the rune that allows the advanced minds of the Galðr and Seiðr masters and mystics to face the unknowable.

ᚠ Ansuz is also the receiving rune; its ability to open various levels of the Self to incoming knowledge and information surpasses all other runes. Its force is able to blend your essence with the vast waves of cosmic intellect and connect you to vast sources of direct knowing, unfolding wisdom beyond your wildest imagination.

Even though this rune is not the rune of the Hamingja, it does have a deep and important connection to it, for it allows the flow of megin throughout the Self. Without it, it would be impossible to direct megin into anything and breath is one of the main vehicles for megin. More on this when looking at advanced Hamingja work. The rune is key for any type of communication, be it spirit to spirit, energy type of communications, or even speech. It is about the sum total power of such communications, sharing of ideas, inspiration, freedom of thought (which in human beings is directly related to freedom of speech, for speech is the carrier of thought and ideas).

Spirit & Spiritual Reality

This rune represents and influences the absolute freedom of spirit. It is the wings upon which it flows and flies upwards. ᚨ Ansuz is the rune that governs the transformation through growth of spirit, its growth from inception until it reaches its final state of existence. It also governs the scope of the spirit, as well as how it expresses its own inherent unique characteristics. All inspiration flows in from the spiritual reality and this rune is used at this level of existence to direct it, amplify it and enhance its effectiveness. Using its power, you can direct the flow of inspiration into yourself or others by simply channelling this rune's inspiring force through into the energy body and then back up into the spirit.

When it comes to the spirit, this rune is a very effective one when working with dreams. Activity within the dreams, interactions and dream recall can be strengthened. This is a whole sub-field of specialisation in Seiðr work and will hopefully be covered in its own work.

ᚨ Ansuz powers are able to influence all aspects of the intellect and perception; it governs not only the intellectual capabilities but also the related functions of understanding, gathering of wisdom through experienced knowledge and, most importantly, ᚨ Ansuz facilitates the development and mastery of pure knowing. This is the direct gaining of knowledge from universal sources without the need for study, interaction or experience. It allows you to experience such waves of knowing because it is able to connect you to universal flow(s) of knowledge. Naturally it goes without saying that until you have fully mastered this aspect of the rune, all knowledge so received must be verified and proven to be valid, else you risk falling into illusion and falsehood. By the same hand, ᚨ Ansuz is also the rune of illusion; getting lost in the clouds and fantasies is a real danger for the spirit working with this rune. Always try to keep your intent pure and aim for a specific goal, or the ecstasy of ᚨ Ansuz will carry you away. The tendency of over-intellectualising things, over-thinking, over-analysing and getting lost in words are all results of unstable ᚨ Ansuz energy.

Mind & Mental Reality

As far as the mind is concerned, ᚨ Ansuz expands its scope of action. It opens up its ability to receive, and enables communications across realities. Most importantly, it is the rune of trance – more specifically ecstatic trances. The Seiðr trances, Oðinnic ecstatic trances, the trances of the Spá women of old, even those of other prophetic traditions, all fall under this rune's influences. No mind can rise, no thought can exist, no idea can flow or exist without this rune's power carrying it or its capacity to cause minds and awareness to be its receptors.

An important part of this rune's influence on both the mind and the mental reality is vital for our survival; it is the rune of freedom. Freedom of mind and freedom of spirit. It is exactly as Oðinn reveals in the *Hávamál* when he discusses his fourth spell (more about the runic secrets revealed in the Hávamál later on in this book). ᚠ Ansuz's ability to lift your mind on its winds (like a Hugr raven taking flight) is unrivalled. Whether you need inspiration, clarity, or sheer thinking power, this is the rune to use. It provides a unique ability, which is to carry over knowledge gained in other realities back to your own, for ᚠ Ansuz not only influences knowledge and memory in the traditional way, but it also does so energetically. It can carry entire volumes of knowledge in the tiniest energetic fragment, for those who know how to read this are indeed able to extract it and make the same use of it as they would have by reading hundreds of page from a printed book.

It is likewise the rune of thought beyond thinking, the runic force which inspires and promotes creative undertakings, and it is the rune of innovation, new ideas, new concepts, new realisations. It is the rune of the free-flowing dance of the mind as it goes wild and free of all constraints, creating, perceiving and processing things in an endlessly ecstatic and elegant movement.

ᚨ Ansuz is also the rune of all languages, be they ancient or new. Its force enables the encapsulation of ideas, concepts and other abstractions into form (language, image, etc.). It is this rune that gave our minds the ability to understand the runes themselves!

When you want to read the universal threads of awareness, ᚨ Ansuz can facilitate that – not only in terms of capability and skill but also in terms of accessing them. Much more could be said about these light threads of creation, but this will suffice for now. Use the rune and mediate on them to start learning.

The power of speech asserts itself through ᚨ Ansuz at this level and below, its influence and expression moves from ideas and abstract concepts from the Archetypal to thoughts at this level. The exchange of thought is how minds communicate, and all this falls within the remit of this rune (including the manipulation of thoughts). It also governs the intellect, speed of thinking and overall capabilities of the mind. By modulating the ᚨ Ansuz's influences in others and the self, it is possible to speed up or slow down the activity of our minds.

Energy Body & Energy Reality

The element of air, neutrality, balancing of energies and freedom of all energy (and energy forms) is governed by ᚨ Ansuz. At this level, speech becomes the silent or almost silent, a whisper which influences and shapes energetic reality. Both the shadow and energy bodies (Sal and Hamr) fall within the scope of ᚨ Ansuz and whispered Galðr. Remember this! It is an important key! The power of communication here extends into hypnosis and autosuggestion when the rune's powers are applied at this level of existence.

Another interesting power of ᚠ Ansuz in relation to speech is its ability to embody intent and power within spoken words. All the mysteries of magnetic speech, mystic speech, word weaving, song, invocations, incantation, calling forth universal forces with sound itself (including the runes!), the mysteries of names and much more falls within the remit of ᚠ Ansuz (the Skaldic Arts). With its help, you can acquire all such abilities and for the Spa-endowed, prophetic speech is also awaiting to be awoken with it. This is the ability to realise prophecies as they are spoken into reality, in effect making the prophet(ess) a channel not only for the information but also the realisation of given foresights. Additionally, all creative forms of word use belong to this rune's force, as do all the mysteries of words of power and Skaldic work. Much Seiðr work relies on the songs of old, which when spoken, alter the state of the mind and allow it to fly free. This too belongs within the set of skills on offer to those who master ᚠ Ansuz.

Using this rune's forces, you can balance out and harmonise any set of energies, be they runic or not. ᚠ Ansuz is especially effective when it comes to increasing non-physical hearing, or the hearing of energetic beings, shadows, energy whispers and so forth.

When it comes to the control of the air element, a whole range of abilities can be awoken and connected to it via this rune's power, including communication and control of energetic air beings.

The free flow of energy is enhanced in the energy body, as is the strength of the shadow self. Remember, the shadow is formless, and flows like the air for higher-frequency shadows, or bleeds/oozes out like oil (or blood) for the denser ones. The former ones can be influenced by ᚨ Ansuz and the latter by ᛚ Laguz. These bodies can be sent into a type of ecstatic trance of their own. It is a very different yet somewhat similar state to the mental and spirit trances; here, it is a trance of pure sensation/feeling, while the others are intellectual ones.

Physical Body & Physical Reality

On the physical, ᚨ Ansuz controls breath in all its scope, be it the mystical powers of breath along with all types of breathing techniques, down to influencing breathing itself. All mysteries of the megin breath fall within its remit, as do the important trance-inducing breathing techniques (some of which were covered in this book, see p.97). It allows use of the breath to carry not only energy from the physical to the other energetic bodies, but also impressions and nourishment. ᚨ Ansuz is the king of breath, breathing and air.

In terms of the physical, it also exerts a great influence on consciousness. Its ability to free the conscious from the immediate physical and elevate it to other modes of functioning is undeniable. It also has the ability to purify it. What this means is to make it more subtle, more refined and cause it to expand the breadth and scope of activity, both in terms of how receptive it is, down to how active it is and where this activity is focussed. It improves the speed, the effectiveness and range of functionality of consciousness.

It is an excellent rune to take control of the air element's physical influences, as well as helping with all types of healing in respect to breath. It is an excellent rune to help soothe the nerves and settle into a state of non-agitated alertness, promote relaxation and assist with breathing difficulties. It can also be used to influence the sense of smell and hearing as it influences soundwaves and the carrying of scents through the air. It also governs oxygen, be it molecules of oxygen flowing through the blood or the level of oxygen in the air we breathe.

Other interesting abilities linked to the ᚠ Ansuz rune are sending whispers over the wind, control of the air currents and even after extremely long practice, it is possible, in theory, to cause things to become very light or even float.

The Rune Raiðo – Reið

Sound: r
Vocal Scale: Sol
Numerology: 5
Natural Polarity: N - M - M - F - M
Energetic Colour (Universal): Slightly dim red with a hint of transparency within it.
Primal Power: Movement from one state/place to another, journey through life/existence, evolution.
Sensation(s): Lightness, flowing movement of air, this version of air is denser or more compact than the Ansuz one

Archetypal Level of Existence

ᚱ Raidho embodies all the forces of movement. It is the journey from one place to another and from one state of being to another. It is the directionality, the movement and the journey itself. This rune's forces will always result in some form of change and motion (as it manifests down), be it positive or negative. The ᚱ Raidho force and powers are not only limited to movement, they also embody the initial primordial rhythm and, to a lesser extent, cycles. When two or more concepts move in a common direction, their vibrational patterns have a tendency to harmonise this interplay and interaction; it gives rise to rhythms, and those rhythms then help propel those journeying together further and faster. This is one of the runes which gives rise to the need of journeys made in company of others. By this point in the rune row, the Self is here and is becoming aware of the Other (or not-Self, if you prefer). At R Raidho, we see the first interactions of the Self and the Other, leading to the more quasi-permanent settling of the Self with the Other found in P Wunjo. To put it simply, Raidho's forces will bring about temporary joining of more than one for a common goal but P Wunjo's will bring them together long terms or for a lifetime.

Because this rune's powers induce harmonic rhythms, is it also the rune that sets patterns and processes in place. It governs how various forces, energies and even powers interact, brings them together and then splits them apart as their goals are achieved. This is the rune that guides evolution and fate along a proper path in order to achieve a goal. It is very important to keep this in mind: R Raidho always has a goal, an end point, the end of the journey. Archetypally, this is where the 1 becomes 2, the beginning and the end. As such, it is both the journey, the ones travelling and the means by which they travel, leading to a common association of this rune with the chariot, boat or vehicle, and building a strong relationship to the M Ehwaz (horse) rune. An important distinction between those two runes is that R Raidho is the journey, which M Ehwaz is not, and R Raidho is non-living transportation vehicles, whereas to M Ehwaz belong the living forms of transportation.

Within R Raidho's remit belongs the transformative gaining of experience, the growth through the slow process of journeys undertaken on all levels of existence. Changes made through the means of this rune's power are fundamental and deep; it has the power to change the way your very Self expresses itself throughout reality, it brings to light new possibilities and forces old ones to be matured, perfected or forgotten and discarded. You can think of ᚱ Raidho as making the worker and his tool the perfect companions, as if they were one. Expertise is what is born out of the journey within one's own skill set. You go on a journey from apprentice to master, and in this way, ᚱ Raidho is a key for runic perfection and mastery. Learning, using and mastering the runes is the longest of journeys, yet it is also the most fruitful. Remember though, each journey comes at a price; there is always a cost for both embarking on a journey and for seeing it through. You need the fuel to keep propelling yourself forward. Without it, you might well find yourself stuck in the middle of nowhere, unable to move forward or back.

Spirit & Spiritual Reality

In the spirit, ᚱ Raidho represents expansive movement with purpose and goal. By now, the spirit will have gained the capacity to expand and the power to do so; this rune gives it the 'where' it will reach out to. Without it, there would be no goal or destination. It needs experiences to grow, and it needs to both exchange and affirm the nature of its Self, and to do so, it has to reach outwards from its Self. ᚱ Raidho provides that and directs where and how it will do it. In return, the spirit gains experiences and grows, perfects itself. New ideas, new experiences, new concepts are gathered, new memories form, all parts of the Self grow with the goal of perfecting the spirit, allowing it to grow further to take on more extensive journeys, to reach out further and further. This is the power of ᚱ Raidho at play. It is essentially limitless, other than the limitations imposed upon it by the spirit itself.

In terms of the broader spiritual reality, ᚱ Raidho not only controls the flow of spirits and their journeys but also the boundaries and pathways. It governs the vibrations, rhythms and harmonisation across realms, and allows for certain spirits to bind themselves to certain environments, worlds, realities and so forth. Just as it allows this process to take place, it also imposes restrictions upon it and prohibits those who are not compatible with realms they seek to enter from doing so. It enforces the law of like attracts like to a brutal ruthless degree; there is no compromise, no alteration, no way around on this level of existence. You either are like the destination or you never reach it. The only way to reach your goal is to become more like or vibrate like your destination through the transformative experiences of your journeys. Keep in mind, movement from one state of being to another is also a journey in its own right. On the spiritual, this journeying is what ᚱ Raidho pushes you towards. The need to spiritualise to reach higher realms of existence is dictated to all of existence by this rune.

Mind & Mental Reality

ᚱ Raidho, at this level of existence, strengthens the connection between the true Self (the Spark of Self manifest through the spiritual and archetypal levels of the Self) and the lower manifestations of the Self (the mind, memory, personality, shape, energy and shadow bodies, awareness and the physical including consciousness). It opens the path between the two and allows for the lower to connect with the true. Very few are the human beings who ever even get a glimpse of their true Self, let alone knowledge of it.

Likewise, when it comes to establishing a connection with any type of mind, spiritual being, or even purely energetic being, this is the rune to call for assistance. The eternal dance of all things and lives is governed by its forces. Within our minds, the connection to memory is maintained and reinforced by this rune; forgetting is typically countered by increasing its activity within the mental sphere of the individual. Perceptions can also be connected to end points when projecting out of the immediate confines of the body. Connection to sources of inspiration, seeking out for new ideas, thoughts and concepts is within the rune user's reach through its influences.

Energy Body & Energy Reality

This rune controls the threads of power and energy throughout all of creation. This is an important concept when dealing with the energy body and shadow, be they your own or those of the world at large. All energy flows through those threads along set paths – intelligent energy. Our energy bodies are actually entirely made up of them, and their intersections are found at the hvel (or chakras, for those of you familiar with the mysteries of Eastern origin). This rune allows one to perceive them and utilise them. There is a whole book-long set of methods and arts involved with the manipulation of these threads of existence and using them to evolve yourself. For the time being, know that with the forces of this rune, you will be able to gradually open your perceptions to them, draw energy from them, and start to learn of their functions.

Aligning one's self and energies with greater cycles in existence is possible using ᚱ Raidho (as long as you can perceive the cycle you want to align with). This is used quite extensively in trance work and in Seiðr. In Galðr, we align runes and bindrunes with the forces of ᚱ Raidho and our intent towards specific goals.

All forms of energy body that can take to travel are governed by ᚱ Raidho. You can not only set the destination using this rune, but can also prepare the energy body itself to act as a vehicle for your conscious awareness for the journey. ᚱ Raidho's forces will then propel you to the correct place, avoiding you going astray or get lost (remember to fuel up on energy before doing this! ᚱ Raidho needs fuel). It is also possible to using this rune to bridge what people call the subconscious with the conscious.

Physical Body & Physical Reality

Physically, as far as our bodies are concerned, the manipulation of awareness (through the intersection points of the threads of existence mentioned above) and consciousness (through the biological awareness covered in *The Blood of Lóðurr Awakens*) fall within the domain of this rune's powers. Raising of consciousness, sending it out, evolving it, and changing it all belong to the set of functions of ᚱ Raidho. Remember, consciousness is who you perceive yourself as being, but to the Self, it is a just a tool of experiencing which dies with the body (unless trained to exist without it).

ᚱ Raidho can be used to strengthen one's abilities and one's synergy with all tools of the Self, no matter what they are. The same runs true for all the tools you might use in your daily life. For example, an engineer can increase their capabilities with their computer usage, a scientist with their own equipment, a musician with their voice (which is a tool as well), an athlete with their body (if used as a tool) or even your own mind can be used as a tool by the Self, and so influenced by the powers of ᚱ Raidho.

Just as on the other levels of reality, ᚱ Raidho governs all journeys and modes of transportation on the physical, be it taking trips in the world to taking trips through life itself. As such, when you find yourself stuck or seeking a new direction in life, this is the rune whose force will not only carve a path forward for you but also enable you to take the trip. Just remember that trip will change you; it will force you to grow, which in itself might not always be a welcome or pleasant experience. An interesting way of using this rune is to set your mind on a goal or a state of being you would like to move to, and then unleash the rune's power. People always complain they lack x, y or z. To fix that yourself, think of what it is you need (say, a better job), set your mind on the job you want and visualise yourself as having it (not lacking it!) and unleash the rune's power. The more you harmonise with the end goal via the rune's energy and allow it to carry you forth, the quicker you can get to your goal (in this case, the job!).

One somewhat more mystical journey type this rune governs is through what are typically called leylines. Those energy lines of the planet which are, in essence, part of the planet's energy systems. This is a very extensive field of knowledge well worth looking into. It was also one of the best-kept secrets within Seiðr practitioners (and druids) of old.

The Rune Kenaz – Kaun

Sound: k
Vocal Scale: La
Numerology: 6
Natural Polarity: M - M - F - F - M
Energetic Colour (Universal): Bright vibrant red.
Primal Power: Transformation through transmutation and transference – powers of flame (rather than fire).
Sensation(s): Heat, fiery but contained, sense of aliveness within its fire.

Archetypal Level of Existence

This rune embodies fire as well. However, this is the fire of life and more importantly, its transformative power. It is a more controlled fire rather than the primal raw ravaging flames of ᚠ Fehu. The initial outpouring of life and vital forces is manifest through controlled fire, which falls within the remit of this rune's power. It is the source of all creativity, the passions of life, existence and the drives which push us outwards towards our goals in existence. The power of transformation through transmutation and transference is what ᚲ Kenaz is all about. ᚲ Kenaz provides us with an interesting first glimpse, where the focus of power and runic forces shift from pure fire into fire and light. ᚲ Kenaz is the first glimmer of this association of flame and light; it is controlled light, a soft outpouring of the first glimmers of light from flame in a direct way. Light in this manner is used to illuminate the darkness, the unknown and make it possible for us to investigate what is revealed, pushing it gradually and cautiously into the realm of the knowable eventually, pushing into the known. It is not, however, the overwhelming, unyielding blinding light that is ᛋ Sowilo. In this way, ᚲ Kenaz is used to transform the unknown into the knowable, so that we can gain insight into it and through our efforts, make it known. Because of this, the use of this rune eventually leads to a softer and gentler, more gradual type of enlightenment. But do keep in mind this form of enlightenment is progressive and ongoing; it needs to be sustained, it needs to be worked on in micro-stages until it gains momentum. The more you know, the more you will learn there is yet to discover.

If you are interested in energetic alchemy, mental alchemy, or even spirit alchemy, this is the rune to focus on. The knowledge and power accessible through working and specialising with ᚲ Kenaz offers up many fascinating possibilities to the rune mystic, including the ability to reshape parts of the Self (those parts which are subject to shaping).

The power to create (through transmutation) and the ability to do so are offered up by this rune for those who master it. Creating with runic energy and transforming or re-encoding creation begins with this rune and ends with ᛞ Dagaz. Using ᚲ Kenaz on the archetypal will trigger the skills and know-how for this, which then manifests through the spirit into the mind (perception), dawns on your awareness (energy reality), then finally into consciousness (physical).

In its flame aspect, it represents the powers of purity, or more specifically, purification. All things are broken down in a controlled way until all impurities get burnt away, transforming and regenerating the Self and the not-Self, until their full natures are expressed perfectly, without filters or contaminants. It is the rune that pushes each Self to actualise the purest expression of its nature.

Spirit & Spiritual Reality

Spiritually, ᚲ Kenaz offers up illumination in the purest sense of the word – not an all-encompassing type of burst of light, but a manageable, gradual illumination for each and every one of us. It is like a flower blooming slowly, gradually opening up its petals to reveal the full beauty of its true nature, complete, pure and unfettered. The type of enlightenment it produces is a very grounded, soft and gradual one; it allows all the parts of the Self to catch up with each new stage and brings a fundamental change at the end of the entire process. In other words, it is a cumulative set of micro 'aha' realisations and understandings unfolding on the spiritual level.

With its fiery nature, the forces of ᚲ Kenaz provide boosts in all spiritual activity and ability, both on the individual and the grander scale of things. This in turn leads to a type of transformation allowing the spiritual side of our beings to operate at even higher levels of existence. It is, in this manner, a rune of elevation of spirit, of blooming of one's own and of others' spiritual nature. It is the rune that allows the Spark of Self to shine through the Spirit of the Self. This very process gives rise to new powers, abilities and the realisation of higher concepts. It is the symbolised by the phoenix of the legends of old rebirthing itself and unfolding with its wings wide open, shining forth the true nature of itself in full glory, and just like the phoenix, his light is regenerative and life-giving.

In its positive feminine polarity, < Kenaz acts as a protective rune against the immediate dangers you might be facing. It is the point of light in the dark environments, one which attracts life to itself and whispers of refuge from that which is feared the most. It also provides a relief from the cold, providing a safe space to rest in and to get a temporary reprieve from the constant spiritual battles one needs to face for the sake of growth and realisation of the Self. Its energy helps all recharge the batteries before moving on to the next stage. Do keep in mind that unlike ᛈ Wunjo, which is a more long-lasting resting point in this journey, and ᛟ Othala, which can be a permanent one, < Kenaz is more like a pause just long enough to recharge, gather yourself and resupply, before heading back out. It serves an immediate need and as soon as that need is satisfied, its influence wanes.

Mind & Mental Reality

< Kenaz opens up the mind, and activates all its inherent and dormant abilities. The will is enhanced and empowered by it, the intellect is quickened and its scope is temporarily expanded, and perceptions are enhanced. Mind vision (direct reception of images and vision from

across time and space) is developed and fuelled by this rune's power.

Using the ᚲ Kenaz force, a skilled rune mystic can acquire the ability of thought transmutation, where any thought, concept or idea can be 'shifted' into another. The most beneficial use of abilities along this line is the active silencing of thought. Unlike the usual technique that requires you to slow the onslaught of thoughts within your mind until you can eventually still them completely, with active silencing, you can, by this rune's powers, transform a thought into a non-thought. It can be thought of like clay pigeon shooting, where you shoot down each thought as it arises in your mind before it has the opportunity to take hold. Other applications of this ability involve acquiring perfect concentration where a similar process is undertaken, except here you change the type of any thought which does not relate to the one thing you are focussing on to one which is directly related to it. Upon mastery of this type of practice, you can develop single, pointed concentration to an incredible degree of perfection.

All forms of revelation and insights can be brought about on any topic for a skilled user of ᚲ Kenaz, although as with all runes, not all visions are necessarily pleasant or enjoyable; some truths can be very disturbing indeed. It is the 'sight beyond sight'. Always be careful what you go looking for: you might find things you were not prepared for, no matter how much you think otherwise. Within this rune's force is to be found an incredible amount of knowledge, not only runic knowledge but also knowledge of all other things.

Light, the soft gentle illuminating light which can carry both the mind and memory across realms, is available to the users of ᚲ Kenaz. Enhanced by the effects of perfect concentration, it also ensures they do not get distracted or reach their goal even faster and more effectively limits the amount of mental energy spent.

To those who make progress upon the route of mastery with this rune, at the point where they gain a strong control of the Light and Flame aspects of the rune's force, the flame of knowledge is revealed. A mind bathing in this flame unlocks the knowledge of their ancestry, of their entire lineage and the powers of their ancestral lines. Using ᚲ Kenaz, this can be embodied in their blood (which will act as a receptacle via DNA) leading to the famous (or infamous) saying of having liquid fire in one's veins. It activates and it makes accessible all that know-how (especially when used in combination with ᛞ Dagaz). Most people misinterpret this type of knowledge, which is the experiences and know-how of our ancestors, and which lives on within our very Self.

Energy Body & Energy Reality

In the energy body, the flames of ᚲ Kenaz serve a dual purpose. Not only do they purify and transmute its base structures and energies, but also increase all activity within it. They are also the roots of desire. Unlike other runes, ᚲ Kenaz does not amplify desire as such; instead, what it does is awaken it, activate it and transform it. In other words, it is the source of all desires but also the way to shift the desires from base things to purer ones. Let us put this in context: the most base desires in a human being are survival, food and sex. They are born out of the flames of ᚲ Kenaz, and these are then worked through by each and every one of us and the type of desire is elevated to, for instance, awakening, enlightenment, spiritualisation and so forth. It does not flip from the base to these higher ones; instead, each desire progresses gradually, you will go through the desire for a good life, success in the material world, and so on, until all those worldly desires are exhausted. They then become more energetic-focussed, and eventually move onto the more mental and spiritual. They burn out once you have worked through them and when you reach the archetypal, where existence is so pure that desire no longer exists.

Creativity and inspiration are strongly affected by the < Kenaz rune. They can be awoken, amplified and even directed as one wills. By using the flames of this rune, you can imbue the entire energy body with the seeds of inspiration, causing their fires to burn through you whenever needed.

One of the other important uses of < Kenaz powers is regeneration. When it comes to healing, this rune's forces are able to regenerate not only the energy body but also the physical. The flames of the phoenix are incredibly healing and those very flames are the essence of this rune. Fortunately for us, < Kenaz is a controlled flame and so applying it to healing is very effective (unlike other rune's fire powers, which always go astray, no matter how careful one is).

When travelling through darker realms (such as Niflheim and Svartálfheim), it is useful to tap into this rune's power and store it in one's energy body before departure, to ensure you do not lose yourself in the darkness of those worlds. Our energy bodies are very ill-suited to any form of accumulation, but < Kenaz is an exception because its energy is so gentle and soft, you can store some of it (as long as you avoid overdoing it) within your energy body, without running the risk of damaging it. If you need to store greater amounts of this runic power, do so with the help of ◊ Ingwaz to form a container. Note you will need to use the rune while in Midgard (Earth) to ensure you have its energy stored before you leave because the runes work very differently when used from within the other worlds.

Last but not least, by any means, those interested can learn and develop skills for energy alchemy with the help of the ᚲ Kenaz rune. This is a vast field of expertise, which ultimately leads to the ability to transmute any energy into any other type of energy.

Physical Body & Physical Reality

ᚲ Kenaz is the flame of life made flesh in the physical. All activity in the body, all the fire, passion and drive you ever feel is fuelled by ᚲ Kenaz. It activates the blood, empowers the flesh and controls functions such as thermogenesis. ᚲ Kenaz also controls all the bio-chemistry in the body. It can also be used to control all sexual functions. It is not limited to those; in terms of love and friendships, its powers can do wonders as well.

If its energy is gathered about one's physical body like a quasi-aura, it is possible to generate a field of sympathy and friendship, making communications with others easier and projecting the impression of being a very approachable and friendly person. Using the rune in this manner projects a warmth outwards, which is picked up by people's subconscious minds, causing them to respond in kind.

A somewhat more interesting application of this rune is to use its power and energy to bridge the energies from the hvels (chakras) into the nervous system and blood systems. Doing this can lead to many interesting possibilities.

In the environment, you can use this rune's power to generate a warm environment and remove any iciness between people and even energy entities coming into that space. Another possible use of this rune's power within any given space is to amplify what is already there and bring that into a more harmonious synergy with you. Its energy is an excellent conductor for the formation of groups of people gathering together for a common activity. When that activity ends, the rune power's effects will end.

The Rune Gebo – Gjöf

Sound: g
Vocal Scale: Ti
Numerology: 7
Natural Polarity: N - N - N - N - N
Energetic Colour (Universal): Dark blue.
Primal Power: Exchange, synchronisation.
Sensation(s): Lightness sensation of ease with direction, like a soft breeze of air in midsummer.

Archetypal Level of Existence

The entire spectrum of giving belongs to the underlying force of X Gebo, but is not limited to gifting only. Other principles are included, such as agreements, exchanges in contracts, vows, promises, sacrifices and even those which relate to exchanges between parts of your very Self. All are governed by this rune's power; even fate is subject to the laws of X Gebo. When the Norns take something away, they need to rebalance things by giving something back, be it a new opportunity or an event of pure luck. Every force and counter-force exchange is well within the remit of this rune's force.

X Gebo teaches us when and how much of an exchange is appropriate. These days we are all conditioned to automatically accept the fact that the self is sacrificed for the greater good or the greater whole. Putting everyone above one's Self is not always a good thing. It should never be an automatic response, at least not when dealing with a large-scale beneficiary. Every individual and person has a fate of their own, when sacrificing all of that and the impact they might have on all things is given up. In other words, sometimes the one Self can be far more important than even the whole of humanity. This very statement should be taken with care, for it can lead one down the opposite road towards overinflated ego and delusions (which people are very prone to – everyone wants to be the special one, these days). The only real way of ascertaining the appropriateness of a sacrifice is by wisdom and insight; this is what X Gebo offers to those who master it. Even Oðinn warns us in the *Hávamál* not to oversacrifice. To say the whole topic is tricky to understand is an understatement because on the archetypal level, intellect, feeling, logic and even reason are irrelevant and these are the only tools we have to use in such deliberations. Higher intuition and cosmic knowing are what ultimately decides the appropriateness at these abstracted levels of existence.

Keep well in mind that when X Gebo applies, the exchange is not always equal. You can give something more for something less and vice versa. The wisdom needed to judge whether an exchange is worthwhile is what you should always strive for. Do remember that to never be involved in any type of exchange is to become totally isolated and fall into stasis. The very process of reaching out for something, anything, is the drive of the forces of X Gebo.

Spirit & Spiritual Reality

On the spiritual, ᚷ Gebo is both a force of exchange and a carrier of power. ᚱ Raidho takes you upon a journey from point A to B (or multiple Bs), but it is ᚷ Gebo which, at the destination, enables you to not only to connect but to settle. The very act of settling into a new state or a new place requires an exchange of energy, which harmonises your energies with that of the new destination. By the same account, a similar type of exchange takes place with your old state or place of being, but in reverse. A withdrawal of energy and Self has to happen for you to disassociate from what is left behind. It is very much like pulling up your anchor and moving it to somewhere new. This process of ᚷ Gebo exchanges between the Self and all that is not the Self that enables new experiences and growth. The same takes place between entire realities, as the worlds are contained in the eternal paths within Yggdrasill, all exchanging energy, information, power, lives and forces, up and down its inner paths.

ᚷ Gebo allows for the exchange and gifting of power. The age-old interactions of spirit and human are highly facilitated by this rune in all ways, ranging from the gifting of things (or food) to spirit (for this to be effective, you need to break the objects or cut through the foods to release the megin), down to the building of shrines and templates dedicated to them (serving as a crossroads to that spirit's realm).

Mind & Mental Reality

Within the mental side of things, ᚷ Gebo plays quite a number of essential functions, including memory management, where information and essence of all memories are exchanged from the memory to the mind and vice versa. It also comes into play when several minds come together and, as part of the multiple exchange of ideas, thoughts and concepts, are able to come up with some incredible outcomes which would never have been possible otherwise.

When trying to connect directly from mind to mind, this rune in addition with ᚱ Raidho are used to enable the exchange. Another interesting application of this rune involves the exchange of otherwise unreachable mental states to a given mind and spirit. When you seek to reach something that does not come naturally to you (which isn't within your energetic and mental remit), you can use ᚷ Gebo to initiate an energetic exchange with whatever state it is you are seeking to achieve. For instance, in Oðinnic Berserker trance work, ᚷ Gebo is used to connect to the essence of the bear (typically) or the wolf to induce the relevant trance states.

Likewise, when it comes to mental health, it is possible to make use of this rune quite extensively; obsessions and obsessive thoughts can be disconnected from in order to alleviate and eventually eliminate their impact. Do note, addictions are an altogether different matter; they are dealt with on the physical because they are mostly biologically driven or driven by the biological awareness. Remember, thoughts are power; whatever you think of you are sending power to, and whatever you are thinking of empowers it. The forces of ᚷ Gebo flowing universally enable this natural inter-flow. Whatever applies to thoughts is also true for memories. Always keep that in mind.

Energy Body & Energy Reality

In terms of energy exchange, ᚷ Gebo plays a very important role. It governs a slightly less known type of ancestry in these realities. You see, whomever you give your own energy to and they give theirs to you in exchange, it causes a relationship very much like the ancestral DNA one we know of, in physical terms. This binding of one to the other in such a powerful bond is what this rune rules upon.

At this level of things, the gifting characteristics of ᚷ Gebo come into play much more so than at the higher levels. It is less prominent on the higher levels (for us human beings, in any case) because we humans do not operate on those levels as much. In energetic terms, specifically in our energy bodies, ᚷ Gebo rules over the exchange of forces through the Hvel. It is a crucially important function because these wheels (or centres) then distribute energy back and forth to both the physical and the shadow parts of our Self. When the exchange is weakened, illness and dis-function occur first in the energetic side and then spill over into the other sides. In the same manner, it is not only an energy body to the other bodies' exchange, but works all three ways (shadow to energy, energy to physical, shadow to physical, and back and forth).

As far as our energy bodies are concerned, ᚷ Gebo also offers one of the most powerful mysteries accessible to us, the ecstatic exchange and interflow of every aspect of it with that of another. It is the tool used to achieve the mystical union of two living alike beings in sexual Seiðr. There are complex sets of rules and practices in making use of this, but for those who master this rune, they will make sense (some of them will be covered in a later publication dedicated to the subject).

What has been said regarding the mental applications of this rune's power also applies to the energy realms, but instead of power exchange through thoughts and memories, it is all done via energy bodies and entities as well as energy realms. This should suffice to prompt sufficient insight to inspire you in the right direction. More will be covered at a later point in time.

Physical Body & Physical Reality

Just as on all the other levels of reality, X Gebo functions in exactly the same manner on the physical level and our physical body. It has a considerable influence on us all, be it in terms of friendships, partnerships, contracts, agreements, vows, dedications, sacrifices, sex, ancestral relations, or be it in terms of spiritual, mystic or Seiðr work. All forms of gifting fall within its scope of action, even deep down at a biological level, where we sacrifice the lives of the animals we eat in order to maintain our physical lives.

It is worth remembering that X Gebo's gifts require a gift in exchange. Many assume this has to be a gift of the same intrinsic value as that which has been given. This is not so; there is no rule of equivalence within the scope of this rune's forces (that belongs to ↑ Tiwaz, where just recompense is granted). This is why it is dangerous to over-gift, as it can lead to being highly detrimental to the Self and its evolution, just as it is dangerous to not gift, as it leaves a void which will need to be filled. Usually, we aim to meet an equivalent value where it is possible to preserve the balance, but that is not always possible, as a means of measuring value and counter-value are very limited. A gift of pure abstract energy can be so valuable that it can change the world, and it would be impossible to match that, for example, in terms of a physical gift-back. Typically, it is possible to avoid these problems in ways such as those used in agreements and contracts, where one person exchanges something of value and gets something they want from another – that in and of itself satisfies equivalence, as it is not only a gift but a need fulfilled. A lot more could be said on this topic, but this will have to suffice for the time being.

On the physical levels, sex falls within the remit of this rune, both in terms of simple sexual exchanges to the more exotic and even spiritual ones. It is also possible to use it to bring all sorts of things into your life in exchange for a sacrifice given, or even to throw things out of your life. Polarity is simply revered within those two situations.

The Rune Wunjo – Vin

Sound: v
Vocal Scale: Do (hard)
Numerology: 8
Natural Polarity: M - F - F - M - N
Energetic Colour (Universal): Light blue, very similar to sky blue.
Primal Power: Synergising, co-existence.
Sensation(s): Chilled sensation, comfortable coldness. Think of the first chill you experience after a hot dry summer. It is a comforting pleasant coolness combined with sense of ease and relief.

Archetypal Level of Existence

ᚹ Wunjo is the rune of wishing. It expresses the end point of inner realisation in relation to one's desires for the outer reality. Once you reach the point where you can determine what it is you truly desire to experience (be it a possession, an experience, a change of circumstances), the influences of ᚹ Wunjo set the groundwork for wishing. However, it does not set the realisation of those wishes; rather, it is what sets a desire on the path to becoming a wish, which then needs to be realised. Whether it does or does not become realised will entirely depend on the power of your will. This should have been fuelled by the ᚠ Fehu and directed by ᚲ Kenaz, after having set itself on the path by ᚱ Raidho. You have a realisation that something is lacking or needed (ᚨ Ansuz); this awakens desire for whatever that is. Then that desire gains fuel (ᚠ Fehu) until it amplifies to the point where you need to do something about it, giving it directionality (ᚱ Raidho). Your will pushes it from a desire into a wish (a process of transmutation via ᚲ Kenaz). It starts a complex exchange between the inner you and the outer environment (ᚷ Gebo), where you think of ways and means available to realise it. At this point, it becomes a wish. The important part in this shift from just a desire to a wish is imbuing it with intent. That is the secret transformative ingredient. Providing you have sufficient power behind that intent (will power), the wish will be realised by ᚹ Wunjo. Should there be a lack of power, it will remain a desire, constantly feeding on your energy and trying to gain sufficient momentum to project itself from the wish to realisation stage. Most people's desires shift to wishes and take two steps backwards to become desires again. They loop back and forth most of their lives, due to lack of willpower. This is where the old saying 'one step forward and two steps back' comes into play. Naturally, at this level of existence, nothing manifests; instead, the wish and realisation of the purpose of the wish are proposed outwards into creation until it cascades all the way through the spiritual and mental into the energetic and finally manifests in the physical. This, technically speaking, does not matter much to the wish maker, but it does matter to those who seek to perfect their art and take control of the various stages of manifestation.

    The other important part of this rune is that of synergisation and co-operation. It is the meeting of like and like under a common goal (be it something to achieve or just find a safe resting place on the journey of existence). ᚹ Wunjo is where you meet others of your own kind (those who share a significant likeness in universal terms) and settle down. It is a temporary goal that has been reached, a time of enjoying the fruits of what has been worked for until the next desire and wish manifests within your Self. It is vitally important not to make the mistake of assuming ᚹ Wunjo is a completion rune; it is not, only Ice and Earth runes that can be used for completion. ᚹ Wunjo, with the mix of ice and air, is not an Ice rune – it's an Ice and Air rune. The ice aspect will provide the settling down but the air aspect will push you onwards, sooner or later. It is a rune of rest, achievement and enjoyment for a time. When its airy characteristics pick up, it will be time to go. True completion is found in ᛟ Othala much later on, where after enlightenment of ᛞ Dagaz, you finally realise your true nature and it is only then you can realise what your true place of settlement is (ᛟ Othala). Because of this temporary meeting up with like beings and being together, ᚹ Wunjo also governs all bonds, fellowships and kinships. It allows for the realisation of connections to others and expresses the law of like attracts like on a very profound level of existence. It will actually draw those who are alike together. Remember this: it is also a process of change – meeting others always has an impact on the Self, and sometimes you carry those links forward with yourself on your journey onwards.

Spirit & Spiritual Reality

The spirit and the spiritual level of existence allow the joining of two to take place. Your spirit starts off as one, until it learns to express its nature and reach out, then connect. Now at the ᚹ Wunjo stage, the force of this rune will enable those established connections to be used in order to bring that which is connected together. It draws things to each other for whatever purpose they are meant to be together. This is an important key for those of you who want a change in life. Most will try and complain that no matter how much they try, they simply end up stuck in a given cycle. This is the principle of like attracts like in action. In order to break free from any given cycle, you need to reflect on it and determine what it is about you that keeps pulling you into it. The answer is always internal; the external world and realities simply respond in likeness to the internal state of your being (and fate, but fate acts by changing you to whatever state it needs you to be in, so counter it by changing it to a state you want to be in!). As soon as you change your inner state to remove whatever has you stuck in the cycle you are in, things start to change. The hard part is maintaining the new cycle-free state of being. That is how your will is trained.

The fundamental primal force of ᚹ Wunjo can also be used to an extremely effective setting of end results. By temporarily changing our inner state of being and synchronising with another reality, ᚹ Wunjo will automatically pull us out of the current into the other. This is how spirit travel is achieved. Another important usage along this same line of practices is in the art of Spirit Walking (see: *Spirit Walking for the Rune Mystic*), where ᚹ Wunjo synchronises the spirit and the Seiðr practitioner. In more advanced uses of this art and rune, you can apply this to a space and enable the spirit to take up residence other than in its own reality.

Mind & Mental Reality

ᛇ Wunjo's influences on the mental are highly beneficial; it is a most enjoyable, pleasant state of mind. A sense of achievement, happiness and friendship flows within the rune's very energy. Its power gives rise to contentment and satisfaction. It can remove all worries and struggles because while at this point there is nothing to struggle for, it was achieved, the journey is complete and enjoyment is here. It is a mentally very regenerative rune and removes mental fatigue very easily. ᛇ Wunjo, however, is not just a rune of sitting around in bliss all day and night long. It enables cooperative work, and the building of cities and wonders in our world is the result of the powers of ᛇ Wunjo. Teams of people, beings and minds can be brought into a project in a harmonious and productive manner by this rune, and common goals are achieved through its influence.

In terms of mental health, it can be an excellent healer for states of solitude, alienation and isolation. Even in the hardest of times, it can lift the mind from the darkness and solitude it has a tendency of drifting into.

The rune also plays a vitally important part in the functioning of the Self. It will allow its user to bring together all parts of the Self harmoniously and have them all work towards a specific goal. Most of the time, we struggle to move forward because one or another part of our Self refuses to do so or is in conflict with another, or might just feel isolated from the rest and then puts its foot down in objection (very much like a child going on a rampage because it wants something). ᚹ Wunjo has the power to bring all the Self into a functioning, harmonious whole. Here again, its nature is temporary but even so, being able to function as a complete Self, even if it is to achieve a single set goal, can be incredible effective.

Energy Body & Energy Reality

In the energy realities, ᚹ Wunjo's forces come to their peak. It is only once you come into energetic interactions that its full power can be manifested. Its abilities are hyper-amplified and all that has been said about the like attracts like law not only applies here as well, but does so in a far more direct and immediate way. The bringing together of like forces, like beings, like people, like worlds is very prominent. So much so, that all it takes is for you to have a certain type of energy in your energy body and push its concentration to be more than any other type, and you will be pulled into the energetic realm where that energy is dominant. This might seem like a hard thing to do but it is not really. If you keep all your energies in balance, then throwing one out of balance by increasing the amount only ever so slightly will result in it being the dominant energy in your system, and off you go. This is one of the reasons why keeping in balance is so important; it opens up a whole range of possibilities which would otherwise be very difficult to achieve, if not near impossible.

Not much else needs to be said in relation to the energetic influences of this rune; all the mental and spiritual information also applies pretty much identically here – the only difference being that at this level of reality, the results of those principles manifest; this is where we can see things happen.

Physical Body & Physical Reality

On the physical, this rune governs not only teams working together, the meeting of friends and partners, but also the harmony within the family. Resolving disputes becomes easier and friction can be removed with less effort when this rune's forces come into play. It will bring about an appreciation of each person for those in their lives, and allow them to let go of old disputes, instead focusing their minds and emotions on shared experiences, goals and happy moments. It is the rune that keeps the household, tribe, nation and so forth together, each helping for the good of them all. Just as on the other levels, it is important to keep in mind that this is only temporary; eventually everyone will go their own way, sooner or later. For this reason, enjoy it while it lasts. This does not mean that such harmonious interactions of a group of people will only last a short time – it might be hundreds of years – but at some point, people will move apart, and when it is time for them to do so, it will do. Nor does this mean that once they leave, you will never see them again. We cycle through the runes time and time again; they might well be all reunited at a later point in time again.

Biologically, ᚹ Wunjo's influence is just as important. It governs the cooperation and mutually beneficial workings of the various organs and the biological system. All parts of our bodies are direct manifestations of the Self, and just as ᚹ Wunjo is able to harmonise those non-physical parts, it also harmonises the work of all the physical ones. Someone with energy sight and specialising in ᚹ Wunjo could do absolute wonders in terms of healing should they desire to, especially in combination with ᚢ Uruz. For instance, ᚹ Wunjo is very effective when it comes to regulating the immune system.

Other applications of this rune's power have been discussed in the archetypal and spiritual section, with respect to wishing and to breaking out of unwanted life cycles. Do keep in mind you can push yourself into a more desirable life cyclic pattern by simply inverting the instructions given for breaking out of one. Be creative and experiment; ᚹ Wunjo is a relatively safe rune to get a little creative with (note the 'little' part!). Just avoid getting stuck in another cycle! The ideal is to move from cycle to cycle, learning from each and moving onto the next, once you have done said learning.

The Rune Hagalaz – Hagal

Sound: h
Vocal Scale: Do
Numerology: 9
Natural Polarity: F - F - F - F - F
Energetic Colour (Universal): Pale, almost pastel-like white.
Primal Power: Seeding, destruction.
Sensation(s): Cold and wet, sharp ice.

Archetypal Level of Existence

Understanding this rune is for many problematic; explaining it can be even more so. The force of ᚺ Hagalaz is, from our point of view, catastrophically destructive. It is one of the highest powers in existence, that power which is beyond even any imaginary conception of the human mind (or any other mind in existence, for that matter). It comes crushing down and destroys. It represents the unknowable and the unknown combined in one and as such, it totally obliterates any mind trying to touch upon it. There is nothing to understanding, nothing to perceive, nothing to be illuminated; it is simply unknowable and unconscionable, and even spirit itself cannot grasp even the smallest slither of its nature. This is the beyond everything and all things. Its very nature is what makes it so devastating, because when something known faces the unknowable, it always loses; there are no exceptions, no workarounds, no tricks and no other things to help. It is simply its nature. When the forces of this rune strike, the wise will simply stop and move out of its way, waiting patiently until it has done whatever it has to do and moves on. The true nature of this force is uncontrollable and unusable. What the rune practitioner does is to tap into those parts of the ᚺ Hagalaz force that are at the edge, those parts of it which bleed out of the main force – they are never pure ᚺ Hagalaz but they retain its essential nature. Do be warned: even coming into contact with these 'edges' bleeding out of the rune's force will have a major impact on you, everything you do while in contact with it and your immediate environment. For this reason, many choose to skip it or prepare for a long time, removing themselves from their homes before unleashing this rune. It is simply that devastating, not because it is 'evil' or 'bad' but just because that is its nature. Archetypal, it cannot be used. It can be called but the price to pay for such a call is mind-blowingly devastating. Only the fool calls down that which they cannot control and only the desperate fool thinks about calling down that which is uncontrollable. Each rune has a special method to tap into it on the archetypal. ᚺ Hagalaz's method is best forgotten.

Spirit & Spiritual Reality

As soon as you start working in the spiritual and with each level of reality below it, you will be working with a diluted part of this force and because of that, its energy becomes somewhat accessible. On the mental level, it is even more diluted and by the time you start working on the physical, it will be very much diluted. DO NOT allow this concept of dilution to fool you into thinking it is safe and can be tossed about left right and centre. This rune's forces and powers are never safe; they always produce harsh, even painful end results. Sometimes you need to work through those to make progress, and sometimes you are forced to do so by fate, circumstance or parts of your Self. For those situations, this information on the rune is given. Be wise and cautious in its use.

One of the positive applications of ᚺ Hagalaz is when dealing with foreign influences or interferences. ᚺ Hagalaz's energy can be used to banish anything that is not of the spirit in question. Anything which is not native to its very essence will be ripped away and banished from within it. In this capacity, you can think of ᚺ Hagalaz as a purging power (not a purifying one, as is most commonly mistakenly assumed).

Mind & Mental Reality

Those who work with energy and spiritual seekers can easily end up with mental health problems due to the effects of ᚺ Hagalaz. Many times it is unavoidable because for some, this might be a fundamental and necessary part of their journey. It serves to strip down the mind to its bare bones, throwing out preconceptions, conditionings and unnecessary conceptual blockages; this can sometimes only be achieved by a harsh and overpowering crushing of the mind. The problem is, sometimes the mind breaks while undergoing such process. It will often happen when it lacks the necessary strength and training within itself or another. It is also why in the past, spiritual knowledge was only taught by a master to a student, where not only transfers of power could be made but also the student's trust and submission to the master ensured that in periods of these... let us call them crushing resets, the master could guide and take over for the student until their minds completed those processes and recovered. These days, with the advent of self-teaching and book learning, students have to endure these hardships on their own. Many break. On the plus side, those with the strength needed to come out at the other end do so in an even stronger state.

The powers of ᚺ Hagalaz will not seed a new mind. Instead, what they do is strip the mind and even to a certain extent memory to the core so that their original characteristics and purposes can shine anew. It returns the mind to the seed stage. Often, after such experiences, the mind will turn away from old interests, old habits and patterns and quite often, shift in a completely new direction. This can be subtle or brutal – in the latter case, to any onlookers, that person might seem like a completely new or different person.

Energy Body & Energy Reality

This is where we see the rune being use on a

more frequent basis. Its main function is to strip down someone's life and energy body in order to bring about what is a night-like period. One where everything is lost, and all things with meaning and attachment are taken away by life's circumstances until nothing is left. It is a way to force that person to strip their system bare and return to the Self from where an awakening can be triggered. True awakenings are not comfortably undertaken on one's sofa - they are brutal, some even deadly and devastating. In order to prepare for it, the fates tear your life to shreds until you are alone with nothing and no-one. From that state, the spirit within rises. Some awakenings can be minor, others major and some totally catastrophic. This is why in the old days, you would have been warned that it was best to enjoy life as it was, rather than choosing to dive into the mysteries. You would have been actively discouraged from pursuing them because once your foot took that first step on this path, there was not only no turning back but the effects on your daily life could well be - and would be, at some point in time - totally devastating. Like the mental side of things, the strong ones pull through and as they do, awakening blossoms forth.

The more practical applications of ᚺ Hagalaz powers are very useful in getting to the core or root cause of things. It is possible to strip away illusions, and the lies and deceptions of beings (be they physical or non-physical) by using this rune, just as it is also possible to strip out of the energy systems and energies in general all influences that do not belong to it. If something has been imposed or added or changed and reintroduced, ᚺ Hagalaz will purge it out. All things are regressed back to their core by it and this can be used to your advantage.

ᚺ Hagalaz can energetically not only be devastating but also impose a period of passivity; the onslaught of this type of devastating force is only survivable in terms of submission and patience. It is often a very frustrating period, as energy even within ourselves wants to move, it wants to expand and it wants to be in motion (remember, stasis is its death). However, under the impact of ᚺ Hagalaz, the opposite is required; this can be very testing. Sitting patiently waiting and submitting to a force that is ripping you apart is no simple or easy feat. But remember, there is an outcome to whatever ᚺ Hagalaz causes. It is not destruction for the sake of destruction. Well, actually, it is not a destruction rune at all (that is ᚦ Thurisaz); destruction in Hagalic terms is a side-effect only at this level of existence. It teaches us also that we have limits; everything and everyone has limits and trying to push through them leads to self-destruction.

Physical Body & Physical Reality

People who are trying to deceive you develop the tendency of clearing away from you if you use ᚺ Hagalaz to test things. Simply weave its energy around yourself when you meet up and then watch. Should they become uncomfortable, need to leave your company quicker than usual, or even come up with some excuse as to why not to meet up, you will have your answer. The mystics on the other hand will smile, because to those who have gone through the hardships imposed by this rune, they will shine from their true essence and not be bothered by any force that attempts to strip away anything which is not their core essence.

ᚺ Hagalaz can be used to initiate the pre-cursor events for some radical change, which will ultimately bring out the essential nature of things to the forefront in a clear and unmistakeable fashion. It disrupts everything, brings darkness to life itself and causes immediate catastrophic changes that might seem almost erratic to any onlooker, but all these have purpose and that purpose is to force a shattering change, a total disruption of your inner state and your outer state, and out of those cracks and rubble, it leaves behind your essential nature which can start to shine forth. Just as ᚺ Hagalaz can cause earthquake-like events at the foundations of existence, so too it will do in life. It picks you up and throws you so far out of your comfort zone that you will not only be unable to see where that zone was, but will not even be able to recall there was such a zone.

The same applies to biological process and systems in our bodies (Lik). ᚺ Hagalaz is one rune that is seldom if ever used in relation to the physical body, because the cure brought about by it would be so devastating that the illness is like sunshine in comparison. Find another rune combination/way and avoid ᚺ Hagalaz.

The Rune Nauþiz – Nauð

Sound: n
Vocal Scale: Re
Numerology: 10
Natural Polarity: N - F - N - F - F
Energetic Colour (Universal): A glowing black, almost oily type of texture.
Primal Power: Resistance, reawakening.
Sensation(s): An empty type of heat; an uncomfortable-unsettling warmth, constantly building up.

Archetypal Level of Existence

ᚾ Nauthiz's energies and powers are often either misunderstood or looked at in a unilateral way. It is, in most literature, termed the 'need fire' and to some extent, it is possible to conceptualise its underlying forces in this way but that is not entirely accurate. When looking at things on the archetypal and spiritual levels of reality, it becomes important to grasp the underlying meanings, to know what this 'need' side of things is actually all about. ᚾ Nauthiz can best be conceived of in the following way: imagine a space being filled, be it energy, water, matter or anything else. Then cut out some of it in a shape – say for instance a flame shape. What is left behind is a space filled with whatever you imagined except the cut-out section. This now is a gap in existence, and emptiness. If you focus in, you should be able to understand how this empty gap is trying to pull in whatever you filled your space with in order to fill itself up again, but the boundary of your cut-out shape is stopping it from drawing it the energy, water, matter... this drawing in keeps on intensifying over and over again; the vacuum needs to be filled, wants to be filled. It is this need or want to be filled that the texts of old are referring to when they say that the ᚾ Nauthiz rune is the rune of need. The fire part comes from the fact that this drawing self-amplifies in force over and over again until it is filled. It is an active form of magnetism rather than its natural passive form. ᚾ Nauthiz is not the gap, it is the force in creation acting behind the emptiness that strives for fulfilment and needs to be filled at any cost, with something, anything.

Once this fundamental nature of the ᚾ Nauthiz forces and powers is understood, the derived meanings of the rune start to make sense when looking at them throughout existence. As you will see, ᚾ Nauthiz is essentially a negative polarity rune; the constructive or positive applications of its power are incredibly limited. Its energy takes away things in existence and forces them into stasis (ᛁ Isa). It is these things which give rise to the need so often associated with this rune; it is not the fact that a need is present and then the rune's power comes into play, rather it is because of this rune's forces that the need arises in the first place.

Spirit & Spiritual Reality

Spiritually, ᚾ Nauthiz is both a blessing and a curse. Its influences give rise to various needs on the spiritual. This in turn pushes spirits to seek outwards as they seek to expand themselves outward; think of it as the need of the spirit to fill everything on the spiritual with itself, and any part that is not Self is the equivalent to the gap in creation, as discussed above, from its point of view. Without ᚾ Nauthiz, there would be no drive to interact with anything outside of itself. This can be a positive driving factor for your spirit, providing it can strive towards a good outcome; however, the fact that this need arises in the first instance causes the spirit to enter into all types of challenges and hardships. The spirit then forces its personality (which is you) to sometimes go through devastating and horrific experiences in order to fulfil the 'need' it may have, irrespective of how you might or might not feel about it. Your spirit will even, if it needs to, completely break you in order to satisfy its own needs. This I view as a type of tyrannical imposition of the Higher Self. At this level of existence, there is no emotion, no empathy, no sympathy – they simply do not exist yet (until you reach the energetic level of reality and there is no compassion or love either) and as such, its 'actions' are always totally heartless. People rant and rave about the Spirit and unconditional love without actually understanding what this 'love' at the spiritual level is. It nothing like the chemical-based or emotional-based love we all know of. Love in this context is both a providing of what is needed and a forced fate-based imposition of what needs to be gone through, with the goal of learning and growing. This so called 'higher self' operates (usually) quite separately from what you call 'you'.

The same events occur in the wider scale of the spiritual reality itself. Whatever it needs will be imposed downwards. Ever wondered how horrid things actually are? Look at it objectively: most people are totally lost as to where they are going in life and why; they experience horrific things and end up in devastating life cycles they struggle to survive, let alone break out of; joy and happiness are seldom found and when they are, it is all short lived. In view of all this, you are told that it is for the sake of growth, it is to work through and learn, it is for the 'greater good' (actually there is no such thing as the greater good, since everything runs its course which is predetermined by the fates), or the best of all: there is a reason for everything but the fact is you will be kept in the dark as to what that reason is and will be denied any guidance. The only thing available from the spiritual is a hint here or there, if you know where to look and listen, and that often is given for reasons to get you where this higher part of you wants you to be rather than to alleviate any hardships you might be enduring. Why? Because it does not matter what you do; you are temporary and fade afterwards, as the Fylgja eventually reattaches itself to someone else in the line and the spirit continues to repeat this cycle yet again to grow. The only way to break this horrific cycle is to gain mastery over ᚾ Nauthiz and use those forces consciously. By doing so, you will be able to both neutralise the 'needs' that come from the 'higher' realities and force your own upon them. It is by doing this that you can write your own path and this is where most of the uses of ᚾ Nauthiz, its forces, powers and energies come from. All the practical rune descriptions and outlines will point you in this direction without actually explaining why it is so and what it is you are actually doing. Now you know.

Mind & Mental Reality

In terms of mind and memory, this rune's force offers up a few interesting possibilities. As a default position, it will bring about situations that constrain the mind's freedom or activity, induce distress and want. It is the force that precedes all desires (desires manifest on the energetic level). As such, the skilled rune user can put ᚾ Nauthiz's powers to good use by causing or eliminating whichever roots of desire are not needed or wanted. States of confusion or inactivity can be shifted into their positive counter-states. Memory can be strengthened by the elimination or diminishing of forgetfulness caused by the 'need to remember' and so forth.

In terms of the mental realities themselves, the same applies. Any type of need can be given rise to or eliminated using this rune's powers. Desires can be seeded or eliminated, which in turn directs the flow of forces in the energy levels and eventually the physical. It is a rune of pre-manifestation – if that term helps you grasp its essential meaning and uses better. Using it, anyone who has lost the will to live, a purpose, or goal can be re-ignited and re-set on their path.

This is where the traditional concepts of resistance come into being. It offers up an opportunity to build up momentum and power through the constant pushing and pulling, until sufficient force is built up to break free or break through whatever the obstacle is you might be facing.

An interesting application of this rune's power is to cause the empty 'spaces' where it is possible to absorb wandering thought forms or even deliberately directed thoughts. In this way, a certain type of protection can be gained because applying this correctly to an incoming thought form can completely disable it, trapping it forever (there is no time at this level of reality).

Energy Body & Energy Reality

A great trick, on the energy side of things. Using the resistance parts of the rune involves creating an emptiness with its force, which will then absorb the power you direct towards a given goal. You repeat this process over and over again until that original emptiness has been packed so full that it's brimming with power. Then unleash it with a bang. It is an excellent tool for condensation of energy without having to resort to I Isa.

Otherwise, ᛉ Nauthiz's power can be used to hinder any development or progress in any type of energy (except I Isa, H Hagalaz and ᚦ Thurisaz), providing it is working at an equal or higher level of vibration to whatever you wish to hinder. This is useful in many situations, most notably when events start to unfold in both energetic and physical terms and they start to overwhelm or just be too much to handle at the same time. Using ᛉ Nauthiz will allow you to hinder the onslaught, making things much easier to deal with in smaller chunks. Energetically, it is also possible to use this tactic when dealing with opposing energy types. Let us say you are working towards a specific goal and many things are in your way or trying to counter your goals. You can use ᛉ Nauthiz to hinder those, making it much easier to get to your goal, after which the forces you hindered can be safely let loose. In those cases, they will simply disperse because the intent behind them can no longer be realised (you cannot stop someone achieving a goal if they have already done so – those forces would target a past which no longer exists in this timeline).

Desires and needs have been covered at the mental level but they apply equally here – and even more so. This is where they all start to manifest. It is important to get to grips with one's needs and one's desires, otherwise they can easily overwhelm you. The more resistance you put up against them, the more they will manifest until you run out of steam and sink. ᚾ Nauthiz cannot be denied, but it can be managed. Using its power, it is possible to set the rune in motion to siphon off the most intense and overwhelming desires or needs, and instead chunk them up into smaller parts so that they can be managed either by resolving whatever it is which gave rise to them in the first place, or satisfying them in cleaner and less destructive ways. ᚾ Nauthiz can also be used to rekindle the desires for life and progress, the hunger for energy growth and learning.

Another area where ᚾ Nauthiz plays an important role is one of binding – more specifically self-bindings. Sometimes those are necessary for one's very survival. In the old days, we would have been bound by social and familial traditions and customs (we still are to date, but not as much). Binding the mind by anchoring in the physical or other realities (such as dreams, for instance) can help it from wandering off and losing awareness. ᚾ Nauthiz in this respect is an excellent counter to the 'flying off with the fairies' effects from ᚨ Ansuz.

Physical Body & Physical Reality

In terms of the physical, all that has been said in the previous levels comes into play. Here you have the possibility of unleashing the full breadth of ᚾ Nauthiz's powers. The needs, desires, bindings, protective measures, chunking of life's hardships and so forth can all be equally applied to both the physical body and life in general.

The only additional point to note specifically for the physical level is that dealing with the ᚾ Nauthiz forces at this level requires you to keep a close eye on how you react to them. It is always wise to be extra cautious because this force has a natural tendency of creeping outwards and grinding things down to a complete halt (where it leads into ᛁ Isa), no matter how careful you may be. Always be mindful that even when you need to take a break, it should not be a permanent break. The tendency to procrastinate is phenomenal when working with this rune. Likewise, it also forces those using it to recognise their own limitations; forcing things too fast and too much can cause you great harm as well. This rune's power and energy need to be tampered carefully with wisdom. It is almost like playing with a chemistry mix, where one drop of ᚾ Nauthiz might be more than enough and two could devastate your end product.

Notes

If you read the Eddas' descriptions of Oðinn's sacrifice, you will see that he is said to have sacrificed himself to himself before receiving the knowledge of the runes. It is important to understand what he actually did. We know that he had his heart pierced as he hung upside down. When reading this, most assume that he did not die because he was a god, but from our myths and legends, we know that the gods and goddesses DO die. Oðinn is actually prophesied to die at Ragnarök. So why did his body and he (our personality is rooted in our energy body, which dies after the physical dies) not die? Simply because he sacrificed his 'higher' self to his lower. It is still a sacrifice of self to self, but is critically different from sacrificing the lower to the higher. What he did is take in all the knowledge, power and scope of capabilities from his higher self and absorb them into his lower (current) self. This is the reason why he was able to gain the knowledge of the runes and not only understand them but absorb their wisdom and unlock their power. From that point onward, he re-birthed himself in his consciousness, and he became the matter from which a new spirit is born rather than a physical form into which the spirit descends. The directionality at that point is upwards flowing rather than downwards. He also managed to complete his Self into one whole functioning unit by merging everything he was and all parts of his Self into one rooted in his body (his energy body, to be more precise).

The Rune Isa – Íss

Sound: ī (as in e in english)
Vocal Scale: Mi
Numerology: 11
Natural Polarity: F - F - F - F - F
Energetic Colour (Universal): Primordial black.
Primal Power: Foundation, prima materia, absolute stasis.
Sensation(s): Intense unbearable cold and silence, strong inward pull to it – think of how your finger sticks to the freezing ice cube and then its cold has a burn effect without heat.

Archetypal Level of Existence

The first manifestation of ice, the never-melting, eternal ice, the absolute stasis, stillness and the prima materia. The essence from where matter and the whole manifest reality originated, in the icy realms that were created by the forces of Í Isa. According to the Norse mythology, we are told that fire was created first, and the realm of Muspelheim; many might wonder why the prima materia found within the forces and realms is of ice? It is simple: when discussing the prima materia, what is being referred to is the first manifestation of or the materia from which came matter. Spirit from the fire realms descends into the matter of the ice realms and enlivens it (producing water). It is important to keep in mind an important point when looking at the Ι Isa force: it is stasis, not dissolution.

Let us take a bit of detour. Ι Isa is sometimes argued as being the root of antimatter, rather than primal matter. It is important to clear out this confusion. In order gain understanding, we need to look at two main things: the first is to clarify what matter and anti-matter are and their relation to one another. The term antimatter is used often without actual understanding about what it is referring to. The second is to understand how this runic force changes as it manifests in creation (from the archetypal into the other levels of reality).

Ι Isa is the primal materia, not matter, and as such it is both matter and antimatter because those two are actually the same thing but polarised differently. The scientific point is that antimatter is matter made of antiparticles (which have an opposite charge) to the corresponding particles of the matter. In other words, matter and antimatter are both matter, the difference being that they have particles of opposite charges. This is why they both steam out of the prima materia and both fall within the remit of Ι Isa. Scientists will discover in the future that there is a third state of matter, and that too comes from the prima materia. Just keep in mind that Ι Isa is not a destruction rune, and as such nothing that comes from it or its underlying forces destroys – it is a rune of stasis. Yes, smashing matter with antimatter will destroy them both but it will produce energy (this very phenomenon belongs to the remit of other rune's forces), so you are in fact just changing it from one state to another, not destroying. And yes, before anyone starts saying 'Nothing can be created or destroyed, just transformed', that is based on old science. We know these days that there is spontaneous creation and obliteration of particles taking place at the quantum level.

The second point is that this process of birth of matter does not take place until duality is born and that happens at the border or intersection of the mental and energy levels of reality. This is also where the first, most subtle matter comes into play.

Spirit & Spiritual Reality

I Isa on this level is responsible for both the drive towards and the process of spiritual condensation. Spirit has both characteristics of its nature (the radiation of the Spark of Self) and power (the strength of the energies which make it up). I Isa is responsible for the latter, its power – the condensation of its energies that come from its fundamental nature. This is a somewhat abstract set of concepts, so it might be a bit tricky to understand. To put things as simply as possible, at the cost of a little precision, I Isa is responsible for how powerful the powers of the spirit are and can become. The more this rune's forces exert their influence upon them, the stronger its power, while the less it does, the weaker its powers will be. They will still be there because the power of a spirit is inseparable from that spirit – it is unique and an inherent part of it – but just how powerful that power is will be determined by: the strength of the influence of I Isa and the amount of spiritual energy available to it. As the spirit learns to function without the need for a mental, energy or physical body, the influences of I Isa grow and it becomes more powerful. There are other means to empower your spirit but this is a natural process of evolution whereby all spirits become independent and eventually discard all those additional shells they require during their 'infancy'.

Mind & Mental Reality

As far as the mind and memory are concerned, ᛁ Isa should be handled with extreme care and, if at all possible, should be avoided. The reason for this is simple: those parts of us (Hugr and Minni) are fundamentally linked with activity, usually a high level of activity, be it positive (you are thinking, or coming up with ideas) or negative (in silent mind mode and waiting for inspiration, or using higher forms of perception where no thought is required). Likewise, the memory is either busy when you are recalling things, or passively active when it is recording them (to put it in a highly simplified way). ᛁ Isa's influence is to slow these processes down, which leads to mental stasis. It can impair not only thoughts, but also recall, memory retention and countless other functions. Yes, it is possible to use this rune's power in a semi-constructive manner, but the price to pay with ᛁ Isa is always a slowing down of whatever it influences. An overactive mind can be quietened down just as effectively and with far safer rune combinations such as ᚹ Wunjo and ᛜ Ingwaz (for men) or ᚹ Wunjo and ᛒ Berkano (for women). An erratic mind can be quickly rebalanced with ᛉ Elhaz and ᛖ Ehwaz; there is no need to start throwing in runes such as ᛁ Isa or ᚺ Hagalaz to do the same job in a far more dangerous way.

One of the exceptions when ᛁ Isa is used involves the amplification of memory and solidification of recall. The other comes into play when for some reason the mind has been fragmented. This can happen for a number of reasons but in all those cases, it is possible to use this rune's force to pull it back together and increase the underlying cohesive force that keep it as one, which will enable you to repair the damage done. A very rare use of this is encountered when you get to the point where you have multiple selves in multiple realities and transfer your fundamental essence from inside one to the other, in order to live temporarily in many of them. ᛁ Isa is needed in special practices to keep you from self-fragmenting and losing your anchoring. This is highly advanced Seiðr work. Another example is when trying to enter a trance of stasis: the silence just before the moment of death. These few examples should give you a solid understanding on how its force functions and how they can be used within these parts of the Self.

In more general terms on the mental reality itself, ᛁ Isa is an excellent tool for interrupting the flow of incoming thoughts and suggestions. The how-to is simply this: all you need is to be able to tell what thoughts are internal to you (come from within), and what is being pushed in from outside you. Then unleash the power of the rune in that direction. It will not only interrupt the flow but it will seal it too, preventing further interference from that source.

Energy Body & Energy Reality

In energetic terms and at this level of reality, ᛁ Isa's force is unstoppable. Once you encounter it, you will need to manage it. Its cold is simply indescribable and totally overwhelming. The only effective way to deal with ᛁ Isa is to endure it. In the energy body, it is used to control the cohesive force that keeps it together. By its very nature, it seeks to self-disperse and that is what happens at death (often called the second death). ᛁ Isa here serves to prevent this from taking place by exerting its cohesive influences from the central point of the Self, from where it keeps pulling the countless parts of the energy bodies and our shadow together. As we age, this force weakens, as do we, and eventually along with other factors at play, that part of our Self just dissolves due to the dispersion of its individual components. ᛁ Isa is also, ironically, responsible for the will to survive, or rather its strength, to be more precise. The weaker its influence, the less interested in existing or living one becomes. However, on the other side of the coin, ᛁ Isa is also responsible for leading us into exactly this state of being; it slows down the will and makes taking action, living, exploring and so on dull and unappealing. It can slow your energies down to such a point that total stasis takes over; the more its impact is left unhindered, the quicker the route to death becomes. This is a perfect example of a rune's polarity at play: the first case is the positive and the latter belongs to its negative expression.

Constructively, you can use this rune to enforce the effects of any other rune. Because it is the source of prima materia, its power – or to be more exact, its substance – allows the reinforcement and amplification of power in other runes and of duration of effect. The more prima materia available to any power, the longer it can burn by increasing its substance. This is one of the fundamental reasons why this rune exists. It is not death; death on the higher realms does not exist, and the 'heavens' beyond Ásgarð know not death… but they all know ᛁ Isa.

When put together, you can see that ᛁ Isa is a rune of sustenance and cohesion; it plays an essential role in terms of integration of various systems into a working whole. Scientifically, ᛁ Isa is the root of not only stasis but also of the underlying power behind gravity; think of it as the force with which gravity acts. As such, in energetic terms, it can be thought of as the rune which gives birth to the central point of being for any energy, entity, life form and so forth. It is the root of the circle, both in terms of keeping the circle's shape and in terms of serving as the point of resistance at its centre, from which everything emanates outwards. Without ᛁ Isa, everything would simply disperse all over the place.

If you ever encounter beings of Niflheim, you will quickly come to realise that their nature matches that of ᛁ Isa; they have infinite potential for creation, as the substance used for creation abounds within them and their realms of existence, but none of them have any capacity to create. That is the root dilemma of both Ice and ᛁ Isa: it needs the external force (of fire) to bring about creation, to shape it, to work it into something. This applies to all energy work with this rune.

Physical Body & Physical Reality

This is where most of the forces of ᛁ Isa take a most fascinating turn. Their polarities become very distinct and very easily observable; the difference in effects between the negative-feminine polarity of ᛁ Isa and the positive-feminine are very easy to separate much more so than with any other rune.

Here ᛁ Isa's power is most often very unsettling. It imposes an oppressive silence, making all those who enter it uncomfortable (an excellent trick for protecting a given space). In this negative aspect, it halts all forces, all activity and all motion. It is the encasing ice that takes all activity from life away. Under its negative influences, nothing changes, nothing evolves, and all is at a frozen standstill.

In its positive aspects, it can force a pause in the cycles of life, giving rise to the opportunity of allowing you to stop in your tracks and think or take account of things. This is the time to be used to turn inwards and look for solutions 'outside' the world at large. It is the perfect time to look for the truths within and power of the Self. A self-imposed I Isa sanctuary can be extremely productive but it should be kept as short as possible because these forces overwhelm very rapidly and have a natural tendency of flipping into the negative without warning. It can happen right at the moment you start falling into a slumbering state, slowing down to the point where you no longer feel motivated, no longer feel like doing things.

Notes

Typically, it is relatively safe to work with this rune in the beginning, but once you start making a real connection with its underlying forces, stop. At that point you have a connection and it remains forever; working with it from this point onwards becomes more and more risky and should be avoided. At any rate, it should never be allowed to flow through your any parts of your Self except in extremely rare circumstances. Use the non-Self technique (see p.92) for this rune.

The Rune Jera – Ár

Sound: j
Vocal Scale: Fa
Numerology: 12
Natural Polarity: N - M - F - M - B
Energetic Colour (Universal): Yellow with a light sandy brown hue to it.
Primal Power: Development, (de)evolutionary changes, time.
Sensation(s): Soft earth, wet, solidity very similar to that of mud.

Archetypal Level of Existence

❖ Jera is a very misunderstood rune. Due to its traditional association with the harvest (which is correct), it has been misinterpreted as being the rune of cycles and circular change. This comes about because when we think of crops and the harvest, we are conditioned to think of this entire process in a circular fashion, winter -> spring -> summer -> autumn and back to winter and so forth. When presented in this way, it is all too natural for us to see it as cyclical. The same applies to the day and night cycles. However, it is important to keep one thing in mind: these are not cycles at all; they are sequential (linear) progressions. If you think of these as year 1 winter -> spring -> summer -> autumn, then year 2 winter -> spring and so forth, you will quickly shift your thinking from the imposed apparent cyclical nature of things to a linear one, simply because year 1 winter is not the same as year 2 winter. Just as day 1 and night 1 are different from day 2 and night 2... This apparently cyclical (spiralling) nature of things has been imposed upon the universe by an external force and our thinking is fashioned to automatically accept this. It is not a native phenomenon of our reality – unfortunately, it has become so rooted that unless we take extra effort to weed it out in our perceptions and thought processes, we fall prey to it.

Now that that has been settled, let us take a closer look at ᛃ Jera without the clouding misconceptions. Archetypally, it is the rune of growth, the realisation of things, the rune of plenty. This fits very well with its traditional association with the bountiful harvests but at this level of existence, it plays an even more important role. That is of seeding time itself. Time comes into play at the lowest levels of existence, namely at the border of the energetic matter, for without matter there can be no time. At this level, its force is that of change and realisation of deep essential meaning of all things. ᛃ Jera here provides the groundwork for the first outpouring of meaning. The first rays of each Spark of Self are pushed to manifest by its forces.

It is also the rune of rhythms, the ups and down, the pulse of evolution, the underlying 'beat' behind the soundwaves – all these belong to the scope of influence of ᛃ Jera. It is through this rhythmic dance that it promotes life, movement and ultimately carries creation forward along its set course (or backward in the reverse course).

ᛃ Jera, when associated with ᛒ Berkano, can be used to as a transformative tool: it bolsters ᛒ Berkano's ability to transform, slowing the process down but also enhancing its effects. ᛃ Jera is the underlying power of nature that provides for the transformative processed undergone within ᛒ Berkano. These two runes work in a wonderful synergy, especially when evolution and healing are the end goals of your work. Its force also synergises extremely well with that of ᛞ Dagaz and can be often seen working in tandem in creation. This, I suspect, might be what originally caused the confusion as to the nature of the ᛃ Jera force and the misconception of it as being cyclical. It is ᛞ Dagaz that causes this type of cycling and imbues that pattern into ᛃ Jera when they interact. What this produces is an interesting grinding type of effect, combined with steady constant growth. Such a thing can be both highly advantageous and also, if not properly managed, lead to decay because neither force brings anything new into the process. Neither are creative in their own right, and they both need to be provided with something to work on or work from. Yes, most will argue that the harvests of ᛃ Jera are life-giving, but they all rely on pre-existing life: seeds. Over-culture the same piece of soil and it will lose its ability to produce new crops. This is one of the key lessons of the ᛃ Jera-ᛞ Dagaz cycle.

Spirit & Spiritual Reality

This is where its first influences, in terms of progress and change, come into play. The spirit can and does grow – even if its growth is not what we think of as such, it does change and so the forces of ᛃ Jera play an active part in this. It is important to understand that growth does not mean for the better or for the worse – there is still a clear lack of any form of positive or negative direction here. However, ◇ Jera does give rise to a progress and a regressive growth. You can see this in play within the shape of the rune, one backwards-pointing arrow and one forward-pointing one. The spirit sits as the line between these two. It is the rune of the great NOW, the stillness and centrality of being. It is in this state of active stillness and silence that one's spirit rises. It can rise in either what our minds would term a negative or a positive way, or stay still. Do keep in mind that none of these three ways are good or bad; they just are as valid as each other. The negative is one of diminishing of the spirit, and the positive is one of amplifying it. Both ultimately lead back into the archetypal and to the beginning, which is also the end.

A less well-known range of influences of the ◇ Jera force is that it can be used, and was often in the past, to bring spirits together as well as push them apart. This stems from the fact that the principle of like attracts like will pull and push spirits into certain groupings of likeness, depending on what point in their evolution they find themselves. If a spirit progresses to the lowest degree of likeness to another, they will start to notice one another, and as this likeness intensifies, the pull grows until they meet. During this time, the growth process will be amplified because of the exchanges (X Gebo) between the two until eventually, they start to move away from each other as they transition from development of one facet of their being to another. Should the 'feature' they have developed in one another's company become a permanent form of expression of those spirits, they will retain a bond of sympathy between one another. If not, they will eventually completely move apart. Using the power of ᛃ Jera, it is possible to bring to the forefront of development of any spirit whose characteristics are like those of another and cause the two to move towards each other. Likewise, it is also possible to cause those like characteristics to become defocused (or moved into the background), which results in them moving apart. This rune is used in advanced spirit walking, in order to enable connections to be established with specific spirit types. Thinking of it in another way, what you are doing with this is in effect producing an artificial temporary harmonisation between two or more spirits.

Mind & Mental Reality

ᛃ Jera's influence on the mind, memory and perceptions is both stabilising and enhancing. It is the mind in balance, in harmony, the one that has reached stability through the influences of ᛁ Isa and is anchored in the moment of NOW, able to change into a new state. Only by overcoming ᛁ Isa's stasis and getting out of it do the mental sides of our being gain new strength and power, and when the silence has been endured and the strength has been found to overcome it (rather than sinking into it permanently) it can forge a new path to becoming something more once again. It has taken a step on the staircase of evolution and now needs to prepare for the next.

The runic forces of ᛃ Jera force through the fruition of one's work; it will strengthen the mind and bring it a type of certainty within itself. Likewise, in terms of memory, it is used not only to bring back long-forgotten reminiscences but also to strengthen its capacity for recall. The memory mead of legend is sourced from runic trances combining the ᚼ Jera and ᚠ Ansuz runic forces, along with the influences of ᚨ Othala. The runic power stabilises the mind and gives it endurance, enabling greater persistence in all you do.

In terms of memory, it allows you to give it a degree of not only what can be termed fluid solidity but also enables you to carry memories and concepts between levels of reality. In the same manner, it is possible to weaken memories and banish the unwanted ones as well. Remember, half of ᚼ Jera points backwards! In this respect, ᚼ Jera is an excellent rune for stabilising the mind and interrupting the onslaught and barrage of incoming thoughts. Because of its ability to bring about a state of fulfilment, the effects on our thinking can be quite profound: the worry, the concern, the endless to-do lists, the constant planning all comes to a slow-down and potential a complete halt as the mind settles into a peaceful harmonious state. With ᚼ Jera, it has achieved its goals and its aims, and its needs have for the time being been satisfied. It pauses before moving a new direction. This has a most pleasant side effect of forcing its erratic thinking to also pause. It is almost the equivalent of taking a deep breath and just letting go. Unlike when using ᛁ Isa, it is not a forced pause; it is a pleasant one, far more natural and 'in-flow' than the brutal ᛁ Isa-induced one.

In combination with ᛇ Eihwaz rune, ᚼ Jera can be used to push mental things into materialisation. The two forces joined are very effective when it comes to building up the mental gravity of thoughts (specially large groups of common thought types). They are solidified more and more by ᚼ Jera and finally pushed down into manifestation through the powers of ᛇ Eihwaz. Any form of wishing (in conjunction with ᚹ Wunjo) can be pushed through into realisation. How fast this happens and how effective it is depends primarily on the power invested in the process and whether it complies with fate (or, at least, is not in opposition to it).

Energy Body & Energy Reality

In the energy body and shadow, ᛃ Jera serves the purpose of making its underlying energies and system (including the Hvels) flourish. They are pushed into a state that can be called completion or realisation of potential. You can look at its function in another way, that of manifestation and materialisation of the full potential of your energy bodies. The energy body (Hamr) is after all the crystallisation of the Fylgja's interaction with the sum potential of your ancestral energies, characteristics and potential, with a few other aspects of your Spark of Self's emanations. It will also enable you to complete any of the changes you seed as part of the efforts to perfect your Self.

Likewise, it is possible to use the forces of ᛃ Jera to achieve the same effects not only in others but also in physical places. Everything is imbued with energy of one sort or another; all these energies need to be cultivated until they mature. ᛃ Jera enables you to do so. Casting one set of runes followed by the ᛃ Jera rune will increase the effectiveness and rate at which those runes will be realised. However, keep in mind that ᛃ Jera's influences only bring about the effects within your capabilities and the amount of yourself that you have invested in your Galðr (or Seiðr). When working with this rune, always remember that even after realisation, it is wise to keep some form of end product that you can use for the next movement it will require (be it towards growth or diminishment).

As far as general energy manipulation is concerned, ◇ Jera is an excellent tool for the maturation of a certain energy and can be used to solidify its effects. When combining more than one energy and producing either a join system or a new energy born out of the two (or more) source energies, use ◇ Jera to mature the new energy. Any combination takes time to harmonise, blend effectively and produce a completely new energy with its own characteristics. Most people who are new to all this never realise that such energies need time to become active and fully functional in their own right, and so fail at whatever they were trying to achieve by virtue of such practices. If you simply use ◇ Jera to mature them sufficiently, then make use of it, you will notice a different outcome. This rule is of vital importance when it comes to bindrunes, where a combination of runic powers and forces come into play as a singular new whole (more on bindrunes will be published at a later point in time).

Physical Body & Physical Reality

In terms of the physical body, ◇ Jera brings about cellular maturity, psychological maturity and helps grow the biological intelligence of the body. It is the rune of fertility in terms of realisation of the genetic potential (in this case, by passing it over to the next generation, other types of realisation belong to other runes). It is also a most useful and beneficial rune when it comes to healing ailments of the body. When medication or treatment is used, applying the influences of ◇ Jera can speed up their curative effects. Additionally, the rune can be used to achieve developmental goals, such as in exercises designed to strengthened the body. Combing your gym work, with this rune post-workout will produce some rather interesting and impressive results.

A most fascinating specialisation of this rune's application is that of time. Using the ᛃ Jera rune, it is possible to master time itself, should you with to specialise in this. Even just developing a solid understanding of time is a task in its own right. For the time being, it is just worth mentioning that this falls squarely in the remit of this rune's force and should you be interested in this, then using the rune is the first step upon your path of exploration of time. Remember, time only exists where there is matter. Energy realities, mind, spirit and archetypal levels of existence are totally independent of time. As soon as matter (any form of matter) is brought into the scope of your work, time will play its part.

One of the more exotic applications of this rune is mentioned in the *Hávamál*, where Oðinn mentioned the 12th spell he knows, where he used ᛃ Jera to raise a dead man in order to question him. Here, ᛃ Jera's power over time comes into play. It was a simple feat for a rune master such as Oðinn to move time backwards for a single body using ᛃ Jera. Other interesting things achievable when specialising with this rune are plant and crop-related, they can be quickened to maturity and even kept fresh longer. In the work environment, any project can be brought to successful completion, with not rapid but a slow and steady movement forward, which is needed for maximum quality rather than quantity. Patience and perseverance brings the most success. This should be enough information to get you started.

The Rune Perþo – Perð

Sound: p
Vocal Scale: Sol
Numerology: 13
Natural Polarity: N - N - All - All - All
Energetic Colour (Universal): Reflective black.
Primal Power: Origination, the unknown and the unknowable, formless form.
Sensation(s): Various and wet.

Archetypal Level of Existence

This is one of the most mysterious runes and also one of the most misunderstood. It is also one of the most abstract. Forget about all the nonsense of it being linked to fertility and the female – that is based on guesswork, rather than energetic reality. ᛈ Pertho encompasses everything, and as such includes both the masculine and feminine, their absolutes, their end product and neither of them. It is the source and the end of all evolution and devolution. Everything that has ever been conceived of by any mind, being, or existence is within it, as are things and possibilities which have yet to be. It simply encompasses everything and nothing. It is a very difficult state to explain in words. It carries within itself all that which flows into creation. On the archetypal and spiritual levels of existence, its polarity is completely neutral and does not get polarised until the energetic (and physical – which, remember, is part of the energetic). When it does polarise, it does so in a unique manner which only applies to ⱶ Pertho and ᛇ Eihwaz, as all polarities, none, and not only the combination but the end product of each. These two runes are the everything and every possibility. Out of the two, ⱶ Pertho is the more subtle and difficult to both use and connect with.

Other functions to keep in mind are that ⱶ Pertho is also the rune of the flow of fate. When the Norns weave the fates of all things in existence, it is the underlying cosmic force of ⱶ Pertho that carries those weaves outwards into existence and forces their manifestation. This is the rune of the Spa (Norse Seers), and allows them to enhance their natural abilities and see some of these flows of fate. It is also the rune of intuition and the so-called 'gut-feel', for it guides those who seek answers to the deeper and most mysterious of questions in existence. However, for anyone to work within its remit and with its energies, perfect balance of all aspects of one's Self and one's energies is required. The greater the balance, the wider the scope of mysteries ⱶ Pertho unravels before you. Keep in mind that this rune is not negative or positive; however, since those who have a tendency for the darker side of things cannot reach perfect balance (the very dark requires a lack of it), the mastery of this and the ᛇ Eihwaz runes will be unreachable to them. Take heed not to get lost in light either, as the same will apply.

ᚹ Pertho is the rune which keeps in check and balance all underlying forces in existence. It allows (and guides) them to their end goals and ensures that any disturbances occur only when they are needed and only for as long as needed. As such, its domain is both within the timeless and time, the spaceless and space. This rune never manifests directly; instead, it uses the other runes to exert its influences.

Spirit & Spiritual Reality

Within the spiritual, its functions are practically identical to the archetypal. Additionally, it rules over each and every spirit's total sum of capabilities, always seeking to enhance and expand. Remember, this is one of the forces driving creation and evolution forth. The intuition of each spirit and its ability to be at one with its core essential purpose and being is governed by ᚹ Pertho, it is the link with the all in existence (accessible through Yggdrasil). When you seek to hear the voice of Spirit itself, use ᚹ Pertho, for it opens up that possibility. This rune is one of the most difficult to grasp practically because you can only work with it in a way which it determines. Most runic forces can be twisted and re-polarised or used as a force to counter an event or outcome – not ᚹ Pertho; it simply imposes a higher order of things onto any attempt to change things in a way they are not supposed to be. As such, it is the rune of the divine imposing itself by vast inconceivable force into all of existence. Nothing, be it gods, humans or anything else for that matter, escapes or counters its laws. This enables it to keep the spirits of all sorts in their respective domains and because of this, when working with them, special procedures are required to reach them. This rune's energies keep the spiritual realities and energetic separate (the higher and lower). Much more could be said but this will suffice.

In terms of our own spirit, ᛈ Pertho is responsible for the sense of feeling, or more specifically what has been called sensing (see *The Blood of Lóðurr Awakens*). As such, it will also greatly facilitate the reading of energy, as outlined in the practical instructions for using the runes (see: 'Runic Energy Learning' p.59). You can judge just how powerful your spirit has become by looking at how much and how easily you can sense things. There will come a time where, whatever you focus your mind on, you will be able to read as if you had known that situation/person for ages, and be able to pick up on things even they themselves do not know or admit to themselves. Be careful at this point: people find this type of knowing very unsettling. Privacy in the grander scale of things simply does not exist for us all here in human lives – that very concept is extremely unsettling. Keep what you know to yourself; in time, you will learn not to focus on things which do not interest you and it will be much less of a problem. Nevertheless, keep an eye on how this develops. It will reveal just how far you are progressing and not only how strong your spirit is becoming but also how in-tune you are with ᛈ Pertho and ᛇ Eihwaz (or rather their underlying forces). Those are the only two runes that enable this type of effect.

Mind & Mental Reality

As far as the mind and memory are concerned, this

rune's influence is paramount. It is what one can be forgiven for thinking of as the substance and force through which thoughts are exchanged, received and sent. The ᚠ Fehu rune is the sending rune and the ᚠ Ansuz the receiving rune, but it is through the energy of ᛈ Pertho that whatever is sent or received travels. This rune's force is the carrier – think of it as the lorries and the driver, and the goods to be delivered are thoughts and concepts, and ideas. The dispatch instructions are ᚠ Fehu and the proof of delivery, along with you at home taking the parcel, are ᚠ Ansuz. This is how all thoughts are exchanged. Along similar lines, memory functions energetically in practically the same manner, except before being loaded on our metaphorical truck, memories are retrieved from personal, collective or universal stores.

    ᛈ Pertho enhances the powers of both the Minni and the Hugr allows them to 'fly' further and higher, enabling us to think broader and larger in scope and potential. In terms of memory, it also allows for a more reliable transfer of memory from different trance states back to ordinary consciousness (use ᛈ Pertho in combination with ᚠ Ansuz or ᛜ Ingwaz for this).

    One of the most used – and by the same vein, the most important – functions of the force of ᛈ Pertho is with respect to fate. From this rune's power, all of the Norns work is made manifest. It is the ᛈ Pertho force which takes the individual weaves and makes its threads span creation. These are then 'read' or 'processed' by living beings and determine what those beings perceive, experience, how they grow and so forth. The ᛈ Pertho force is the key to understanding the realisation of fate in all its aspects and permutations. Likewise, using its power enables you to gain understanding of all this and learn how it functions. Those with Spa abilities have those abilities highly enhanced, allowing their minds to flow down these threads and observe how they will unfold. In other words, giving the Spa-gifted an insight into the fate of things. It is wise not to be mistaken when dealing with this rune; it does not bestow the ability to change anything, just the ability to understand and observe (for the Spa mystics and seers). Great wisdom is gained by those who take a keen interest in using and learning from this rune, for its functions and effects allow you to understand how creation works at a fundamental level. This knowledge is then yours to adapt and extend into human fields of understanding (such as the sciences and mathematics), which are all just ways for the limited human mind to glimpse into these fundamental mechanisms of creation.

Energy Body & Energy Reality

ᛈ Pertho is responsible for the cohesion of the various energy system in our energy body. Its function is not only to ensure all the energies, powers and forces flow in a predetermined manner (according to our fates, wishes and ancestral patterns), but also that our Self is able to function through it. It is the combination of our energy body, and the ᛈ Pertho forces, which the personality is formed of at this level of our beings, and by which it is maintained. Eventually, at death, the shell of this body shatters and the overflowing ᛈ Pertho flows outwards, dispersing our personalities into the wide expanses of existence, leaving only the higher parts of the Self functioning. The actions and will of fate flow into us through the universal energies of this rune, and shape or re-shape our beings as needed. They are responsible for the patterns from outside of us making an impact on our beings, as well as for our ability to interact with our environments. Very much like ᛈ Pertho is the carrier and driver of the exchange of thoughts, it acts in the same capacity but in terms of energy. Without it, there would be nothing to channel energy to and from. All energy would be self-contained and never cross the boundaries of its containers. In other words, everything would be in total isolation and fall into stasis moments after being created. Its impact is very significant but extremely subtle because energetically, it is seldom used. All its influences are pretty much automatic and built into the fabric of existence.

ᛈ Pertho's influences on a living being enable awareness to arise. It is the foundation upon which the energies and threads of awareness rely for their functioning. It is with this rune's energy that you can enter into the great vast expanse of the sea of awareness, but only while you are a living being. Once death strikes, the spark of awareness, along with the hvel in which it is seated, dissolve and that once-living form loses the capacity to be aware.

ᛈ Pertho's force acts in a very unique manner on the energy body and the shadow; it helps free the threads of binding that connect these bodies to the other parts of the Self, especially the physical. Using this rune facilitates the separation of these bodies while simultaneously enabling consciousness to be rooted in them. It is an excellent tool for all those who are trying to develop the ability of projecting their individual energy bodies out of the physical and function in them independently of the physical.

When combined with ᛉ Elhaz and ᛋ Sowilo, it is possible to bring about a spiritualisation of the energy body. Such change enables it to embody more and more subtle forces and higher vibrating energies, as well as to integrate the higher functions of each of the runic forces in existence. This in turn elevates it to new heights and allows otherwise unseen and inaccessible regions of existence to open up to it. It also makes it unassailable to any lower forces and is key to obtaining a type of invulnerability, where all things aimed at harming it simply pass on in a reality below it with no effect. Eventually, by undergoing this type of elevation on a regular basis over an entire lifetime, the energy body can reach a point where it is simply beyond all negative influences in creation.

Physical Body & Physical Reality

ᛈ Pertho has an immense influence on consciousness, which is produced by an interaction of awareness and our physiology. Using the energies of this rune, all sorts of trance states can be induced by simply flooding the body with its energy and having the consciousness direct itself to a specific goal. Additionally, ᛈ Pertho is very strongly connected with our blood. It expresses itself through the blood of all living things, and all blood mysteries fall within its remit. The intersection of life force with ᛈ Pertho is what one finds energetically in our blood. All other physiological phenomena can be influenced using this rune, including the body's own biological intelligence (see *The Blood of Lóðurr Awakens*), modulation of other runes' effects on the body and even the effects of other energies. Another interesting domain to consider when looking at ᛈ Pertho is its influence upon DNA - it is responsible for the replication and growth of our genetic codes, as well as their integrity.

Using it, for those who specialise in it, is even possible to access long-forgotten genetic memories (with help from the Fylgja).

In terms of the physical reality, its effects are the same as those listed for the energy reality. ᛈ Pertho is the energy reality manifesting in the physical. The effects of its fate manifestation are highly amplified at this level of our existence, simply because this is where you experience their manifestation. In other words, pre-destination of events, the effects of time and space, the laws of cause and effect, like attracts like and so forth are all forced upon physical existence by the effects of ᛈ Pertho.

From a scientific point of view, ᛈ Pertho is the root cause of Dark Energy. It is this rune's energy which flows through creation, causing it to be maintained within its natural status quo, moving in the destined direction towards its ultimate goal.

Notes

In the cases of ᛈ Pertho and ᛇ Eihwaz, there is no runic power, only runic energy and its underlying force. It is impossible to condense these two rune's energies in any manner and as such they can never become a power.

The Rune Eihwaz – Jór

Sound: æ
Vocal Scale: La
Numerology: 14
Natural Polarity: None - None - None - None - None
Energetic Colour (Universal): Violet, deep violet.
Primal Power: Universality, existence.
Sensation(s): The flow of a subtle force, like x-rays, expansive and magnetic.

Archetypal Level of Existence

This rune is very similar to ᛈ Pertho, actually so much so that many confuse the two. It does have one important characteristic which makes it quite distinct, that of the sense of absorption. This rune's energy pulls you into itself; it absorbs all it touches. This sensation is what allows you to clearly distinguish the two rune's forces. It is also a carrier force, but works in a very different and distinct way; it bends the force and time from source to destination. Additionally, it purifies the forces it carrier within itself. It is important to note that this concept of purity is pure in itself. That means it is not the same type of purity one thinks of as making something more akin to the light (which in itself is not necessarily pure either – well, not until it becomes perfected light). This type of purity is one that makes the essence pure of other non-essence like components. In other words, this rune's type of purity is perfection of a force, essence, power or energy to the exclusion of all external factors. Let us put this in context, as understanding this concept is important in order to grasp the forces and energy of this rune. Take the forces of fire, for example: their purity would be akin to the perfected fire pure of flame and heat, without any influence of anything that is non-fire. Very much like ᛕ Pertho, this rune's force contains the sum of everything; there is no space or time it does not flow through. This is one of the key reasons why it has traditionally been strongly associated with the world tree (Yggdrasil) and its wisdom. It is also why Oðinn mentions in the 14th rune spell that with it, he recounts all the knowledge of the Æsir and Álfar. This rune carries all the wisdom, knowledge and the energies and beings themselves. It connects all things which exist, and all those which do not exist, and is metaphorically speaking the substance within Yggdrasil itself.

Spirit & Spiritual Reality

This rune's energy provides protection in a very unique way. It lifts whatever is protected outside of the scope of whatever is attacking. When something is 'elevated' in this manner, the attack simply passes somewhere below without ever finding its original target. Additionally, for those proficient in its use, they can simply 'send' the energy of the resulting assault elsewhere.

Spiritually, the rune will inspire and enable knowledge of the mysteries in reality. Higher forms of knowledge are made accessible through its influences. It also awakens vision, and perceptions are enhanced through its energy – not only that, but it will also enable you to develop skills to communicate across various levels of reality. Along this line of skill set, using it can enable you to reach the point where your spirit can function in realities that are timeless and spaceless.

One of the key effects, as far as the rune mystic is concerned, is that ᛇ Eihwaz's force is responsible for bridging spirit and matter. It provides that connection link in all its various forms, enabling spirit to descend into and ascend from matter. It also enables matter to be spiritualised and ascend unto spirit. This is especially useful, not only in terms of gaining mastery over the linking threads your own spirit has to your body, but also in any other practices where, for instance, spirits are provided with a connecting bridge to physical items, paintings, sculptures, totems – or even as is very popular in the spirit working community, the anchoring of spirits in gems, jewellery and so forth. All these types of connections are subject to the influences of ᛇ Eihwaz. Mastering them can open up a whole range of important skills, such as a skilled rune mystic in this rune can, by simply touching such an object, intensify the connecting link to an extent that the spirit can be pulled in its entirety into our reality, within an instant.

This linking mechanism of spirit and matter has a very important application in practical terms when working within one's Self. Consciousness is rooted in matter (in the physical body, to be exact), and using

♪ Eihwaz you can manipulate and influence this linkage. By doing so, it is possible to separate consciousness from the physical and transfer it wherever you desire (with limits based on its vibrational frequency). It is a most fascinating thing to do because you are taking a component of your Self (consciousness), which is bound by time (because it is rooted in matter), and making it timeless and space-less (via the link to spirit which is both timeless and space-less), then putting this to use by projecting it somewhere or sometime else. It is definitely an important skill to master and you can do so using this rune's force and power.

A very important practice involving this rune allows for its energy to be used to enhance the sense of freedom of the spirit, with Fylgja and Shadow enabling a spirit to 'fly' out of the physical. It allows you to spiritualise it to the point where it can 'escape' matter. Be warned, though: overdoing it can have quite a few unwanted permanent effects. Use sparingly.

Mind & Mental Reality

Sending the mind and memory portions of the Self up and down Yggdrasil, using its energy moving up and down the Tree becomes a simple feat for any mystic using this rune's force. Additionally, gaining access to the knowledge flowing within its forces becomes possible. The mind is expanded and enhanced, and its capabilities are not only strengthened but widened in scope. The intellect, memory and perceptions are all enhanced under the influences of this rune. New realms of thinking, new concepts, new realities to be explored – using this rune's forces, one crosses into the unknown and starts to glimmer enlightenment from all the novel input received. A danger here needs to be mentioned: stretch a mind too wide, too fast, and it will shatter. This is where perception has pushed too far and the mind is no longer able to keep up: it breaks and insanity results. Within that very insanity, perception becomes unshackled from the norms of understanding, never to return. Facing the unknown can be crushing: only take the first step, if you intend to sink deep into it.

♪ Eihwaz unlocks all types of trance, be it ecstatic trance, projection trances, or any other type of trance. It raises the mind into higher states of awareness and when induced through the physical body, it pushes consciousness into new heights. Special trance states can be induced which push certain aspects of the mind into overdrive, temporarily destabilising internal balance but providing an incredible heightened state of awareness. What one does with and in those states depends entirely upon the individual. It is also possible for two minds to communicate intuitively with the help of this rune.

Energy Body & Energy Reality

The energy body's vibration rate can be increased using this rune's energy, which in turn elevates it to a new level of energy. This process in effect spiritualises it. It is also used to enhance its will to survive; it bolsters the cohesive power which keeps all the individual countless energy sparks and channels which compose its constituent parts together. Additionally, it is possible to increase its endurance, once it is separated from the physical body, by infusing it with this rune's energy.

One thing anyone who manages to separate the energy body from the physical will experience is an irresistible drive, almost a compulsion, within the energy body to explore. Even the smallest particle of dust on the desk can end up being an overwhelming fascination for it, to the point where hours (of physical time) are spent just exploring the energy waves and patterns that it produces. This rune's energy can weaken those compulsions and allow a certain resistance to this compulsive drive. This is due to the increase in power within your awareness produced by this rune. It reinforces your personal motivation, bridging it over into your new form from the physical.

This rune facilitates the changing of the form of the energy body. It is the rune of formless form and as such, it can bestow form upon the formless, and formlessness upon forms. Using these characteristics, it is possible to use the rune's force to shapeshift its form. You will need to learn which forms are used in other realities, in order to function in those realities; once learnt, this rune's forces will enable you to adopt the new shapes or forms and function there. ᛇ Eihwaz's applications are far more numerous than can be completely described.

Physical Body & Physical Reality

This rune's energy is everywhere and in everything. It is the background radiation in existence, ever-flowing and an eternal force. In the physical realities, this rune's force speeds up the realisation of things that are due to happen. It follows the commands of fate but also includes all other energetic causes and effects. It is the energy of this rune which brings about manifestation of their end product. When you set something in motion using runic power (using the other runes), adding this one right at the end of whatever runes you have used will cause a far speedier manifestation than would be the case otherwise. It is also possible to use this rune in order to cause a shift from one set of circumstances to another. That is one of its energy's natural functions, and by combining it with another rune, it is possible to direct that shift purposefully. For example, using the ᛉ Elhaz rune, you can shift the events into the spiritual; using the ᚹ Wunjo rune, you can move them towards a more socially harmonious set of circumstances; using ᛟ Othala, you can move into a beneficial situation for the home and so forth.

This rune facilitates the induction any type of trance the rune mystic wants to achieve, either in himself or herself or in others. By directing the runic power into the front of the head, consciousness is rapidly sent into a passive type of overdrive and opens up to the higher levels of reality, resulting in a complete state of trance. It is also possible to induce this rune's energy to flood the blood of any living thing, which results in a total biological trance, with full alertness of conscious awareness. It is a very strange state of mind, where it is both in trance and not in trance simultaneously. The body, on the other hand, experiences the full effect of the rune's influence. What is actually happening in this state of being is that biological awareness and intelligence is sent into the trance effect; this in turn has an effect on the brain and causes the part of our consciousness which is dependent on it to also go into trance, whereas it keeps the part which is not dependent on the brain out of the trance. The two states synchronise and it results in a very expansive bodily trance, which carries consciousness along with it. Use this trance wisely, for it unifies the physical and non-physical parts of the Self. Even temporarily, such a union can both be the greatest blessing imaginable or the worst curse, depending on how you use it. ᛇ Eihwaz used in this manner enables a stronger connection to be established between the conscious mind and the biological awareness (subconscious), facilitating the communication and interaction between the two. It is also possible to use the effects of this rune in order to awaken dormant parts of the Self. To do so, simply direct its force into whatever part of the Self needs to be awakened.

The Rune Elhaz – Ýr

Sound: z
Vocal Scale: Ti
Numerology: 15
Natural Polarity: M - M - M - M - M
Energetic Colour (Universal): Golden light, shivering metallic gold.
Primal Power: Divinity, spiritualisation.
Sensation(s): Sensation of spiritualisation, total realisation of divinity within, lightness and sharpness combined, all penetrating rays of divine light like radiation beams flowing through everything.

Archetypal Level of Existence

Absolute divinity burst into archetypal existence with the first outpouring of perfected abstract light – that is what this rune's force is about. From that single event in the great sea of nothingness, divinity sprang into being, and reflections of pure perfected light birthed absolute divinity, which then manifest in the most subtle forms of existence. This divinity shines forth into creation, for it is a reminder of the initial act of creation: its source, its cause, its end goal and its outcome. Many wonder: well, what is divinity? Or associate it with the gods. Yes, they do indeed express divinity, but they are not its source; instead, they are archetypal embodiments of one or more divine characteristics and power. What are divine characteristics? Powers? To put this in as intelligible concepts as possible, do keep in mind this is a severe oversimplification: a divine characteristic is the purest, most abstract, and highest vibrating expression of the totality of all aspects and forms of expression of said characteristic or power. Far more could be said about this rune's force(s) but they are rather complex and far too intricate to cover in a single paragraph or two. We will cover this rune in much greater detail elsewhere in terms of its archetypal powers, influences and forces and how they apply themselves in creation.

Those who master this rune's force will be able to imbue all expressions and manifestations of their Self with one or more aspects of divinity. The rune brings about a gradual spiritualisation of all parts of a fully realised Self, to the point where it starts to touch upon divinity itself because it develops a likeness to it. By virtue of the divine laws and like attracting like principle, it is pulled towards it. At first, it touches briefly upon it, then more and more until a fragment of this divine force bleeds into such a Self. Because it has become fully realised, it is able to withstand its overwhelming power, which would have shattered any other Self by its simple presence. Eventually, over timeless time, such a Self eventually changes further and further and becomes more and more able to withstand greater contact with divinity, until its energy can flow freely through it. At that point, it becomes able to spiritualise its own characteristics and start to merge them with their divine equivalents. The process continues beyond time itself, but the end result is a divine Self. In our human terms, even step one of such a process can take millions of centuries.

This rune's power is often used when working with the Hamingja. It is not only used to increase its protective capabilities, but also strengthens the boundaries of the Hamingja itself, allowing it to contain a greater amount of megin (see *The Breath of Oðin Awakens* for more info on the Hamingja). Not only does this rune's force affect the Hamingja, but it also has a greater impact of the total sum of all the life force within any being. It is possible to strengthen the life force itself using it.

Spirit & Spiritual Reality

In terms of the spiritual, ᛉ Elhaz is the rune that establishes connections to the gods. Using the bifrost bridge is possible when applying the powers of ᛉ Elhaz. In order to cross that bridge, a certain degree of spiritual evolution is necessary and so this rune not only opens the gateway but also spiritualises the spirit, allowing it to travel smoothly over the bridge. Besides the bifrost, ᛉ Elhaz is also able to open pathways throughout Yggdrasil, allowing you to travel the nine worlds.

Its force helps you develop what can be termed cosmic intuition. Yet again, this is one of those concepts which is notoriously difficult to put into language. It is a type of intuition which is ever-expansive and all encompassing. It is not focussed our physical existence but on all of existence and flows throughout all of creation. Such a type of intuition is very different to what the word's usual interpretation is. It is a type of absolute knowing, perfected prophecy, and even pure essential action-based knowledge, running through all realities, flowing through everything ever created and every manifestation of it.

Spiritual protection is well within the remit of this rune. Calling upon the Valkyr with this rune provides unyielding spiritual protection. Should its user have power within this rune's remit, entire armies of Valkyr will respond (depending on the mystic's spirituality).

Spiritualisation is the speciality of this rune's energy, but more importantly, the arts of the spirit song belong within its remit. The sound of spirit(s) creating life, in the great song of life, is what this rune unlocks. Those who hear it are blessed; those who understand it are wise, and those who wield it are gods.

Mind & Mental Reality

This rune's power facilitates the union of the mind with the higher parts of the Self – in other words, it allows a connection and eventual union with the archetypal Self. This is where the full power of the Breath of Oðinn is realised by the spiritualised mind. It rises high and carries with it the very essence of your conscious mind guided by the Fylgja. Powered by the Hamingja, the Self rises beyond the boundaries of the created into the pure abstraction of the archetypal YOU. This is the real you; the undefinable essence of you is made accessible to your mind using this rune. Once mastered, you will be able to cross the boundary of existence and become a pure concept of the totality of your Self, leaving all the material aspects of you forever. All other work with this rune serves to gradually elevate your mind little by little, until eventually you can reach this elusive state of being.

In terms of the mental reality as a whole, it can be used to bring the divine out of concepts, and the understanding of the intrinsic meaning of all things, and to learn of it. Perceptions are enhanced by it, and all the mind's capabilities are broadened and heightened.

This rune's energy has a very special and seldom known use, it is able to unite the Minni and the Hugr (memory and mind) with the Óðr (spirit), bringing about the creation of a complete Self on the mental and spiritual levels of reality from its fragments on the mental level. Undergoing such stitching of the Self from across different levels of reality is not usually possible, because each of them has what can be thought of as un-breachable barriers separating them. Using this rune in order to achieve this is one of the few rare exceptions to this state of affairs.

Its ability to spiritualise can be applied to any mind, be it your own or someone else's. Maintaining the produced new state of mind, however, is not a guarantee. It is up to the individual mind whether it has the capacity to do so or not. However, it is possible to use this rune's effects on a regular basis and in that way, achieve this capacity to maintain the spiritualised elevation and its associated enhanced mental functions. In such cases, the initial effect would be very short-lived and rapidly fade, where the mind would resettle back into its usual modus operandi. By repeating this elevation of spiritualisation over and over again, the mind adapts and familiarises itself with this new state of being and eventually learns to ground itself in at the new level. It does take a lot of practice to do it in this way, but it is definitely possible.

Energy Body & Energy Reality

The very energy of this rune is both protective and

teaching. Over the ages, it has traditionally been linked to the concept of the Valkyr, as she is both a warrior (protector) and a teacher (bestowing knowledge of mysteries and higher forms of reality) upon those who awaken her. ᛉ Elhaz's energies fit into this concept exceedingly well. Its force carries unbound levels of knowledge of higher (or more subtle, to be accurate) realities and of the inner nature of things.

Likewise this rune's powers are some of the few which enable the spiritualisation of any and all energies both within the Self and outside of the Self. This in itself gives unlimited protection. Why? Simply put, when something is assaulting or attacking using this rune's powers, it will instantly spiritualise it and awaken a higher purpose within whatever is striking out. This changes the very nature of the forces striking out at you. The other side of this protection stems from the fact that imbued with this rune's energy, you start to shine in a golden light. Spiritualising your energy body, it rises it beyond the reach of whatever is trying to harm you.

One important passive effect which occurs whenever this rune is used within your Self or someone else is the opening of awareness to the existence and communication with non-physical beings of all types. It provides a type of natural extension of awareness and gives the awareness hvel a certain fluidity that enables you to shift your perceptions into the non-physical, which in turn enables you to perceive whatever non-physical beings are there. Used on a regular basis, you can enhance your awareness to the point where it spills over into consciousness with its new range of perceptions, allowing you to develop a conscious non-physical focus that is like a lens you move from physical into non-physical, depending on what you desire to perceive. In terms of the energy bodies, it appears like a shift of the hvel from one of the energy bodies into the other. As soon as the hvel slide to the opposite body, your awareness is shifted (from its default physical into the other).

Physical Body & Physical Reality

This rune also offers up protection in the physical world. It is not simply a protection from energetic harm. Those who are proficient in its use can expand the power of this protection to prevent harm from diseases, fate and so much more. Additionally, a high level of proficiency allows the divine within to bleed over into the physical environment. It awakens what we can call 'true blessings', not only to its wielder, but also to all around them.

Physiologically, consciousness can be greatly enhanced through its energy's interaction with the physical body, and awakens the ability within it to catch glimpses of things beyond the physical (usually from the corners of one's eyes). Bridging everyday consciousness with dream awareness and shadow awareness is possible by using this rune.

In terms of shielding, this rune's energy is paramount in importance; there is no equal to its capabilities. Its influence can also be extended to protect all the blood relatives of a family, and the possessor of the Kin-Fylgja can further extend that power to protect an entire family group, depending on his strength and power. A mystic who is also in possession of the kin-Fylgja can by its power extend his protection to not only all living members of the bloodline, but also those within the Helheim and beyond.

Remember, using this rune will always have a significant influence on its user. It is impossible to remain unchanged when the actual runic force of ᛉ Elhaz flows through the body. Using it on a regular basis will result in the body becoming a conduit for manifestation of the divinity within.

Notes

It is important to note, when dealing with ᛉ Elhaz and ᛋ Sowilo, that their effectiveness and the strength of power one is able to draw from these two universal forces depends on how abstracted one's Self has become. The more so, the stronger one's work with these two runes will be. They are very special runes, as are ᚠ Fehu+ᚢ Uruz and ᛏ Tiwaz+ᛒ Berkano. These six runes form the apices of the spear of the Self Seiðr working. This spear is used by the mystic to pierce the heavens and step beyond their boundaries. More on this highly complex method later. Just keep in mind that these six runes' forces have different universal runes that apply to them.

Keep in mind, no matter what level of reality this rune's energy and powers are used on they will always dissolve all negative energies and powers no matter whether in or outside the Self. It is an unavoidable effect as it forms part of the very essence of the rune force.

The Rune Sowilo – Sól

Sound: s
Vocal Scale: Do (hard)
Numerology: 16
Natural Polarity: N - M - B - M - B
Energetic Colour (Universal): White, pure blinding light.
Primal Power: Self, power, realisation.
Sensation(s): Piercing light, like a cold laser beam radiating through everything; explosive ominous power.

Archetypal Level of Existence

This rune has what could appear to be two facets to its essence, the first being light and the second the Self (or to be more precise Spark of Self), but in fact they are one and the same. The original outpouring of light in creation is nothing more or less than the Spark of Self of creation; within us, this is replicated on a smaller scale but the underlying principles are exactly the same. ᛋ Sowilo is the rune of light, but light itself can be many things, depending on who experiences it and where. On the archetypal level, it is the purest outflow of light, the initial spark and ray which streamed forth into existence. It is also the perfected light, one that has evolved to the point of perfection (yes, light evolves). At this point, when it has become both pure and perfected light, it becomes absolute.

Why discuss this light? Because it allows you to understand the Spark of Self; ᛋ Sowilo is the root essence and the totality of Self. The spark eventually evolves to grow into a flame, into a sun and into a universe of its own. Each is totally unique and individual (there is no duplication in existence on the spiritual levels or above). As this Spark of Self shines forth, it manifests its core characteristics and powers, and those in turn shape the spirit it embodies, which in turn gives rise to the mind, energy body and eventually physical (if appropriate). When dealing with these outpourings of the Self, one is dealing with the highest possible level of the Self and its most abstract one too. At this point, there is only the Self and nothing else; each spark has all the space to only itself and everything in existence is only that which is also part of itself. As it manifests into the spiritual, there appears the first duality of Self and not-Self.

The forces of ᛋ Sowilo not only express this but also allow it to be strengthened, amplified and directed into very specific directions. For instance, Seiðr practices exist that enable additional outpourings of the Self to take place, embodying you in other realities at the same time or as separate beings completely. Others exist to bring about different characteristics of the Self that might not be present in the current you, and so forth. These are all extremely advanced uses of this rune but are worth keeping in mind. Once ᛋ Sowilo is mastered, all sorts of possibilities open up.

In terms of the greater scope of things, ᛋ Sowilo is the primal primordial light, the outpouring of the first act of creation. It brings about all states of enlightenment, illumination and understanding, and is the ultimate power as a concept of the all-power. In other words, it is the essential meaning of power itself. From it flows all of evolution, success and insight. Additionally, within it flows all knowledge and information. However, on this level of existence, it is a pure concept without any substance; this means that to make any practical use of it, the manifest parts of reality have to be relied on rather than the archetypal.

Spirit & Spiritual Reality

This is where ᛋ Sowilo starts to manifest. It is important to distinguish it from physical sources of light (fire or the sun), as confusing the two can lead to many practical errors and problems. Light here is a manifestation of an essential duality; it is the active polarity of the masculine end of the spectrum, and it generates life, wisdom, knowledge and insight. It is always active in some form or other – there is no such thing as passive light because it needs movement and motion and all things it comes into contact with activate. Spirits are made of this light; it is part of all spirit's essential nature. Each light is unique and different (as determined by the Spark of Self) but it is nonetheless light. There is no such thing as a darkness spirit as is often assumed. Yes, there are darker ones, but those are just spirits whose nature as not as light as others'. All things are either light in some shape or form or not-light.

At this level of existence, ᛋ Sowilo determines the power of each spirit, its vibrational capacity, its scope and the sum total of characteristics it can express.

Its light can be used to not only enlighten but also to amplify the will and to call forth those who are alike. It makes your spirit shine and acts as a beacon to those who can see it. Another interesting application of this rune's force is to use it to increase your spiritual capacity before calling forth other spirits. Amplifying your power in this manner allows you to pierce the dividers in existence and ensures you can be heard and seen by other spirits.

ᛋ Sowilo has a strong impact on what is called spirit sight and should be used when attempting to develop this skill set. It should also be used when delving into the darker side of spiritual reality. In those circumstances, it allows the essential nature of your spirit to persevere against any confusion, illusions or manipulations, and can be used to prevent falling into darkness. Remember, those of pure heart and spirit can sink into the darkest depths without losing themselves to the dark and continuing to shine in shimmering, blinding light. Those are the ones who gain control over the darkness itself by virtue of their light (the dark craves the light and the light shines at its strongest in the dark).

ᛋ Sowilo is also a very good runic force to use when modulating one's spiritual manifestation. What is meant by this is simple to understand, if you think of a spirit in terms of the light it is emitting. The type and intensity of light determines the type of spirit, and by using this rune you are able to shift this light, making yourself temporarily into a different type of spirit and, because of the like attracts like universal law, immediately be shifted into the reality occupied by spirits of your new type (for as long as you hold onto this new emanation within yourself). Many more applications exist, but these few should suffice to give you a more solid understanding of the importance and power of this rune.

Mind & Mental Reality

As mentioned above, willpower is governed by ᛊ Sowilo, but not only that. It also governs the intellect and higher forms of intelligence (such as silent knowing). With its power, you can widen the scope of your mind and the speed at which it is able to process (think); not only that, but you can use ᛊ Sowilo's light to reach new types of thinking. Adaptive thinking is vital when it comes to communicating with thought or with non-physical beings. Everything is transmitted as pure thought and shimmering lights at this level of existence. Those who master this will develop the skill to understand all life forms, ranging from the fungus growing on the tree, to animals, other people and even non-physical beings. There are life forms made of pure light, others of pure energy (which live within the solar orbit) and so forth. Essentially, learning to communicate in this manner opens up a massive range of possibilities. It is extremely difficult to learn this, but not impossible, by any stretch of the imagination – it just takes time and effort.

One of other important possibility this gives rise to is learning to communicate with our own bodies. Using the light energy of this rune, one is able to directly interface not only with the intelligence of our individual cells, but also with our nervous systems. Definitely an important thing to learn to do. Not only is this limited to the physical body, but communication with the energy body and the shadow is only possible directly by the help of ᛊ Sowilo. Using it is the equivalent to merging your mind with the higher self and then talking to the lower parts of the Self.

ᛋ Sowilo's light can be used to light up a path to take or a decision to make; it is often use to break through illusion and obstructions – where there is doubt or uncertainty, its light can literally shed light upon the matter(s) at hand. It has an uncanny ability to show you totally unexpected ways through problems by a flash of insight, an epiphany bursting forth, a new way of looking at the situation and so forth. Unlike ᚦ Thurisaz, which shatters obstacles, ᛋ Sowilo breaks through them or shows you ways around them. It has no need to shatter anything.

In terms of thinking, this rune can not only bridge the gap to new ideas and concepts, helping you understand them, but is also used to activate certain thought patterns or groups. Some thoughts and ideas dim away from your reach because they are not used often (the thought, figuratively speaking, runs out of power), and because thoughts attract like thoughts, you can use ᛋ Sowilo to flare up a certain thought (or train of thought), which will then act like a beacon for more of the same type. This is an excellent way to trigger waves of inspiration. Other thoughts can also be stripped of drive using this rune – a good example are those that provoke worry or concern, obsessive thoughts and so forth. With a little work on this rune, and as you gain mastery, turning thoughts and thought types on and off will become an accessible skill set for you.

For those of you working with thought-forms, ᛋ Sowilo can be a most powerful and excellent tool.

Energy Body & Energy Reality

In terms of the energy body, ᛋ Sowilo is one of the main activator runes. It not only makes it more active but also brings it forth into the grasp of the conscious mind. It allows you to reach your energy body, which can be annoyingly distant most of the time. In addition to this, it empowers it and awakens dormant parts. ᛋ Sowilo increases all forces and energies with the energy body, no matter whether you want it to or not. Should you wish not to have those activate, and live only a day-to-day ordinary life, avoid using this rune. Higher functions and possibilities are always targeted first and foremost by this rune's force. This is unavoidable and does run the danger that overuse can lead you to being overwhelmed, so use it wisely and cautiously.

In terms of the Hvels (energy centres), it will awaken them, activate and strengthen them. Whether you target the ᛋ Sowilo powers into a minor centre or a major one does not matter – its effects are the same on both.

One thing to keep in mind when working with this rune: it strengthens not only the energy body but also the shadow. All light casts shadow at this level and the stronger the light within you, the more powerful a shadow it will cast. Be prepared for this.

In terms of all energies, ᛋ Sowilo increases their vibrational frequency, and it uplifts them, clearing them out and banishing any 'murkiness' within them. All energetic contaminants are immediately purged away when using this rune. It happens automatically. For those of you who work with the light and the dark, be aware of this. ᛋ Sowilo will purge the dark and it will purify the light itself. Used reasonably and not overdoing it, this rune's power will always generate a successful or positive outcome – it is its very nature to do so. However, when overused, it purges everything to the colour of light. Because of these effects, a healer can make excellent use of this rune in order to bring about health in both energetic and physical terms. Its increase of life force and the power of that force are not to be undervalued! One effective way to use is to flood the energy body with its power from the archetypal, letting everything purge away that is not-Self.

Very much like ᛉ Elhaz, ᛋ Sowilo is a protective rune but works in a slightly different manner. It can keep at bay any and all negative and dark forces. They simply cannot reach into its light and survive. This rune renders powerless all things that its forces come across, providing they are incompatible with it (they are not like it).

ᛋ Sowilo is also a critically important rune in terms of awareness. Awareness steams from the crystallisation of this rune's power in your energy body. It is also rooted in one of the off-body hvels. All forms of awareness can be enhanced by this rune, be they personal awareness or the universal equivalent.

Physical Body & Physical Reality

ᛋ Sowilo will quicken any positive outcomes in your life that it can activate. It enables you to face things with greater power and certainty because using it causes your Self to express itself through your action and your body in the physical reality. It brings about success in whatever you actively engage in and is an excellent rune to use when facing a challenging time. A good practice I use personally is to allow its power to wash over all the food I might eat or drink – there is so much negative energy amassing in our food and drink that it would shock anyone who actually looked at it.

ᛋ Sowilo here is linked to the light emanating from the sun. It is the life-giving light (not the sun itself! The name of the rune was used in ancient days only to serve as a trigger to the actual mysteries of each rune, not for its literal scope of action and powers). It brings about a sense of wholeness of completeness. It also reminds all those who come in contact with it of the spiritual side of things, elevating and bringing a pleasantness to all it touches.

In difficult situations, this rune's power can be used to find a way out of various problems. It provides the necessary ideas and inspirations needed to make progress and is an excellent tool to use when trying to determine the truth in difficult situations, or when a crucial meeting is about to be attended! It also shines the light on matters that might be concealed or missed otherwise.

In terms of the physical body, it is an activating rune. It will enliven and speed up any physical processes or metabolic (re)actions. It is also an excellent rune to use in moderation when it comes to the nervous system and the eyes. Imbuing the eyes with it for short periods of time will allow for energy sight in the physical eyes to be developed (do not overdo this, or you will put your physical sight at risk!).

The Rune Tiwaz – Týr

Sound: t
Vocal Scale: Do
Numerology: 17
Natural Polarity: M - M - M - M - M
Energetic Colour (Universal): Red, smoky reds.
Primal Power: Victory, success and righteousness – the primordial patriarch.
Sensation(s): Harsh sharp firm flow of air (and winds).

Archetypal Level of Existence

↑ Tiwaz is the father rune. It is one of the two special runes of this Ætt (the second being the mother rune ᛒ Berkano). Usually, the Norse god Tyr is associated with this rune. However, as mentioned previously, linking a god to a rune obstructs understanding of its true nature. In fact this is the divine rune of the gods, rather than a specific god per se. It is the rune of universal law, the cosmic order rune and the rune of cosmic justice in its more abstracted form. From this essential meaning of justice, ↑ Tiwaz's rune force is also strongly link to authority of all sorts.

This rune has a very important connotation with the concept of the pillar and spear. It is a war rune as well, although not in the same context as ᚦ Thurisaz. Here, the battling is very tactical, driven by purpose typically for the betterment of some situation. It is a rune of guided targeted strength for a specific goal. ᚦ Thurisaz, on the other hand, is raw power being unleashed; it strikes what is needed and everything else as well, ᛏ Tiwaz is far more directed and will only strike at the aimed goal. It is the wise man (father) striking out to protect his family, land and territory. It is matured strength and tempered power, guided by experience. These are the essential conditions required to use this rune's energies and power, doing so leads to success. Do not mistake this for a tamed power – that could not be further from its true nature. It is a highly masculine force, but this time, that force is controlled and used correctly. The main difference is that it is used wisely and constructively rather than just unleashed. The wisdom needed comes with age and experience (maturity). This is the father force that stands up for what is just and for those who cannot defend themselves; it is the protector as well as the judge. It is the rune of the ruler and warrior.

Spirit & Spiritual Reality

This is the rune of perfected strength of will. The will has been tampered, moulded and conditioned to its utmost potential. The force of this rune intensifies the power of your intent and gives knowledge of one's true strengths. It will guide you towards the inner truth which is you. In universal terms, a spirit has to manifest its inner truth or self-destruct – those are the only two options open to it.

↑ Tiwaz's force is responsible for the impact of the principles of creation, such as the like attracts like principle and its variations, such as like influencing like, and so forth. It is the rune of justice in the cosmic sense of the word and this applies to all levels of reality, including the spiritual. Its force and powers enforce this without fail, for it is the rune that governs the laws of existence itself. As such, it also is indirectly the rune of the laws of fate; it is by its influence(s) that whatever fates are woven by the Norns are brought into realisation by ↑ Tiwaz without compromise. Not only are the fates linked in this manner to this rune, but so are the more fundamental laws which hold the fabric of creation in place and pre-date the arrival of the Norns and their work.

In terms of the spirit, this rune allows it to become a pillar of power, enabling forces to flow down into the lower realities through your own spirit. This spiritualises your own spirit and imbues it with some of the characteristics of its force. This builds a permanent unbreakable bond between your spirit and the force(s) you are working with. Likewise, for those spirits with a physical or energetic embodiment, the opposite is also true. For them this pillar forms bi-directionally, where powers from below are given the opportunity to rise, and those from above are able to descend by it. This is an essential function of exchange and intercommunication, where runes, forces, powers, energies, knowledge and even living beings can shift from one mode of existence into another through such pillar structures imbued with ↑ Tiwaz. It is important to keep in mind that before undertaking such an upwards or downwards journey, the very movement in this manner will cost a tremendous amount of energy. The pillar structures only provide the means, not the 'fuel' needed to make these type of shifts.

With ↑ Tiwaz being the ancestral father rune, it is possible to use it in order to connect with the entire paternal ancestral line, be it for guidance, for insights, or for other activities, where the masculine side of the ancestral heritage is needed. ↑ Tiwaz will call forth all the patriarchs of the line – if you want to call the matriarchs, use ᛒ Berkano instead. Each rune is very specific and their functions do not overlap.

Mind & Mental Reality

This is the rune of rationality, stoicism, self-knowledge and even self-sacrifice when it is truly needed. It is the rune of the elevated mind, cognition rising to new levels and defeating the opposing forces in existence. ↑ Tiwaz is the victorious intellect in extension, rising to new heights.

This is where righteousness and honour come into play; by keeping a strong true moral compass, you can unlock the full potential of this runic force. Do keep in mind that your moral compass has to be synchronised with the universal fate, for going against it puts you against the right path of creation and in direct opposition to this rune's underlying force. Fairness and detachment from irrationality are two essential weapons for you to wield – forget not that balance is a key requirement in rightful action.

The mind imbued with this rune's power is able to pierce the heavens themselves; breaking through limitations of understanding, perception, and intellect is possible, using it. Pushing through barriers is facilitated when using the powers of this rune. ᛏ Tiwaz is an excellent rune to use when seeking out guidance; it is the rune of the ancestral father, the ruler of the clans, and even the wisdom of the All-Father flows within its force, for it was all realised thanks to its power. As such, in mental strife or uncertainty, or when you lack direction for a solution to problems which seem to be overwhelming, or simply where you cannot find a way out, then referring to this rune can help you find ways in which to overcome those problems. Simply call upon its power and remain in a mental silence; let your intuition activate and this rune will be able to shed some guidance through direct inspiration to you. At times when you truly need a fatherly helping hand, rather than just being lazy and running to it because you cannot be bothered to find an answer on your own, it can be a most valuable guide. Keep in mind that it might be the rune of the ruler and ancestral father in its positive polarity, but it is also the rune of the hermit and wandering Seiðr man in its negative one.

Remember the rule of like attracts like: the more you work with this rune, the more you will pull towards righteous thoughts and, eventually, people who think along righteous and just ways. Likewise, you will also, as time goes by, isolate away those who do not. If there is no unfairness in your life and thoughts, it is extremely unlikely for you to pull a person who is unfair in (except when it is dictated by fate).

This rune promotes order; as such, it is possible to make use of its energy whenever things get messy in terms of recall, thinking, or even gathering of ideas and concepts. When you are trying to think your way through a problem or other, its influence can be a blessing indeed.

Energy Body & Energy Reality

↑Tiwaz is used at this level to cut through energy and emotionality. It is the cold hard realisation of the facts of things and a response in kind that leads to a just outcome. The turbulent emotional states can all be struck down with a logical approach. An illusion or emotional deception can be cut through with a sharp mind using ↑Tiwaz. Remember, the person who lives by the whims of emotion has an erratic life; imposing order into a messy environment and life requires clear thinking and consideration of facts of a given reality. ↑Tiwaz will assist you to do this, and when in other realities, it will allow you to understand the underlying truths and facts in operation there.

Just as with the mental side of things, on the energetic level, it is possible to use this rune for the pillar effect. Becoming a central pillar for a given force in creation allows free flow of its energies and influence through your energy body (Hamr). The important point to note in terms of energy is that you will need to submit to the flow and then, providing you have sufficient strength, impose order into the incoming energies (without trying to control) before they continue their path outwards into the energetic realities at large. Doing this allows some very interesting application such as channelling of power directly from the universal into the personal sphere of action, filling a space with universal energy and so forth. Do keep in mind that if you use a given force in this manner, the force will also get to use you in the same way. Be prepared! It is a give and take that keeps things going smoothly along the universally (not the human) righteous path.

Another important function of this rune's force in our energy body is that using it, you can set right any disruptions or mis-configurations of the energy body and its organs (Hvels). Often times, beings and things attempt to change, add or even prevent energy flowing correctly at certain points or along certain paths. They do so for a wide range of reasons, whether to limit it, to alter how it functions, or even to force its development down the route they choose, rather than what its right way would have been. This rune's power can reset things to their proper ideal pattern. Do keep in mind that if you have gained certain energetic abilities through the interference of third parties, resetting things will result in you losing those. Likewise, it is also possible to do the same thing with entire energetic environments.

When energetic confrontations take place, using this rune can lead to victory. It enhances the expression of your own will, allows you to establish control and dominion in the matter and bolsters not only your battle skills but also, by virtue of your connection to universal justice, your victory (providing what you are fighting for is meant to be).

Because this rune is also the rune of sacrifices – specifically self-sacrifices – it has dominion over them. Not only does it govern them but it also leads you towards the understanding of what is too much or not appropriate to self-sacrifice. It is foolish to give away so much that you harm yourself as an end result.

Just as with all the other levels of existence, ↑ Tiwaz governs all energetic promises, oaths and agreements. Under its dominion fall all energy exchanges, or rather their impact. For instance, when you give and take energy from another energy being, it leaves a permanent imprint in the both of you for as long as you exist. This is a type of bonding very similar to that of members of a family. You become 'related' to the being with which your energy has been exchanged (the actual exchange is governed by X Gebo, but the impact of it falls within the scope of this rune). The universal laws are enforced ruthlessly, according to the actions of this force. Sometimes you can see the outcome and become horrified at it, because from a human point of view, it might be outrageous and totally unfair and unjust – but if universally it is just and fair, then it will be that way. Always keep this in mind when working with this rune: the human morality and perceptions of order are totally irrelevant in the grander scheme of things.

Physical Body & Physical Reality

↑ Tiwaz is a force to be reckoned with in terms of business, legal cases, and any type of proceedings, as well as in professional sports. It leads to success, where the right actions lead to the right results. This is also the rune of promises, contracts, agreements and even oaths. Be careful to stick to your parts of any deal made; the price for breaking a ↑ Tiwaz-enhanced agreement is dear. The God Tyr lost his hand for breaking his!

What has been said about the pillar effect and with respect to battles, justice and righteousness all apply to the physical reality as well. This rune is also a warrior rune. Unlike ᚦ Thurisaz, which is the youthful explosive warrior, this one's forces are more akin to the matured highly experienced warrior or general of an army; it has gained mastery of the arts of battle and war, and as such it is also far less compromising and harsher in its actions. The wisdom, ability and power it acquires as a result of this is phenomenal and less prone to collateral damage. It is also an excellent rune when it comes to learning self-control and discipline; it banishes all the tendencies towards the erratic and makes it easier to distance one's self from the emotional instability. It is the force which makes men able to ground emotions and process them, effectively refocusing the mind on practical solutions and the next step to take, rather than get distracted by emotional inputs or things which might bear no relevance to the matter at hand. It is also the rune that will drive all that which is masculine into a protective and caring role: it seeks to ensure order and stability, safety and security, and likewise, it is also the rune that will promote the need to build a foothold or a base of operation – when combined with ᛟ Othala, this effect can be greatly amplified. It is not the rune of the adventurous, which belongs to the domain of ᚢ Uruz and ᚦ Thurisaz. With ᛏ Tiwaz, the time for adventures is over, and the time for building a stronghold is here.

Additionally, ᛏ Tiwaz has the ability of elevating consciousness upwards. It will spiritualise the entire sensory system of the physical body and propel it into the energetic awareness. Remember, this rune causes the universally right effects and for human beings, this is to evolve out of a state of physical solidity into the realm of energy and power. Using this rune, it is possible to force through this elevation in a gradual manner and to counter any opposing forces, purely on the basis that what you are pursuing is a universal per-determined fate-driven goal for the human race. Victory is assured because it is destined in this context, and using this rune's power, you can piggyback on this, in order to propel yourself upwards.

The Rune Berkano - Bjarkan

Sound: b
Vocal Scale: Re
Numerology: 18
Natural Polarity: F - F - F - F - F
Energetic Colour (Universal): Dark green, the rich green of mature pine trees.
Primal Power: Nourishing, transformative, primordial matriarch.
Sensation(s): Warm moist earth, sensation of weight and temperate warmth combined.

Archetypal Level of Existence

ᛒ Berkano's force is that of the primordial mother. It is the end goal of the feminine at its peak – both nourishing and nurturing, yet firm, relentless and resolute. This rune's energies sustain and maintain the powers of other runes. It will augment all the effects of whatever it influences and ensure they are longer lasting. It bolsters the growth and development of whatever it interacts with. ᛒ Berkano balances out the harshness of ᛏ Tiwaz and offers the hand of temperance to its forces. ᛒ Berkano's force is very feminine – extremely so; as such, men should be very careful when trying to make use of it. It will have a feminising influence on whoever works with it or comes into contact with it. The advice is exactly the same as what was given for ᛏ Tiwaz and ᚦ Thurisaz to women: if you are a man, avoid having ᛒ Berkano's powers, energy and forces flow through your Self. If there is an absolute must, keep it extremely short and use as little power as possible.

ᛒ Berkano's power is generative and regenerative. ᛒ Berkano embodies the full spectrum of the nurturing darkness. It not only signals the emergence of new existence from its foetal stage but also protects it and conceals it from harm. When it comes to the powers of silence, to protective concealment and subtle coaxing towards a certain goal, there is no equal to ᛒ Berkano.

ᛒ Berkano is, in a similar manner to ᚲ Kenaz, a transformation rune, the main difference being that it is more of an end-goal type of transformation, rather than ᚲ Kenaz's transmutation process drive one. This might seem a little confusing but is rather simple; with ᚲ Kenaz, you have a starting point and you perform x, y and z transmutations on that starting substance. It is the substance plus the effects of your x process, your y process and the z process that determines the end results. Whereas with ᛒ Berkano you have your starting substance and a set goal, what processes are undertaken to take you from the start to the end do not matter – what determines the outcome is the starting substance and the end goal. Whether that substance undergoes one process or one million processes is entirely irrelevant, as are all the stages it undertakes during its transformation. You can also think of it as a foetus undergoing ᛒ Berkano transformations until it becomes a baby. The individual stages are irrelevant because you will know that if you begin with a foetus, you end up with a baby (providing all goes well), whereas with ᚲ Kenaz-type transformations, say trying to get lead to gold, the ultimate goal is irrelevant other than being informative – what matters is the individual processes you take from the base lead to the next and the next and so forth, until you get to your end product (the gold). Each stage, each process is fundamentally critical in importance and your immediate purpose is to get through the first process with the required result, then use that as the basis for the next start for the next and so on. It is also a far more error-prone type of transformation because the failure at any point in the chain of individual steps will result in total failure and force you to restart at point 0. However, with ᛒ Berkano, you can have in-between process failures in your transformation but still end up with a successful outcome. Use ᚲ Kenaz only when you need to fine-tune what your outcome will be to an extremely precise degree. For the scientifically minded, it would be accurate to describe ᚲ Kenaz's transformations as being transmutative and ᛒ Berkano's as adaptive.

    Another very important function of this rune is its ability to absorb the negative and consume it in order to use it as nourishment for its regenerative and nourishment functions. Its association with trees comes to the forefront when observing how its powers function; its effects are very similar to roots being wrapped around each individual power and bringing them all together, as well as preventing them from dispersing. It ensures safety and is very useful when something needs to be cared for. A good example would be at the birthing of a new Spark of Self, where this rune's force is hyper-active. It also plays an important part when it comes to all types of transformation; when moving from the old state to a new one, ᛒ Berkano comes into play just as the new state is being adapted and until it becomes stable in its own right. It is a rune of becoming and blossoming.

Spirit & Spiritual Reality

On the spiritual level, this rune is highly protective; it will both act as a concealing power and a shielding one. Do be careful just much of it you use, as it has a tendency to overstay and becomes hard to banish. This rune's tendency of overdoing things is what caused the 'helicopter mum' expression to come into existence. Small doses of this insanely powerful force are more than sufficient.

An important use of the ᛒ Berkano force is to effectively rebirth a spirit. It allows for the ashes of any existing spirit to be taken and nurtured into a new spirit, with its old characteristics and powers as the basis for its new being. ᛒ Berkano will be able to hold the fragments of a dissolving spirit and then re-fuse it together with whatever new elements it needs. It is a most complex undertaking to initiate and is rife with possibilities of failure – but it is possible nonetheless.

ᛒ Berkano connects the conscious to the spiritual. It will allow you to elevate your mind to these more subtle layers of existence. It will strip all that which is meaningless (from the spiritual perspective) away, and synchronise your consciousness through your own spirit to its realities.

ᛒ Berkano's transformative methods are very well suited to spirit transformations because it is practically impossible to determine each and every individual stage of a process, when it comes to spirit changes. There are just too many factors at play and too many unknown and un-knowables. Getting a glimpse or two into the nature of spirit is possible, but understand that the very nature of the core of a spirit is not. Because of that, <Kenaz's processes will practically always have an overwhelming failure rate, whereas ᛒ Berkano, which is tolerant of unknowns, does not suffer from such problems.

One of the more interesting effects of this rune is how its force interacts with the kin-Fylgja. Upon becoming pregnant, ᛒ Berkano's force will bind the future mother to the kin-Fylgja (family spirit). This amplifies the powers of the mother, depending on how powerful that family spirit is. This is one of the great advantages women have, and one of the reasons why they are so sensitive to the non-physical side of reality. They are protected by their own family's spirit and when they become pregnant, they also gain the power of their unborn offspring's father. This new power gained is at its strongest until the child becomes a fully-fledged adult, at which point it starts to fade and transfers to the child instead.

ᛒ Berkano's other vital role on the spiritual is to absorb the negative spirits, spirit energy and spiritual influences. It converts them into something else entirely (depending on what is needed, it can be but is not necessarily positive). As with ᛏ Tiwaz, ᛒ Berkano can be used to call forth the ancestral line's influences; however, it applies to the maternal lines – in other words, calling upon all the matriarchs of the line.

Mind & Mental Reality

All the arts of persuasion of the mind and the will fall under the scope of ᛒ Berkano. This rune's force and power take a gentle yet firm grasp, and have the ability to bend things ever so slightly, but just enough in order to reset their course completely to what it intended. In this manner, it can manipulate the mind totally effortlessly – the precision and the subtle touch it imposes is practically always missed, unless one is very sensitive to it.

The full impact of the moment, the great NOW is fully expressed by this rune. It is the womb of time itself, the start of the illusion that binds all things in matter. By using this rune's power, its effects on our mind can be enhanced, providing stillness, returning it to the point just beyond time. It causes some very odd containment of the mind; by closing off the mind from time, it has a very liberating effect.

In terms of memory, traumas and other difficult painful events in your life can be released by the effects of this rune. It can burrow down deep inside the mind to the point where all is uprooted, nothing is left unturned and all that needs to be released is.

All types of memories and thoughts (as well as thought forms) can be transformed from one state to another using ᛒ Berkano's force. When it comes to the transformation of thought forms and memories, ᛒ Berkano comes into its own here. This rune's power is ideally suited for them (thoughts, on the other hand, are better suited to the ᚲ Kenaz type of transformations).

ᛒ Berkano can also be used to precipitate ideas into manifestation; just as it can be used to facilitate the birthing of energy systems, it can do the same with moving ideas past the mental and into the energetic. Remember, just as is the case with birthing of physical life forms, ᛒ Berkano cannot create anything – it can just take a seed, nourish it, and bring it to fruition.

Energy Body & Energy Reality

ᛒ Berkano is the matured emotion, the emotion tampered by experience and wisdom. It balances out perfectly the powers of reason, logic and the stoicism of ᛏ Tiwaz. It facilitates the working of the emotional mind and the logical mind together as one cohesive unit, blending the two into a unified whole. It takes the strengths of the masculine mind, its ability to process emotions rapidly in a non-overwhelming and stable manner, and combines it perfectly with the feminine mind, which is able to use emotion in order to free itself of the rigid structures imposed by logic and reason, stretching out into unchartered territories. The two working in balance produce a wonderful, solid type of energy state and correspond to the calm, powerful mind. The resulting effects on the energy body are critical to the formation of a cohesive, stable and free-flowing energy system.

ᛒ Berkano's powers can be used to weed out of the entire energy body's system any blockages, negative bottlenecks and unwanted changes. Its power will root itself deep into the energy systems, organs, pathways and energy centres, purging them or maturing them, depending on what is needed.

This rune's force is key to solidifying the energy body and making it able to function independently from the physical. It becomes able to carry consciousness. Do be warned: the intensity and amount of ᛒ Berkano power needed mean that only women can use this rune in this way. Men would be too negatively affected and our energetic biology interferes with this rune's effects on the energy body. This rune is the principal driving force beyond the Seiðr mysteries of the womb and its energetic functions.

A powerful effect of this rune is related to the universal energy gateways and springs of power. ᛒ Berkano rules upon them all. Its underlying force gives rise to them and offers up the possibility of tapping into these universal springs, wells and nexus. Unlocking the flow of deep ancestral power is possible through this rune and nourishing one's own energy system from those can provide countless benefits, which will depend on the source you wish to use. For instance, Oðinn used the well of Mimir for knowledge of all past creation – the very existence of that well is a result of ᛒ Berkano's influence. Additionally, such sources of power and energy also exist in our own energy bodies, or rather are directly linked into them via the hvels. They are not only a processing centre in the energy body, but their secondary function is that of a wellspring or gateway (depending on the hvel). Those that function as wellsprings have a direct outpouring from universal streams of energy and power. Unfortunately, they are closed by default and need to be activated in order to release the free flow of said power. ᛒ Berkano helps with this process and also ensures that the outpouring of energy can be allowed to flow in a harmonious, integrated manner.

Physical Body & Physical Reality

When used within the physical body, this rune can help reconnect to the feminine forces within. It will automatically feminise and mature the biological intelligence (see *The Blood of Lóðurr Awakens*). This makes it a fundamentally unsuitable rune to use for men! If you are a man, you should avoid the energy of this rune flowing through your body at all costs (use the non-self technique on p.92 instead). It is for the same reasons that ᚦ Thurisaz and ᛏ Tiwaz should be avoided by women, but this one applies to men.

Other than that, ᛒ Berkano can have a powerful regenerative influence on everything within the body and outside of it. Its power is one of renewal and is highly generative; it nourishes all the systems which are starved or lacking. It has an important link to ancestral knowledge and experiences; these stored in our genetics can be quickened by this rune's power and brought to life in the body. However, it is worth being cautious because just bringing back anything from past generations can be as detrimental as it can be helpful. Intent will be the deciding factor, and fate will determine what the impact of your attempts to do so will be. Act wisely with a pure heart when doing this; your intent needs to be strong and your intensions pure. Knowing one's own limitations and abilities is vitally important in this type of practice – overestimating yourself can be very detrimental. You have been warned.

ᛒ Berkano's influences and roles in manifesting the archetypal matriarch come into full force here on the physical (and, to a lesser extent, on the energetic). All that has been discussed above with respect to this archetype applies here physically. Please refer above for this information.

In the wider context of daily life, this rune's impact is one of new beginnings, and the fruition of something that was long in the works and needs to finally manifest. As such, its powers can be used to accelerate this. It can also be put to good use in love aimed at reaching an ongoing relationship. It is not a rune for a quick explosive spark and affair – rather, it is the 'love' that keeps a family together and stable.

Additionally, if you need to keep things concealed or secret, such as in business dealings, you can take advantage of this rune's power. Likewise, it is also possible to put it to good use when trying to regenerate a 'dead' project or endeavour. ᛒ Berkano will inspire you as to how this can be brought back in a new way that might help you in its realisation.

ᛒ Berkano rules over the energetic part of the womb and governs all women's sexual mysteries. It is also strongly linked to the sexual hvel in women. This energy wheel is found slightly higher in women than in men. Its functions are far more extensive and powerful in women as it opens the gateway to awareness within the energy body. Unfortunately, most literature describes only men's sexual energy centre. To those with energy sight, it pulsates a bright cyan energy when positively charged or a dark cyan almost dark sea green when negatively charged or dormant.

The Rune Ehwaz – Eykur

Sound: e
Vocal Scale: Mi
Numerology: 19
Natural Polarity: B - B - B - B - B
Energetic Colour (Universal): Pale white (like chalk).
Primal Power: Awakening, symbiotic relationship.
Sensation(s): Earthly, dense but a softer type of earth, comfortable solidity which holds you stable but does not bind you down, has a cohesive effect like gravity but it is smooth and gentle.

Archetypal Level of Existence

This is the rune of symbiosis on all levels of existence. By this, what is meant is two compatible or alike life forms, or concepts, or emanations into existence coming together in a harmonious union in order to move forward as one. In such relationships, each maintains its fundamental 'self-ness' but works as part of a whole with the other. In such positive unions, the two can move forward and progress much faster than each could on its own. Additionally, any challenges that could have been disastrous to one of the two are managed by them both together and become not only easier to push through, but can become a non-event entirely, depending on the strengths of the other. The weaknesses of both are countered by the strengths of each other and their strengths are amplified by each other. This has often, for this reason, been associated with marriage but this is not a marriage rune – not by any stretch of its force, simply because the two parts coming together in such a symbiotic energetic and archetypal relationship need to be alike. The masculine and feminine are too different archetypally to allow for this type of symbiosis through ᛗ Ehwaz. This is also one of the key reasons why ᛗ Ehwaz is the rune of the unity within the Self. Here, all the parts of the Self are parts of the same Self, and such symbiosis is easily established at all levels. Ancestral symbiosis is also possible using this rune. However, here again, since there is commonality in the nature of each blood member in a family, a linking achieved by it is not always maintained. The individuality and differences in personality have a tendency to weaken the effects of this force in such a context. This is why ᛟ Othala is the ancestral rune and not ᛗ Ehwaz, just as ᚷ Gebo is the rune of marriage rather than this one. They both require same-ness, but ᚷ Gebo's forces focus on even the smallest like-ness, whereas ᛗ Ehwaz's focus on what is not-alike, and once that becomes a more than insignificant quantity, it rejects symbiotic unification.

 Understanding the forces of this rune's other characteristic – that of travel – requires a little conceptual work. Archetypally, this is not the rune of travel as such (that would be ᚱ Raidho); rather its forces are those of movement. When travelling, you have the power that drives you forward and the motion of the movement. ᚱ Raidho is the former and ᛗ Ehwaz is the latter; it represents the motion of the movement in a forward direction. Yes, it is a very subtle distinction between the two runic forces, but archetypally these very subtle differences make an enormous difference. If you prefer, you can think of it as ᚱ Raidho being the driver and the engine, whereas ᛖ Ehwaz is the movement which carries you from A to B. Using universal motion, you could very easily move from point A to B without even needing the driver or the power of ᚱ Raidho's engine. Using this type of spiritual kinetic flow is how the Seiðr practitioners move between worlds. This is the reason why ᛖ Ehwaz is deemed to be the awakening rune; it is not only the bringing of all parts of the Self into a unified harmonious system, but also the movement of that unified Self forward along the path of realisation through evolution itself.

Spirit & Spiritual Reality

In the spiritual level, this rune's effects are very specific: they deal with the interaction of spirits, groups of spirits and one's own spirit with the spiritual realm itself. Unlike in the other levels of reality, in this one, the rune itself is the vehicle for motion aimed to get from point A to B. It is important to understand here that since time and space do not exist yet, there can be no travel from A to B because A and B are at exactly the same 'spot' – they are both at the timeless and spaceless NOW. This fundamentally changes the manner in which this rune's force manifests and functions; instead of the motion through space, it moves the spirit(s) from one state to another. It too is a journey, one of evolution or devolution, but movement it is. This shifting from one state of spirit to another can be thought of as a change in vibrational rate of the spirit. By using this rune, you can move from one state to the other as needed in order to connect with a different spiritual realm or entity. However, just as always, here the rule of like attracts like applies – it acts as a scope of potential states you can move into and from. In other words, if your spirit does not have the capacity to be in, say, state C, it will not be possible to use ᛗ Ehwaz to move a spiritual realm where spirits are in the C state of vibration. Likewise, it will not be possible to form a symbiotic relationship with C state spirits. If your spirit is capable of functioning in, say, the A state of vibration because it is very like its own nature, then it is possible to use this rune's forces to 'move' in that realm and connect with other spirits functioning in the A state.

This can indeed be very confusing to understand at first, but makes sense if you keep in mind that only those things which are alike can be together; the more alike they are, the deeper the connection. This is why human spirits all exist together: they are alike and it is why, for example, very few human spirits can exist in the animal spirit realms because they do not share this likeness of being. Even if they share some characteristics, it is not sufficient that their very natures need to be alike. This explains why the shamans and Seiðr practitioners of old had to shapeshift and adopt animal types of form in spirit, in order to travel to their realms. ᛇ Gebo would allow them to work with those spirits without sharing such deep likeness within their own natures – but that is limited to working with them, more often than not, here in Midgard (Earth) where all mix and interact. Moving to their realms requires this deeper inner likeness in nature. This is why in Spirit Walking (see *Spirit Walking for the Rune Mystic*), the adoption of the typical form of spirits and their energy signatures is taught before traveling to their realms. Yes, spirits are formless, but by adopting the same forms they appear in, you can change the way your mind and spirit manifest, providing you practice enough, until they start to express very similar, if not identical characteristics as the spirit in question, even when being formless. Remember, form and shape is a symbolic representation of the underlying powers and characteristics of a given spirit.

Mind & Mental Reality

Here the fun begins with this rune! ᛖEhwaz on the mental level is essential when sending the mind or memory ravens flying. Using it, you are able to develop a very deep synergy between the two parts of the Self, and then even move this bond to other parts of the Self in order to achieve things such as deep recall of dreams, energy body (Hamr) outings, physiological recall of ancestral experiences and so on. Using ᛖEhwaz can open up an interesting possibility of deep union of the biological intelligence (see *The Blood of Lóðurr Awakens*) and the conscious mind, even going so far as to merge the biological (or what is commonly called the subconscious) with the conscious. All sorts of states of hyper-awareness result from such a unification, as the animalistic (or child-like) part of the Self is united with the conscious in a perfect harmonious relationship, propelling the two together into new heights of awareness and perception. ᛖEhwaz promotes the understanding and acceptance of the inner parts of the Self with each other, and provides the push they need to work towards common goals. It is an incredible rune to use in healing when trying to deal with a whole range of mental health problems, the vast array of which can be attributed to some sort of conflict between two or more parts of the Self.

As far as interactions of two minds are concerned, yes it is possible, but is extremely difficult and rare. The two minds would have to be not only in perfect harmony but think alike to a greater extent. That is the main difficulty to overcome. It is possible to have a situation where one mind is submitting itself to another, and in doing so, sharing in the essence of that mind. This often happened with the ancient yogi and spiritual master – student relationships where the student practically worshipped his or her master, and in doing so, developed a deep likeness to them. In those cases, ᛗEhwaz's forces would bridge them and allow knowledge, experiences and powers to be shared between the two. But such types of teaching are too open to abuse in the modern day, so know they are possible in a very limited situation – but we shall not go into how these can be practically achieved.

ᛗEhwaz is also used when trying to send your mind or memory forth into other places than your immediate physical surroundings. Using its power to send forth the Hugr raven, it is possible to experience a range of enhanced mental perceptions and abilities ranging from waves of inspiration, acquiring of knowledge by purely intuitive means, experiencing other types of thinking and even shifting your mental perceptions to other forms of universal thought. For instance, when trying to perceive the universal threads of existence, this rune will facilitate these types of shifts and adaptations.

With memory or rather the part of our mind that deals with active memories (those acquired, used and managed by you in your lifetime, not ancestral ones, which is the domain of the Fylgja), that seat of memory can also be sent to other places, people and even realms of perception using this rune's powers. However, do be cautious: while it is away, it is possible for it to get lost. Actually, this is one of Oðinn's worst fears (losing his raven(s)). All the practices describing the sending forth of the Minni in *The Spirit of Húnir Awakens (Part 2)* are enhanced by this rune's forces and its powers facilitate success with them. All you need to do is fill the Minni with this rune's energy before sending it forth; the perceptive outcome should be quite noticeable.

Energy Body & Energy Reality

This is where this rune's power comes into its full expression. What it can help with is very vast. One of its primary uses involves influencing the connections or relationship between the energy body and the shadow, which in turn influences the physical body (which is the third energetic body we all possess). Its force works meticulously, ensuring that the energy body and the shadow are kept separate at all times during life. They almost form two entirely individual bodies, one occupying what can be thought of as the left side, and the other the right, only connected by the forces which flow and interact through them. Pushed and pulled by the biology of the physical. Using this rune's power, you can gain not only an insight into these parts of yourself but can also learn to control these inner forces and their flow. Once you do learn this control, it is possible to separate these parts of the Self and journey out with either or both of them using the force of this rune. Its powers, combined with ᛚ Laguz, enable the reshaping of the energy body, and combined with ᚱ Raidho, can propel it forward into new realms.

As on other levels of reality, ᛗ Ehwaz can be used to quicken the vibrations and stretch the frequencies of all energies, including those within the energy bodies of the Self. Additionally, gaining control of energy using this rune's power is also possible and by having such control, you should be able to manipulate and project it as needed. The same rules apply here as they do on the mental level of things; ᛗ Ehwaz's power to bring together two like forces/energies is strong, and it enables the rune mystic to blend them into a symbiotic unity. The fascinating thing about its effects on energy is that those are not only brought into a symbiotic relationship as individual powers but they are united; they interact within and without each other, not only preserving their individual characteristics but also causing them to produce a third, which is greater than the sum of the two, and that third power is propelled forward into action on a path of its own.

Similarly, this rune is used when the blending of two entire energy bodies into one novel being takes place. Such fusions are extremely rare, but their end product is immensely potent, assuming the two survive the procedure.

Physical Body & Physical Reality

ᛗ Ehwaz offers up some rather interesting possibilities to the rune mystic on the physical level. In order for integration of the Self to take place, the physical body needs to be integrated into the rest of the Self. This rune can be used to awaken the spiritual nature of the individual cells in the body and then integrate their awareness into the whole. It has the potential to reveal the true nature of our physiology. When viewed from the quantum state, each cell is an independent point of energy, and that point is also a line. Those lines weave and interweave in order to form matter, and our cells, organs and all the matter they are made of. Each of these lines vibrates and by doing this creates a vibrating energetic waves. As these waves combine, they form what is typically called the astral body or the 'soul'. Each vibration emits more energy and in turn produces what people have often referred to as the 'aura'. This is inherently a physical phenomenon – it is energetic but material. This vibration of billions upon billions of waves and their effortless unions/combinations is what ultimately produces our consciousness. It is also one of the reasons that those who are not trained to do so will lose their consciousness when not functioning physically. In this way, ᛗEhwaz is not only the rune of harmonic symbiosis with the cellular or atomic side of our bodies, but also the rune of consciousness itself. By using it, you can gain an understanding and the capacity to witness this part of your most physical Self, as well as influence it. It takes a lot of practice, but over time, simply allowing its energy and power to flood your body from head to toe is all that is needed to stretch one's ability to perceive – providing you keep persevering at it. How long it takes depends entirely on the individual. Likewise, it is also within the realm of possibility to extend this type of perception to the universal whole. Things do get very overwhelming very quickly at that scale of things but seeing these threads of intelligent energy flowing throughout the environment is definitely a possibility this rune can guide one to.

This rune's power and its underlying forces can have a positive impact when trying to achieve what is true astral projection, which is nothing other than the separation of these energy systems from the physical. When doing so, the body grows cold and pale, and breath slows down to the point where unless you pay extremely close attention, you would not even notice it breathing at all. This is an extremely dangerous type of separation, and for this reason, will not be covered in practical methods and is only mentioned for theoretical understanding.

Beyond this type of subtle application, the rune's power can also be put to good use when it comes to dealing with daily worldwide matters, such as ensuring trust and cooperation in various ventures and friendship (especially that of buddies); it can increase loyalty and truth between two people and can bring out tendencies for sharing concerns and deep-seated truths. It also governs travel and journeys, not only in terms of moving from one place to another, but also in moving from one situation to another.

The Rune Mannaz - Maður

Sound: m
Vocal Scale: Fa
Numerology: 20
Natural Polarity: N - Your Own - Your Own - Your Own - Your Own.
Energetic Colour (Universal): Deep red (ruby-red).
Primal Power: Unification, realisation.
Sensation(s): Sensation of warm air currents, gentle and harsh warm breeze; summer breeze.

Archetypal Level of Existence

With ᛗ Mannaz, there is an important bit of confusion we need to iron out at the outset. Many sources describe this rune as the rune of 'man' or 'mankind', and although its forces do represent humanity on the physical level of reality, it is vitally important not to mistake it for the rune of mankind. No rune is specific to any race of being in existence; these are universal abstracted forces which apply to all of existence, and in most parts of existence, there is no mankind. With that out of the way, let us take a closer look at this rune's forces and powers.

ᛗ Mannaz has a strong relationship with the ᛋ Sowilo rune; they are practically reflections of each other. ᛋ Sowilo is the rune of the Spark of Self, or the initial outpouring of one's abstract essence outwards into creation. ᛗ Mannaz, on the other hand, is the realisation of that Self within creation. You can think of it in this way, ᛋ Sowilo is the start and ᛗ Mannaz is the 'end' product (even though there is no end as such). This rune's force brings together absolutely everything, every part, every glimmer, every shred of every manifestation of the Self and unifies it into a complete whole. It is, in this capacity, what one can call the great unifier. Unlike other runes with similar effects, this one will automatically exclude that which is not the Self – anything which does not belong, which is not rooted in your most abstract essence, will be purged out of this union. As such, it is not a rune of partnerships like ᛖ Ehwaz or ᚷ Gebo, or a social rune like ᚹ Wunjo. It is the Self which has become complete and is now standing on its 'own two feet' in the great vastness of existence. For this reason, it is also an excellent rune to use when you need to reaffirm your Self, or you need to brush off anything that is clinging or attached to you. Its power will automatically purge away any and all influences that are not from deep within the Self. When we talk of the purity of Self, this rune's power is what is being referred to. It brings out the divine within the Self. Remember, according to the Norse mindset, even human beings have the divine within, as it was gifted to us by the Oðinn, Vili and Vé (or Oðinn, Húnir and Lóðurr, depending on which name set you prefer), when humanity was created. Likewise, the ᛗ Mannaz forces bring out the divine in other beings in existence – well, their specific manifestation of it.

When the Self is working as a unified harmonious completed being, countless other possibilities open up for it. The ability to fully express its own power – or to be more accurate, the radiation of its Spark of Self, including all possible variations and manifestations of that power – is gained. It shines within the archetypal, and that emotion affects all those it comes into contact with in creation. It is at the point of ᛗ Mannaz that human beings can start to walk the worlds and their inner light shining out, reminding all those they come into contact with of the higher nature of existence. It has a strengthening quality to it as well as a reflecting one. It is very much the equivalent of a touch of something divine to all those who have not yet reached this state of their own inner being, and this touch elevates them ever so slightly towards their own realisation. It can also be used by the rune mystic to quicken the development of any other whom they come into contact with, be it spirit, human, animal, or any of the billions of non-physical life forms out there.

Having reached the point of ᛗ Mannaz, the development of the Self is complete. All the other runes after it carry the fully realised Self forward – even ᛞ Dagaz, which is the so-called 'enlightenment' rune, as that too acts as a catalyst to carry things forward rather than to complete the Self or any part thereof, for that work has been done in ᛗ Mannaz.

A useful application of this force is to project it into the Spark of Self of someone else, in order to help them on their way. You should be very careful before doing, so unless they really want to walk the path of spiritual development. It is a harsh road, where many hardships are faced on a daily basis. The life of a warrior is not for everyone, but for those who do opt for it, a pure projection of ᛗ Mannaz by someone who has mastered this force can do wonders to speed things up, open to new realisations, and break through any blockages along the way.

Spirit & Spiritual Reality

On the spiritual level, this force is a rather interesting one. The rune's power pulls the spirit inwards. An outside observer would notice immediately how the initial effects of this force are strikingly similar to those of ᛁ Isa. However, unlike with ᛁ Isa, stasis does not occur; instead, once all of the spirit is concentrated at one point (that point links it back to the archetypal where the two flow freely into one another), it undergoes a total unification of all that it is. Since time does not exist here, all that it is also includes all that it ever was and ever will be, from our human point of view. It is a totality of being, to be brought back inwards in order to be completed. Once that happens, both the spirit and the force of ᛗ Mannaz cause a type of implosion followed by an outflowing. This time, unlike what occurs in the first Ætt, the spirit does not expand outwards; instead, it is contained by its very core (the point where it imploded in and re-connected to the archetypal). There is no longer any risk of over-expanding and dissipating into everything, which results in the wiping out of the spirit. ᛗ Mannaz gives it that single point of cohesion back into the Spark of Self and so when it does flow outwards, it radiates rather than gradually thinning out, until there is nothing of it left. This thinning out is what happens when a spirit tries to be 'at one' with everything – it basically becomes thinner and thinner until it is no more. Ironically, by trying to evolve into everything, it ends up losing its Self and becomes nothing. A spirit which has undergone progress through the runes and reached the ᛗ Mannaz point will, by mastering ᛗ Mannaz's force, gain this anchor and become something separate, unique and fully realised. From that point onwards, it can expand without risking losing its Self. And so it does, first by flowing through ᛚ Laguz, then solidifying its gains in ᛜ Ingwaz, radiating its own light and changing its environment through ᛞ Dagaz to build its foothold in ᛟ Othala, from which it can shift into the next cycle.

Likewise, the mystic who has mastered this rune can, if caught in time, pull back any spirit which has started it thinning out. With it, you can stop this process and re-establish the connection between any spirit and its archetypal Spark. It is also perfectly possible to help spirits who have lost their footing, direction and have forgotten their Self to re-establish what they were and who they are (in other words, their individuality and uniqueness is reaffirmed by this rune's powers and underlying force). It is the best tool you have available to counter the tendencies of stasis and the collective. The rune reaffirms (and strengthens) the uniqueness of each spirit, its underlying purpose and characteristics.

Mind & Mental Reality

As far as the mind is concerned, ᛗ Mannaz unlocks a whole array of extremely helpful effects. It can be used to help with single-minded focus. Minds which run riot and become distracted left, right and centre can be brought back into check using this rune's power. Like on the spiritual level, here its effects of reaffirming the mind are strong. It can be used by all those who have the habit of thinking of others and forgetting about oneself in the process. Yes, being thoughtful of others is helpful and to be recommended, but not when it comes at a cost to the self. Any sacrifice to the so-called greater good is a most damnable thing to occur, for it can potentially wipe out a unique creation and negate the very purpose for which that being was created in the first place. ᛗ Mannaz strengthens our understanding of our own minds as direct manifestations of the Self. Its forces help you detach from the hustle and bustle of society and the collective thinking, in order for you to perfect your own mind and gain a solid grasp of its total potential. Anyone who seeks to master transferring of consciousness, enhancing of perceptions beyond their daily lives and bridging into universal awareness needs to perfect their minds and memories using ᛗ Mannaz. Not only will this rune's power enable you to undergo this perfecting, but it will also be a great assistant when it comes to detaching from the daily life. It changes, evolves and reignites long-forgotten potentials within, both in terms of mind and memory. This is one of the reasons why it is often associated with an increase in intelligence and awareness. It does not increase them per se, but rather consolidates them and awakens their potential, which results in a realisation of what they were meant to be all along. This is often perceived as an increase in intellect, even though the inherent characteristics of it have not changed.

This rune's force plays an interesting part when it comes to consciousness. It is not the rune of the harmony of various parts of our mind – that has been already achieved (through ᛖ Ehwaz) – instead, this rune is the product of the merging of the conscious, what people call the subconscious and even the unconscious into one coherent whole. This rune allows us to achieve what one could be forgiven for calling the super-conscious, where consciousness merged with everything else becomes something entirely different, and its scope is increased to unfathomable degrees, so that its reach becomes so vast it is mind-shattering, and its abilities become the total sum of all abilities of its parts and something more. This rune's force expresses the divine structure within the mind itself. By using it, you can slowly and steadily move into such a state of consciousness. Likewise, once mastered, it is possible to induce temporarily this same effect in others – how long it lasts depends entirely on how progressed their minds are, and can range from just a second to hours. When combined with other trance-inducing runes, ᛗ Mannaz ensures preservation of consciousness and recall. It is also an excellent tool for projection practices; using it effectively can ensure that you do not become mind lost (or, put in traditional terms, that your Hugr and Minni return safely!).

ᛗ Mannaz's energy can be used very effectively to induce seeing in the mind's eye. This is typically referred to as a form of clairvoyance, in new age literature. In fact, it is the opening of the spiritual eye that is perceiving through the mental. The way it works is that you 'see' fully formed images. It can be very confusing because there is no use of the eyes whatsoever – the fully formed image just 'pops' into your head, as if it had been observed. It is impossible to distinguish between a normal observation and a mind's eye observation of this type. The two are just as real, just as un-malleable as each other. I suspect it is received directly in the visual cortex of our brains, rather than originating in the eyes, and then being transmitted to the visual cortex.

In any case, filling ᛗ Mannaz's energy in the central region of the head and the back, while focussing on seeing through the Hugr raven (mind), is a good way to facilitate such 'seeing'. Note: it is not only an image; you can also receive sensations and even hear sounds in this manner.

Energy Body & Energy Reality

ᛗ Mannaz is a very interesting rune to use in your energy body. It allows for the influences of the Spark of Self to radiate outwards through your energy bodies (Hamr – energy body, the Sal – shadow and Lik – physical). It acts as a type of bridging mechanism for the highest parts of the Self (the archetypal) to the lowest and merges them. In this way, this rune is the rune of awakening. Its power allows you to fuse the various parts of your Self together. Do keep in mind that if you are going to use this rune in this manner, it is important to determine the end result before you begin. Here again, Oðinn's sacrifice comes into play: are you going to merge (sacrifice) the lower into the higher parts? Or the higher into the lower? There are implications and consequences that are incredibly far reaching to either of those choices, and there is no pulling back once it is initiated.

For other applications, this rune's power can be used to perfect any of the energy bodies and bring them into synchronicity with their original purpose. In other words, to cause the divine parts within to manifest and become the central operating mechanism for whatever body one is working on. In this manner, you can perfect these bodies and open the channels for the divine to manifest through them. Additionally, you can fuse them together: for instance, merging the shadow into the energy body results in a complete non-physical vehicle for your awareness. Those mystics who are very strong in this rune's mastery can also fuse their physicality in the resulting vehicle and make it able to carry full conscious awareness with its physical matter. In this manner, for them, it is possible to leave this Earth (Midgard) with their physicality. Yes, this is extremely advanced, but within the realms of possibility offered by this rune's underlying forces. However, specialising to that extent would be at the cost of other runes' mastery.

One important use of ᛘ Mannaz is for empaths; those with strong energy reading capabilities have a natural tendency of also developing very strong empathy, which can at times be extremely difficult to manage. Just imagine walking down the street and feeling the waves upon waves of emotions, or meeting someone and just by looking at them, getting flooded with all their feelings, all about them, their energy systems, their personalities, all the energies floating around them… and the list goes on. Such information overload from one person is then multiplied by dozens, if not hundreds of people daily. It can quickly become a crushing burden to bear. ᛘ Mannaz can help tremendously here. Using it to establish a type of 'pillar of self' can help keep you grounded in your Self and tone down the information overload, even to the point where it eventually becomes nothing more than a murmur in the background. That, combined with limited social interaction, allows the strong empath to live a near-normal life. In this manner, ᛘ Mannaz effectively becomes a shielding mechanism against the non-Self. It balances out (not harmonises) all the energies within and can be used to do the same with others.

A final important use is that of perfecting the energy body itself. Using it allows the original form to be regained and made use of. Someone specialising in this would regain the ability to use the very source form of this part of themselves. This results in what looks like a set of millions upon billions of orbs of light floating together in cohesive unity. In fact, each of these orbs is nothing more or less than the biological awareness of each of your physical body's cells – it is from these orbs of light, held in a given pattern, that each cell originated in the first place.

Physical Body & Physical Reality

Just as on the other levels of reality, in physical terms, ᛗ Mannaz helps us realise our full potential. When seeking to perfect the physical body, be it through exercise, or mediation, rune work, dieting and so forth, this rune can help. Be careful though: at this level of reality, it can express itself negatively too. In such circumstances, it would include what the body considered harmful, such as surgery, cosmetic surgery, drugs, chemical treatments and so forth (see *The Blood of Lóðurr Awakens* for a detailed discussion on these topics). The other uses here involve awakening the biological awareness and intelligence. As mentioned above, these cellular characteristics are the core of our bodies. Just as you work on developing the other parts of yourself and spiritualising them, so should you focus on your biological components too, for your body is you as well as any other part of the Self.

In a broader set of influences, this rune's power can be used to enhance personal development not only in spiritual terms but also through life, work, relationships and achievement of goals. It is also a very good rune to use in circumstances where you are being drowned out by life's circumstances or your social circle. When you feel as if you are simply being dragged through the motions and losing yourself or your voice in the process, ᛗMannaz can help.

ᛗMannaz is the rune of expression or manifestation of the Self, and this applies to the physical world as well. How you project yourself, and how other people see you and judge you is a result of this rune's force. Remember, the image of 'you' that others see is what you project outwards. From your appearance, to your behaviour, your reactions and your even you way of communicating and thinking. These are all things you get judged by on both the conscious and subconscious levels, in other people. Becoming aware of this and changing those things about you is what ᛗMannaz teaches those who listen. Mastering one's appearance, in terms of controlling what other people's perceptions and opinions of you will be, is well within the remit of this rune's lessons and skills. Use it wisely. The world is not here to change for you – you are here to adapt to the world. That is how your biological awareness learns, becomes more fluid and hence freer, eventually no longer needing the rigid structures of the physical. ᛗMannaz facilitates learning these skills and gaining these perceptions. They are of utmost importance, especially once you gain the ability to travel beyond Midgard into new totally unfamiliar realms.

Notes

An interesting thing for you to ponder on: the Germanic name of the rune we suspect is ᛗMannaz translates to man, while the Icelandic is ᛗMadhur, translating to mother. Look for the actual meaning behind this inconsistency and find a few mysteries of ᛗMannaz.

The Rune Laguz – Lögur

Sound: l
Vocal Scale: Sol
Numerology: 21
Natural Polarity: M - B - B - F (when stagnant) or M (when flowing) - F
Energetic Colour (Universal): A greenish-blue, not quite cyan but rather a deep green with a slight blue undertone.
Primal Power: Transference, fluidity.
Sensation(s): Wetness, cold and damp, sense of vastness of universal seas.

Archetypal Level of Existence

Undeniably, this rune's strong association with water is not without reason. It represents fluidity in all its aspects and manifestations. Not only in terms of water, but other fundamental forces as well. ᛚ Laguz rules over even fluid fires and ice. As you might suspect, this rune's power governs all mobility, energy required for it, purposes behind it, its pathways, processes and even its end goals. Due to this, along with its associations with waters and the seas, it strongly influences and is responsible for the life force. Keep in mind, we are talking here how life unfolds and flows, not its source. The source of all life is found in fire; it is when it melds with ice (prima materia) that it can manifest (as water). However, do not confuse how it manifests with its core fundamental feature: life itself – that belongs to the realms of fire. Why make the distinction? Because in other realities, the process of manifestation of life is very different and it does not involve ice or water at all. In ours it does. ᛚ Laguz, however, governs it in all of them, since it is the primordial principle of fluidity and even the densest matter can be made into a fluid (think earth/metals and lava). In addition to this dominion over the fluidic elemental natures, ᛚ Laguz also controls and gives rise to all things belonging to the mysteries of reflection, mirroring and illusions, as well as shifting from one state to the other.

ᛚ Laguz archetypally is manifest as the vast red sea of life-force. In the Eddas, we learn that only Thor is capable of swimming through the violent cosmic waters, and Oðinn uses Sleipnir to run across them. The other gods and goddesses require the bifrost to cross them. Using ᛚ Laguz, the eternal seas of life can be touched upon (providing you can transfer into the archetypal) but not crossed. However, their essence can be made to flow downwards through the Self (once it has passed through the ᛘ Mannaz stage) then made to flow outwards. In the old days, these vast seas were also referred to as the blood of the dragon and indeed, they do have a strong association with the world serpent Jörmungandr. As such, it also holds the mysteries of life itself within its vast boundless body; the realm of all possibilities, all manifestations and all experiences flow through it, as do all the desires and goals of every form of life it has ever taken across every possible realm of existence.

Because of this fluidic nature of life, ᛚ Laguz is also the rune of death. Just as life is drawn from its vast reservoirs, so too when death strikes and the Self splits and dissolves, the forces of ᛚ Laguz collect the very essence of life itself back into its vast body. This is where all the experiences you accumulate from life end up; this is where all the spirits, energy bodies and minds dissolve into at some point or other – even the gods and goddesses do. Only the truly immortal never return, but even they do gift the essence of their life experience into this vast red sea in exchange for their immortality. These forces are what is behind the common references to the cosmic collective unconscious or the primordial unconscious. The underlying forces of ᛚ Laguz are what bridges realities, for wherever there is life, its forces exist and through this connection it is possible to bridge into wherever life is. There are inherently two mechanisms of shifting from one reality to another: flame and water. Flames carry your awareness upwards, waters downwards. This is why ᛚ Laguz is often associated with the realms of the dead, because its use allows you to sink down into those realms.

A final primordial characteristic of this rune's force is that of magnetism and the power of attraction. It is part Ice, and from there, it acquired this power. All the mysteries of the magnetic, from both scientific and energetic points of view, are governed by this rune. Whether you seek to gain something, perceive something, attract something, this is the rune to use.

An important note is due here. ᛚ Laguz governs all waters, actually anything and everything which is fluid. As discussed above, it should now be clear why it is the rune which also governs the well of Mimir and why this is the well of memories. This is a perfect example of how ancient truths can be ironed out from illusions and misconceptions, by applying logic to the underlying fundamental knowledge understanding flows. Now that you understand the basic characteristics of the forces of ᛚ Laguz, understanding why collective memories are linked to the waters and contained within the well of memories becomes clear. The same principles of reasoning can be applied to any concept of abstract nature.

Spirit & Spiritual Reality

ᛚ Laguz governs the sense of feeling (not to be confused with feelings!). The ever-expanding touch of the spirit as well as its withdrawal are both enabled by this primordial force. Not only that, but the spirit finds nourishment through the impressions and experiences it collects from its perceptions, and those are all carried to it by this rune's power. The spirits very fluidity originates in ᛚ Laguz, as does its adaptability, but even more importantly, its waters carry over the extremely subtle substance it needs to keep itself as one whole spirit. Out of all the runic powers, this one is the most difficult for spirits to connect with because they are so rooted in heat and fire that it takes hard work to make a sustainable direct connection to ᛚ Laguz. Do note the 'direct' here! Indirectly, everything in existence has a connection to it; however, a direct connection is so vital for your spirit's growth that it incarnates in order to seek it out. ᛚ Laguz is the flow between the spirit and the flesh. The physical has a natural aptitude to the life force; it is actually the optimum natural receptacle for it and through the spirit's embodiment into flesh, it seeks out to acquire this connection and learn to maintain it. This is why, in the old days, you would have been instructed that upon death, you lost the ability to feel. Because the spirit lost its connection with the ᛚ Laguz flow and started to decay or go into stasis. With regular training, it is possible to learn spiritually to preserve not only the sense of feeling but also this vital connection. Doing so enables you to push your spirit into a permanent connection with the flow of life itself. Spirits who achieve this become cohesive in their own right and gain form as and when they will, as well as no longer needing to bother with physical life at all. By the same route, ᛚ Laguz acts as a bridge, a connecting link, allowing the spirit to be in flesh and to experience life. It also enables the flow of experiences and meaning from the physical to the spirit, which it then uses to nourish itself and grow. It is thanks to ᛚ Laguz that it can incarnate – ever wondered what the root cause of a child gestating in the womb filled with liquid was? Well now you know; that liquid/fluid is the manifestation of ᛚ Laguz which in turn acts as a gateway for the spirit to embody into the growing child.

    This rune also governs interactions between spirits, as well as all forms of exchanges, be they energy, experience, essence and so on. It is not the exchange itself that falls within its dominion but rather the flow of forces as it occurs. ᚷ Gebo, being the rune of exchange, is the facilitator for it, like the mechanism or engine, whereas ᛚ Laguz is the underlying force that propels the one into the other at the intersection. It is a very subtle distinction but an important one to grasp because ᛚ Laguz can pull things to itself rather than cause a full-blown exchange of force, but it can also enhance the ᚷ Gebo-initiated exchange and amplify its results. By the same rules, if you seek to reconnect with your spirit or are having difficulty sinking deep within yourself and making that connection, ᛚ Laguz will prove to be a most helpful ally.

Mind & Mental Reality

As far as the mind ravens (Hugr and Minni) are concerned, this rune's power and force play a critically important role. It is what allows them to flow outwards and back; it is the force of creative intelligence and creativity in their full scope of action. Inspiration is also governed by it and can be influenced to a greater degree. ᛚ Laguz will not only amplify the flight of the mind but will also ensure it returns with stronger memories, for it bridges the two with normal consciousness. Perceptions are all enhanced by this rune's effects because they are provided with more substance to work with. Mental agility and breadth are increased by its effects, as is the ability to fly in the mind ravens (see *The Spirit of Húnir Awakens (Parts 1 & 2)*). Combining this rune's powers with those of ᛗ Mannaz and ᛖ Ehwaz will permit the two ravens to be merged into a single one, bringing about the unity needed for the manifestation of ᛞ Dagaz within the mind. Combining it with ᛏ Tiwaz, on the other hand, enables the mind to break through any hindrances or obstacles to perception. Bridging the conscious mind with the unconscious is a perfect application of this rune's force, but do be careful when you do so: the dark depths of all our unconscious minds harbour not only wonders, but also terrors and horrors that are totally unimaginable to us (under normal circumstances, the conscious mind and to some extent the subconscious act as gateways keeping those under control).

From a mental health perspective, ᛚ Laguz can be used to help reinvigorate a fatigued mind. People who are focussed heavily on intellectual activities can at times feel as drained and tired as those who engage in vigorous physical exercise. Using this rune's power, it is possible to revitalise a mind when it has become exhausted – the same applies to memory. When you are just too tired to remember, this rune can help if directed into the Minni.

Energy Body & Energy Reality

ᛚ Laguz rules the energy body and the shadow body. As such, its influence and scope of use on these two parts of the Self is downright phenomenal. Here, we will focus on some of the key applications. Using ᛚ Laguz, it is possible to channel life force into these parts of the Self (as well as into the physical) and perform energetic healing as well as reinvigoration. Charging up the energy body is essential if you want to make practical use of it, as carrying consciousness out of the physical requires a tremendous amount of spare energy. This rune can help (in combination with ᛜ Ingwaz) in the accumulation needed. The resulting life force needs to be very cohesive and concentrated, and you need to have large quantities of it. Pretty much the equivalent of what the physical body provides it, plus whatever you are going to be using up in heightened awareness. If you manage to sustain this charging until you learn to breathe in the energy body itself, you should be able to ground yourself within it. The more energy you have the longer this separation will last.

Another important application is that ᛚ Laguz is essential when it comes to awareness. Since this part of us is born and exists in the energy body (until it too dies and our awareness flickers out of existence), its power can be used to control and culture awareness itself. This is a highly complex set of skills which relies on mastery of the energy body and its mobile hvel (chakra). Suffice it to say that this rune's power will facilitate all experimentation within this field, both in terms of know-how and ability as well as power.

Its use in dreamwork is essential. It is the primordial rune of the dreamer, allowing you to cross the veil separating the realities (the solid material and the fluid non-material) and opens up the gates of the dreaming. As such, it provides any who cares to use it with the possibility of using their dreams in order to expand their awareness and experiences. All the most interesting phenomena of dreaming, such as becoming lucid in dreams, shifting from within one dream into another, building the dreamer's body and so forth fall within its dominion. It provides for a completely different type of fluid rationality when developed through dreaming, as well as a different type of awareness.

An important application is its ability to make the energy body more fluid and adaptable to change. This was used in the old days by the Seiðr practitioners in order to shapeshift, but can also be used to shift the shape of only the energy body. I personally like shifting it into a small boat upon which you can use your spirit to travel to inner realms or different energetic realities. Some might wander what the difference between using the Fylgja and doing it this way is – the answer is simple. Using the energy body to travel is limited to energetic realms in which it can function, but using the Fylgja, one can truly shift inter-dimensionally. Both methods are valid in their own right and both enable you to carry back certain experiences; which you use depends entirely on the destination and how 'present' you want to be there.

In terms of emotion and feelings, ᚱLaguz is the master key. It controls them all, for they are all born out of the manifestation of the red seas of life. It is possible to calm or still them (use the masculine polarity) or excite them (use the feminine polarity).

A final scope of application of ᚱLaguz when you want to bridge the emotional and sensory space between yourself and someone you care for, or someone you want to exchange emotions with, use ᚱLaguz to bridge the space between the two of you. Much more could be said about this rune's influence on energy systems and the reality as a whole – for the time being, this will have to do. Additionally, ᚱLaguz will enhance the senses in the energy bodies, amplifying their sense of feeling and improving sensitivity to energies, thoughts, perceptions and much more. It is a rune well worth focussing on.

Physical Body & Physical Reality

Both our physical bodies (Lik) and physical realities are primed receptacles for the red waters of life: the life force or vital power of ᚱLaguz, inflowing from the archetypal and universal. Actually, to a certain extent, all matter is. How this life force is polarised and how it becomes expressed will depend on the attached mind, spirit and the matter into which it is poured.

Since consciousness is born out of our physicality, ᚱLaguz has a great scope of influence upon it through our bodies. By using this rune's energy, it is possible to sustain consciousness for longer periods of time and also to change it and make it more fluid, as well as grow its scope of activity by the application of this rune's power. Additionally, when trying to project it out of the physical boundaries, this rune's power can be of great assistance.

All the functions of the fluidic components in our bodies are governed by this rune's influence, ranging from blood, to acidity, water retention, the eyes, the sensitivity of the skin and its perceptive abilities and so forth. This rune can also be an excellent conductor, for tension modulation of its effects can both cause muscular tension to build up or to loosen; the same can be said for nervous tension. Many wonderful effects can be induced with this rune: some highly specialised, others more practical in daily life, such as enhancing perceptions by amplifying the sense's receptive powers. It can also be used to make things more fluid and has a special effect on time when combined with ◇ Jera. We will leave the healing aspects of this rune's power for the appropriate literature. One important physiological application is with respect to the biological awareness and intelligence (see *The Blood of Lóðurr Awakens*). Using ᛚ Laguz before undertaking any practical work with that part of yourself will amplify the results you can achieve and its secondary effect is to nurture and grow that awareness and its corresponding intelligence.

In more daily matters, this rune opens up new opportunities. It is an excellent 'wash away the old and carry me onwards to the new' force. It promotes adventures and trips, be they short or long, and experiencing of novel things. When trips across bodies of water come into question, know that this is the call of ᛚ Laguz reaching out to you.

This rune's power has the ability to take some of the most entrenched things in our lives and cause them to flow again, introducing movement into their very essence and functioning.

A final practical note is that ᛚ Laguz is one of the best runes to use when you need to clear out things. It flow is like that of a great river that will carry away blockages and things in your way. Additionally, because of its tendency to make things more fluid, it will do so when needed and then carry whatever was causing trouble away. This effect can be applied to situations, people, energies and even thoughts that might be lingering about and being detrimental to you.

The Rune Ingwaz – Ing

Sound: Ng
Vocal Scale: La
Numerology: 22
Natural Polarity: M - M - M - M - M
Energetic Colour (Universal): Deep dark yellow.
Primal Power: Solidifying, crystallisation.
Sensation(s): density, gravity, solidity. This is the density of the elemental earth it is the solidity of the earth you feel when you hit a wall. Unyielding and unforgivingly solid.

Archetypal Level of Existence

This rune rules masculine sexuality, or in other words, the act of creation and the power for creation. Do not confuse this with the origination of the power of creation, which it does not possess – instead, it holds that power within itself by having absorbed it when it flooded forth at point zero. ◊ Ingwaz's power is to crystallise or solidify power into manifestation, for either immediate or later use. This is why archetypally ◊ Ingwaz contains the initial burst of creative power. Additionally, ◊ Ingwaz acts as a containment for any form of power directed within it. Potential energy can be stored within the rune or any structure that pulses its power until it becomes fully matured or it is time for it to be put to practical use.

From an archetypal point of view, this rune is called the rune of seeding or the rune of the seed. From it, not only does the seed take root but it is also formed by this rune's force. When combined with the ᚲ Kenaz rune, it gains the possibility of transforming the energy or power contained within the ᛜ Ingwaz one. Combined with ᛒ Berkano, the ᛜ Ingwaz seed can be brought to germination.

Another vitally important function of this rune's force is preventing integration into existing systems and structures. It pulls things out of the collective state of being and reinforces or builds the individuality. It is this rune that pulls the sparks of creation from the collective flow of life into individual Sparks of Self, which are in effect seeds of creation. These, if matured before those life forms in which they are embodied perish, can bloom into an existence of their own. It is a rune of evolution, but in its dormant state.

A final point about this rune to discuss here is its connection to the concept of centrality of being. Its forces have a very powerful, sometimes even overpowering drive to take things to their centre points. For the mystic, this is essential since reaching the centre of their own Self then allows them to expand outwards into all of their being. The same principle applies to all things in existence since everything has a centre including forces, powers and even loose matter. Once you gain the ability to sink into the centrality of something, you can then extend to every single point in whatever it is you have become centred within. It is from this very concept that the intellect gained a grasp of what is often referred to as being all-present and ever-present. That word illustrates this type of achievement of awareness implosion and expansion. It does so in a very limited way because this state of being is simply beyond the scope of even an 'enlightened' intellect, but it is all we have to work with when trying to grasp what it the underlying state is.

Spirit & Spiritual Reality

On the spiritual level of things, this rune's power is generative for the future. Its force will govern all spirits' need to become, to realise their very essences and to gather resources, and to accumulate until the point arrives where the said spirit(s) can propel themselves into manifestation. It pushes forth the spirit to not only conserve essential energy and spirit essence, but also to make use of it at a certain point, in order to become what it is meant to become.

Because of the lack of time and space at this level of existence, this rune's force and powers in general will ensure that spirits do not merge with others. It acts as a barrier to this very process, because the tendency of losing itself is very high at the level of existence where everything has a natural flow into blending into one another, and all forms of independence and individuality are eventually lost in a blur of existence. This is where we gain the concept of all being 'one', which is nothing more than the dissolution and loss of the Self and how spirit matter is ultimately recycled.
◇ Ingwaz prevents this and is a powerful safeguard of Self against this type of ending. One of its key practical uses is to ensure the Self remains viable when one

does get involved in such mergers and fusions – in other words, when you actively seek out this type of blending of Self and non-Self, ◊ Ingwaz can be used very effectively to ensure that at the end of whatever goal you had to experience such a state of spirit, you can separate out and regain your full scope of Self.

Another important use of this rune's power is its capability for increasing in consciousness and the maintaining of its functions. Consciousness is a fickle thing and has the tendency of not only being easily disrupted but also of consuming enormous amounts of resources. In order to support this entire conscious eco-system, ◊ Ingwaz plays an important role in not only its preservation but also in terms of supplying it with whatever it needs, and determining the breadth and scope of its functioning. If there are sufficient resources available to the spirit, the ◊ Ingwaz forces will expand the functions of consciousness, and if there are fewer resources, it will dull it down. It is ◊ Ingwaz, or rather its force, that determines just how conscious you can or cannot become. This rune's power is the principle cause as to why some people never experience anything beyond their daily physical lives and, conversely, why some experience multiple levels of reality. Do not be mistaken by thinking it is because this rune's force acts as a holding back mechanism; it is rather the opposite. It determines whether you have sufficient resources to use consciousness in a given manner or not – if you do, it will unfold its capabilities, if you do not, it won't.

Mind & Mental Reality

Mentally, this rune is primarily used for centring the mind. It greatly facilitates the pulling within when attempting to enter into either a meditative or trance state. It also stabilises the mind when it is being swayed by emotion and provides the stillness needed when dealing with volatile situations. Mastering this rune on the mental level will allow you to keep your calm in a wide range of situations and stop it going erratic. It is highly masculine in polarity and an excellent tool to have available when logic, reason and the stabilising of emotional tendencies is needed. Emotions destabilise the mind, irrespective of whether they are positive or negative – even love, which people are so obsessed with at this point in time, has severe negative effects on one's capacity to think clearly. Neuroscientists know that a brain addicted to love experiences the same effects as a brain addicted to cocaine. The same runs true of negative emotions; their impact is even more noticeable. Fear, for instance, is a complete debilitator for the free-thinking and is used very effectively to force changes in modes of thinking, and abused heavily when it comes to manipulating us. ◊ Ingwaz is an excellent tool when it comes to countering all these emotional influences on the mind. It stabilises the flight of the Hugr and solidifies the effects of the Minni.

The other important function of this rune's force is its ability to help us break free of established patterns of thinking, conceptualisation and belief systems. Its powers are very influential when it comes to separating the individual mind from overriding currents of the collective. In other words, it will tear the Self away from things such as the group-think, the enclosed bubbles of conceptual limitation and even from traditional or familiar set patterns. It is especially useful when it comes to attempting to free oneself from socially imposed norms of thinking or behaviour. Men are particularly bound to these social norms, even in our so-called 'modern' day and age; using this rune, we can unlock ourselves from all these pointless self-sacrificing patterns but can also unlock deep masculine mysteries of the mind, from which we have been conditioned away.

In a wider field of application, this rune's energies and powers facilitate the crystallisation of thoughts, through forms and concepts. It allows thoughts to gather in energy and power, making them more influential and condensing their essence in preparation for manifestation into the energetic realms of reality.

Energy Body & Energy Reality

On the energetic side of things, in terms of the energy body, this rune is found at the core of each hvel, where energy is accumulated, churned and released. It is thanks to this force of ◇ Ingwaz that such centres of energy could be formed in the first place. By virtue of this using ◇ Ingwaz's powers, it is possible to fix any dysfunctions and even fractures in any of these hvels, as well as amplify their effects or awaken them. The mysteries of the energy body are very vast and some are extremely delicate and complex. More on the energy body as a whole will be covered in other literature – suffice it to say that this rune holds the knowledge of these types of applications, and if you want to specialise, this is the key to it.

An interesting advanced specialisation in this rune's force manipulation allows you to form what can be thought of as crystals in the energy body, which act as energetic stores. Naturally, any surplus of energy will be processed and dissipated back into your immediate environment. This body is not suited to the storage of energy in any way, shape or form. Actually, it struggles to hold onto any surplus, even when it needs it. This is one of the reasons why, when you do energy healing, the patient feels great and sees an immediate improvement (assuming you are skilled in this area), but that benefit fades very rapidly. What most healers will do is pile on more energy in an attempt to make the beneficial effects last longer. This puts enormous strain on it and eventually is also processed out, after having taxed the ill body even more. It is possible after gradual increases in energy use to amplify the amount of energy the body can cope with, but that is a slow and tedious process often requiring years of practice. As a general rule, 10 years of daily gradual practice will increase its storage capabilities by about 0.5-1%. Using ◇ Ingwaz to form condensed energy nodes or crystals within the energy body will enable you to store surpluses and then either gradually, or in one swoop, release that when it is needed. For this to work, you need to consciously direct the entire process and release using this rune. Much more could be discussed on this fascinating application of ◇ Ingwaz, but these few hints will have to do for the time being. Do note: when a foreign energy enters a man's energy body, it causes sexual arousal (our energy bodies do not know how to process new energy, which is alien to it in energy type, so it processes as sexual energy). When you experience this, use the ◇ Ingwaz rune immediately and draw this excess into storage. You will then be able to use it later on for any creative purpose you wish. It does happen to women as well, but it is very noticeable in the case of men, who are very prone to immediate physiological reactions. For women, you will have to learn to look within and keep an eye out for triggering of this type of reaction; it is, I am told, much more subtle, but once you learn to observe for it will be able to spot it quite easily.

Physical Body & Physical Reality

In terms of the physical body and reality, I will have to keep this brief or I would write an entire book. ◇ Ingwaz is the rune of pleasure, and all things which are delightful, pleasurable, or enjoyable fall within its remit. Yes, sexual pleasures (especially for men) are included for the highly masculine polarity of this rune, but it is not limited to just those. It also includes within its range of influence all the things you would deny yourself or you deny about yourself.

Its powers can best be conceptualised as standing on the line between winter and spring. It is both the storage of energy and resource during winter, and the release in spring of all that which has been stored. It is the rune of new life, of creation and most importantly of manifestation. All energy, concepts, thoughts and desires are solidified by this rune's effects; once it reaches a certain threshold, it then forces them into realisation. Do note, this does not always happen in the exact manner you would want or expect it to. All these realisations will flow according to the laws of creation, customised for the reality in which they happen. This is why energy work for many turns out with a whole array of unexpected 'side-effects', especially when wishing for something. Be very careful when using it to create, which is one of the key mysteries men should specialise in, for this is the rune of masculinity in all its scopes and forms. Always keep in mind that ◇ Ingwaz is also a very immoral force; it cares not for the social norms, for humanity's conceptions of right and wrong, legality of things or any of that. It is especially symbiotic in energetic terms with the Vanir in this respect – they too are immoral entities, and those who study the myths and legends will be able to ascertain this for themselves.

Applied to the world at large, ◇ Ingwaz can be of use when it comes to create atmospheres of comfortable stillness. That silence, which is alike a deep breath in the flow of life, that sweet pause in the hustle and bustle of life where nothing needs to be said, where movement is not necessary, where there is a sense of total peace and detachment from the world. Where a need arises for doing your own thing and disconnecting from others, and the overwhelming drain of social interactions needs to be moved away from, then ◇ Ingwaz can help. It reaffirms the Self within and without. Without its influence, we would all become nothing more than ants in a hive with no purpose of our own – in other words, total automatons. All social interactions and hierarchies are born out of the influences of ◇ Ingwaz; all forms of order and structure are influenced by it. When combined with ᚹ Wunjo, it gives rise to social structures and ordered hierarchies, which are needed for society to function properly (◇ Ingwaz's feminine polarity, producing the feminine-masculine positive pole), but likewise, ◇ Ingwaz also in its reverse polarity (the masculine-masculine positive polarity) enables the individual to be reaffirmed and separated from all hierarchies. Ever wondered why men process their emotional needs silently and mostly on their own? Why they pull away to do their own thing when things get too chaotic around them? It is this precise effect of the ◊ Ingwaz force that dictates this; it is part of every man's not only biology, mind and energy system, but of our archetypal Spark. It is also this very force that makes all masculine forces, beings, energies... foundations upon which all can rely on in times of instability, and which enables us to build upon those very foundations.

Finally, let us not forget to mention that ◊ Ingwaz is the rune of all male sexual mysteries, ranging from the creation of the seed from which new life is born physically, to all the way up to the highest mysteries which enable the evolution of the spirit itself.

The Rune Dagaz - Dagur

Sound: d
Vocal Scale: Ti
Numerology: 23
Natural Polarity: N - N - B - B - B
Energetic Colour (Universal): Electric blue.
Primal Power: Awakening, enlightenment.
Sensation(s): Expansive radiation with occasional static flowing through it.

Archetypal Level of Existence

This rune's force is a fascinating one. It is responsible for refinement as a slow repetitive process, like that of a mill refining flour rather than a rapid transformation through transmutation of ᚲKenaz. Its effects are also purifying, in the sense that it purges out all imperfections as well as impurities, until the very perfected essence of meaning is reached. This can be both positive and negative, as ᛞDagaz will purge out all variations, all permutations and all diversifications from the core of something, until that very essential meaning of what is at the core is manifest in its purest and most powerful manifestation. Note the shape of this rune: it is very much alike the symbol commonly used for infinity. It is a slow and repetitive cycle, which is typically unbroken. When you find yourself stuck in a loop, a repetitive cycle, a set of ever-repeating life circumstances those are all the work of the ᛞ Dagaz force. This need not be negative, such cycles with the up and down (or positive and negative, hence the two nodes to ᛞ Dagaz, rather than just it being circular) are needed for growth and experience gathering. In this sense, it is the rune of enlightenment, for it is a learning cycle as well as a purifying and perfecting one. At some point or other, you will find all processes and all lives gain balance, harmony and stability; when this occurs, they find themselves at the central point of the rune's shape, where the two sides of ᛞ Dagaz merge in perfected expression. This is the greatest of all mysteries and it is fully embodied at that one point in the rune. The ability of gaining centrality from ᛝ Ingwaz is now enhanced and amplified in ᛞ Dagaz, where it becomes a harmonised and balanced one, a pure centrality that enables transition out of the cycle itself. For at the central point of a balanced ᛞ Dagaz, one is elevated beyond its scope. It is this rune's power which can free the spirit from the cycles of existence whilst it exists and elevates it to a new existence (from spiritual to archetypal, where it establishes new roots in ᛟ Othala and becomes eternal, it becomes a new fully realised archetypal concept, radiating its own essential meaning throughout existence).

    Many associate ᛞ Dagaz with light, but it is not light per se – that belongs to the remit of ᛋ Sowilo – instead, the enlightenment experienced through the influences of ᛞ Dagaz is this elevation beyond all cycles, beyond the patterns of existence, this one breath which propels your very awareness to new heights, from which you can see back down and realise what it was all about. You can watch the cycles and understand them as you observe the goings on and processes of the lower states of being from this new heightened awareness. Until you realise the ᛞ Dagaz state fully, you eventually sink back down from this height because the cycle pulls you back into itself, but with this new realisation gained, you can experience it in a different way – you know it, you understand it and you can manipulate it. By doing so repeatedly, you are then able to weaken its influence over you; you reach that point of harmonised balanced centrality over and over again until you can finally root yourself (ᛟ Othala) in the higher state and permanently become a resident of the new reality, thereby abandoning the cycles themselves. In this process, you can see why this has been termed the rune of dawn.

Most people look at this dawn connection and link it to our day and night cycles. Yes, it does exist here, but it is important to keep in mind that the runic forces are universal. Universally speaking, dawn, night and day are not the same; a single day can last hundreds or thousands – if not millions – of years in our time-equivalent thinking. A universal or cosmic dawn need not even be a manifestation of light or day. The dawn and dusk associations of ᛞ Dagaz represent the forces of polarity themselves. Learn from both poles to reach centrality and balance. Master each, become light, then descend into the dark, then rise once more into the light, carrying the power of the dark under your belt. For without both, you can gain power over neither. In this sense, ᛞ Dagaz can be used to master polarity as a whole. It is a rune where you learn of each pole, their individual effects and how they are counterbalanced with their opposite. But always remember, ᛞ Dagaz requires purity of Self – that means purity of intent and only those of the purest being can descend into the dark, and over them it will have no power. It will not be able to corrupt their core, for those pure Selves do not see its power and only those who truly do not desire the power of darkness will obtain it, whereas those who even have the smallest glint of a hidden desire for it will fall unto its corruption and either lose themselves or have to undergo the grinding processes of ᛞ Dagaz further and longer. Not only is this purity of Self achieved through ᛞ Dagaz, but the rune mystic can use this rune to force a purification of what they please, be it ideas, concepts, emotions, or even thoughts. The slow-grind purification of this rune and its influences are as wide ranging as one can imagine.

It is the underlying force of ᛞ Dagaz that allows the kin-Fylgja to finally become fully realised. Where all ancestral influences are realised and the entire line stops incarnating into new familiar hosts, as it all parts from that familial line, it becomes rooted in the archetypal and spiritual in its own right, dissolving the need for physical incarnations of its members.

Spirit & Spiritual Reality

On the spiritual level, ᛞ Dagaz governs the rising and descending forces, it acts as both a balancer and as a force that pushes spirits into experiencing opposite sides of polarities in the lower realm. It is also the force that traps spirits in a given pattern of expression until they have perfected their mastery of those very patterns of spiritual energy and knowledge, to the point where they can rise above them while holding onto their essence. In other words, the spirit needs to learn from its own patterns and as it rises out of their grip, it will need to keep hold of the essential significance and influence of those very patterns and integrate them into itself. Only then has it sufficient mastery and power over those facets of existence that it becomes able to free itself from their influence and move onto whatever next set of patterns it seeks to explore. In this manner, each spirit moves from realm to realm, existence to existence, learning and growing from these patterns of manifestation, extracting energy, knowledge, and experience from each and every one. Since at this level of existence it functions in a timeless and spaceless capacity, there are no restrictions to it, except those of its own nature (for instance, a lower vibrating spirit cannot move to a higher realm unless it has heightened its very core nature, and it does this through completing these ᛞ Dagaz cycles of evolution, but it can lower itself to an even lower one since it has already mastered those, and so forth).

    ᛞ Dagaz's power, on the other hand, allows a shift in vibrational rate to occur for the movement of one reality to another (keeping in mind the universal rule outlined just above). It can also be used to increase or decrease the intellect and will, in order to induce temporary elevation of any spirit. How strong this turns out to be or how long it will last depends entirely on how far you have mastered the rune. By the same principle, it is possible to use ᛞ Dagaz to induce a flip in the darkness vs light cycle it governs. When you find yourself stuck in, say, a state of stasis, be it in the light or the dark aspects, ᛞ Dagaz can quicken the move into the other. This is especially useful when you need to shift your own spirit between these two universal polarities. It is also useful to induce such a total change of perspective in order to experience reality from the other point of view. Inducing it at the spiritual level will enable you to become completely and totally like all the spirits of whatever of these two poles you select because it will immediately start to manifest those changes in reality, eventually even cascading into the physical. Before someone starts experimenting too much, no, you cannot achieve this effect in cases of others, unless they intend it to happen. Without the pure unfettered intent of a spirit, it will not be able to change its own core nature to conform with the opposite expression of its nature – instead, what takes place is the current nature of that spirit is enhanced and pushed forward along the path it is already following.

ᛞ Dagaz is an excellent rune to use when you are trying to enhance the will and how strongly it is expressed in life. Keep in mind that the type of willpower ᛞ Dagaz gives expression to is deeper and more subtle than the other fire runes (ᚠ Fehu and ᚦ Thurisaz specifically). This manifestation of will is the long-lasting, persevering will that expresses the very nature of your spirit. As you learn and move through this rune's force, that will gets strengthened and becomes more and more unshakable, as does belief in yourself.

Mind & Mental Reality

Here we enter the domain of the more commonly known applications of this rune's powers. ᛞ Dagaz is responsible for all the 'aha' moments, all the flashes of inspiration and all epiphanies of the mind. Its influences are wide in scope, in terms of the intellectual side of the mind. It quickens it, sharpens it, gives it the ability to grasp constantly increasing levels of subtlety and abstraction and most importantly, it intensely invigorates it. Many Hugr mysteries are unlocked and practically accessed through the use of this rune, including sending the mind soaring into the unknown. Those who master ᛞ Dagaz have brilliant sparkling Hugr ravens that are a sight to behold: it simply takes your breath away as your mind's eye gazes upon such a manifestation.

In terms of the Minni (memory), ᛞ Dagaz's influence is somewhat different and rather fascinating. It initiates a type of purging of memory, or rather an extraction of the essence of the memories. This process is automatically initiated upon death and is responsible for people seeing their lives streaming in front of their eyes upon dying. This churning of the memory systems allows the source of our awareness to gain the essence of those memories, as our own awareness explodes in blinding light for that one last moment, before being permanently extinguished in the energy body. Mystics can use this rune in order to initiate this process in stages, to clear out all the debris from the mind and free themselves of the weight and burden of those memories, while simultaneously enabling their memory system to advance to a higher level of functioning. This in turn enhances your ability to recall dreams, out-of-body experiences and flights of the mind away from the boring daily lives most live. It enables you to de-anchor from the here and now and step into a more subtle set of functioning, as well as bring back memories of those experiences so that you can recall them consciously. Experiences beyond the physical are rather pointless if you cannot even remember having them in the first place. Natural tendencies dictate that women find this shifting of memory locales much easier than men do because men's energy bodies are designed to forget. This is something all men will need to work at improving or they will have much less awareness and little or no consciousness on the non-physical sides of reality.

When mastered, ᛞ Dagaz can be used to not only enhance the mind but also to enable your mind to expand practically anywhere it has the energy or inclination to do so. Unlike with the spirit, where you can only switch to the highest point equivalent with your spirit's vibrational capacity (and maturity), on the mental level, this limitation does not exist. The only real limit is as far as you can imagine. If your mind can grab hold of a concept of a place or realm or state of being, ᛞ Dagaz will be able to propel it further into those. This is one of the incredible advantages we all have, living in Midgard (Earth). Since it is the central point in creation, you get to interact with all sorts of life forms, concepts, people, ideas and manifestations you would never be able to otherwise. Any such interaction can propel your mind into the conceiving of new and exciting things, and that in turn is the key needed for ᛞ Dagaz to open up new avenues of exploration for you. Take full advantage of it while you have time to do so.

Energy Body & Energy Reality

Energetically, ᛞ Dagaz's influence in purging and purifying as well as perfecting your energy systems is undeniable. It can be used to great effect in consciously evolving the energy body, shadow and energy in general. Here, it will force you to experience the energy body and shadow self, from the one to the other and vice versa, until you reach a balanced and harmonised state between the two. It is very important to do so because without mastering ALL the parts of your Self, you will fail to fully integrate them into a whole Self – and without this whole Self, your Spark of Self cannot manifest directly. In other words, the divine parts of yourself are locked until you have a fully integrated Self. Using ᛞ Dagaz enables you to achieve this through a long grinding and perfecting of the individual parts. Your two energy bodies need to work together, then when you move into that all-too-mysterious middle point between the two, you will find a type of 'chamber' which leads to freedom and the next stage of evolution of this merged Self.

Importantly, this shifting between the one and the other can be facilitated by ᛞ Dagaz, but can also be interrupted by ᛁ Isa. Those who master both of these runes will gain some very interesting possibilities and when interrupted with ᛇ Eihwaz, you can propel your entire energy system upwards or downwards. These are both done by combining and unleashing the forces of both runes with either ᛁ Isa or ᛇ Eihwaz, cutting straight down through the centre point of ᛞ Dagaz.

In terms of perceptions, ᛞ Dagaz can be used very effectively when it comes to opening the energy sight. The eyes (and ears) within the energy body are very potent receptors for the powers of ᛞ Dagaz and they respond well to it. This type of sight is always tricky to achieve, especially for men. Using this rune (and if need be, combining it with ᚦ Thurisaz for some extra power when it comes to men, or combining it with ᚠ Fehu for women) will facilitate the awakening of sight and hearing of non-physical realities (remember, you need to have a fully repaired and active heart hvel to connect to these realities – you need the crossroads within to gaze across realms). Just for the sake of your own wellbeing, go slowly and steady with this. Use these powers when you want turn the energy senses on and remove all trace of them when you want to turn them off. Go slow, one step at a time, or you will get overwhelmed. You have been warned.

Other applications range far and wide. Entire fields of ᛞ Dagaz energy can be used to counter all types of forces that drag you down energetically, or can be used to enhance quickening of your energy systems. ᛞ Dagaz is also extremely useful for dreaming and becoming aware within dreams. With spirit walking (see *Spirit Walking for the Rune Mystic* for more info), the perception and harmonisation of your energies with that of the spirit is achieved, as is the elevation of your awareness to its level. In other words, it amplifies the like attracts like through its churning and purifying functions.

Physical Body & Physical Reality

The entire nervous system falls under the influence of ᛞ Dagaz, from its formation, its growth, and whatever shape it will take down to the control of the functioning and synaptic firing which takes place with it. As such, those of you with the specialised knowledge in this field can find ᛞ Dagaz a most helpful companion in your work. For those of you who also want to specialise in the physico-energetic interactions in our bodies, it is possible to extend these nervous impulses even further.

The eyes fall within its scope of influence and using this rune, it is even possible to expand your sight to include seeing of energies physically. Phenomena such as the luminescence of the body can be seen by simple relaxation of one's visual focus or by gazing at the body from a new angle. The ability to notice small shifts and changes in our fields of vision, which are usually lost from childhood, can be regained and so forth.

One important thing ᛗ Dagaz does for all is the freeing from imposed norms on self-expression. With its help, you can gain a deep insight into how the environment you live in limits you in your expressions of your Self. There will always be limits while in a physical life – that is unavoidable, but knowing them and realising their impact on yourself is an important key to eventually freeing yourself from them. It not only helps you realise that structures and norms are there for a reason but will also guide you to shedding their impact on you or even allow you to manipulate them. This is an excellent skill to obtain when trying to go into acting, for it enables you to slip into a different mindset, governed by different norms and social expectations to those you would normally, with relative ease.

A somewhat more obscure function of ᛗ Dagaz is that of time. This is most difficult to explain but a concept well worth contemplation. Time exists only where matter exists; on the energetic, mental, spiritual and archetypal levels of existence, there is no time. Yes, the mind can perceive time, but only because of our physical roots. Take away all interactions with the world and all watches or clocks, pull the blinds, and suddenly, you will notice that your perceptions of time become very fluid, until you get to the point where you can no longer tell what time or day or even week you are in. In order to understand time from the ᛞ Dagaz point of view, a metaphor is needed. Think of a white square cloth made of intersecting threads woven together. Now, to this image add, say, a few horizontal and a few vertical threads spaced out every few inches, crossing over each other. Gravity pulls and wraps this cloth, it curves the lines as it pinches the cloth, and pushes them outwards as one or another corner is pulled. ᛞ Dagaz comes into play in the following way: picture someone trying to stich this cloth. As the needle pierces your red lines of time, it interrupts them and then pierces through them, pulling a thread through and then attaching it in the same manner at another point on another line or even the same one. This folds the fabric, or introduces a lose thread, connecting two or more points through time. This is the influence of ᛞ Dagaz on time. It is the needle piercing through the fabric, it is the new thread, it is the resulting new pathway through time and it is the fold in the cloth (which represents space). Think on this and you will learn how to apply ᛞ Dagaz to time itself. It is the twilight, the in-between states, the vastness of the possibilities of time (and by correlation to space as well). It is also the compression of all of existence, as the fabric is stitched together from one end to the other, until it becomes the equivalent of a black hole, and it is the shattering of all that stitching and the connecting threads as space unfolds out again, reaffirming its essential nature: existence and expansion. Compare this to what we are told in the Norse myths and legends, when all creation is swallowed back into the Ginnungagap and then explodes forth once again into a new (hopefully) improved configuration, ready for new life to germinate from within it.

The Rune Oþala – Óðal

Sound: o
Vocal Scale: Do (hard)
Numerology: 24
Natural Polarity: N - B - M - M - M
Energetic Colour (Universal): Dark yellow or sometimes it can appear as a sandy brown with a yellow hue.
Primal Power: Becoming, ancestral realisation.
Sensation(s): Solid earth, dense rock, force of gravity.

Archetypal Level of Existence

This rune's force, powers and energies are all about anchoring – or, as a more popular term, grounding (although they do imply some key differences). The enlightenment and elevations experienced in ᛞ Dagaz need to be anchored at a new level of existence; this is what this rune facilitates. It allows the foundations established in ᛜ Ingwaz, and rocked in the processes underwent during ᛞ Dagaz, to finally be remoulded and anchored in ᛟ Othala. Once this is achieved, the Self is ready to use this new foundation to propel itself further into new heights and to build upon them. Without a spot to anchor the Self upon and gaze forth into the vast boundless unknown, it would lose its footing and get lost in the vast expanse of existence. It is from here that it can choose its next path forth and know that this new foundation will be there to return, if need be. It is at this point that the flow of ancestral power can be accessed freely and both nourish the new emerging Self, as well as provide it with whatever support it needs. It has broken out of the cycles of ᛞ Dagaz and has in ᛟ Othala established the new groundwork for the next step forth, into a higher manifestation of the runic currents. At this point in evolution, the Self needs to decide not only its next step forward but also the direction in which it will move. Will it procreate? Will it hyper-evolve? Will it act as a vehicle for the evolution of the ancestral line? Will it continue to develop new facets of its Spark? Any and all decisions made by the Self at this level of existence in its work, with this rune's force, will determine the type of Self it becomes. This is a tricky situation because this decision is not up to you or any of us; it is a decision made for us by the Spark of our Self, in co-operation with the kin-Fylgja (fate has no power or influence on the archetypal – instead, essential meaning and core purpose are the building principles).

This crystallisation of the Self is important because at ᛟ Othala roots are established in order to anchor this new Self in existence. Using this rune's power at this level, you are able to direct the development of the Self; building anchors across realities and in different realities is not only possible, but a very good way to diversify your development. Additionally, this rune's force allows you to create additional manifestations of your Spark of Self and from it, additional spirits, energy bodies and even alternative physical bodies in other realities.

It also allows you to re-establish roots along pre-existing paths, especially those built by your ancestors. This bridges the ancestral knowledge and full power of the legacy within your Self and causes your perceptions, awareness and even consciousness to partake in it all.

Spirit & Spiritual Reality

The similarities between the ◇ Ingwaz and ᚷ Othala runic forces are striking. Not only because they are essentially a continuation of one another but also because they serve similar functions. In terms of consciousness, these runes can almost be used interchangeably with one notable exception: when applying the ᚷ Othala powers, they will also anchor consciousness in whatever location or state you select. This is something you cannot do using ◇ Ingwaz powers; not only can ᚷ Othala anchor consciousness, it also has the capability to spread these anchors along either pre-existing paths or new ones. You can use this to not only increase spirit travel to other realms and worlds, but also anchor in them there, upon arrival. A good metaphor to use here is that of extending the roots of conscious.

When working with your own spirit, you can establish a very useful balance through ᚷ Othala's anchoring capabilities and its preservation of freedom functionality. For this rune helps you establish a spiritual base from which you can set flight and to which you can always return. This gives you the equivalent of a permanent residence at your disposal and opens up a wide range of possibilities as a permanent resident in the spiritual. It is, ultimately speaking, a natural extension of our very natures, for the human being is both matter and spirit.

Matter first and spirit second; your first permanent base is found in your physical body, and having a second one for your spiritual Self gives you the opportunity to live a spirit life as well, where you have a semi-permanent residence to enjoy as and when you desire to inhabit. By 'living' in the spiritual realms, you facilitate the gathering of further knowledge, experience and most importantly, spirit energy with which to grow your spirit even further. This will in turn enable you to acquire or develop new perspectives and views on creation, life and existence in general. This is the point from which your ordinary existence and life in Midgard (Earth) changes fundamentally and you gain a base of operation for a new type of life, which is part spiritual and part physical, until eventually you will be able to shed the physical altogether. You begin and keep on building your new home on the spiritual, and maybe for the lucky few, a new type of spirit family. This becomes your own personal sacred space, your castle within creation, your temple – for this is where your spirit lives.

Just as you go about building a spiritual space of your own using ᛟ Othala, the same can be said about your spirit itself. Seeing as you do not need to build it from the ground up, what this rune's force enables you to do is realise it fully and enhance it with all the ancestral influences and energies. All inherited abilities, powers and characteristics are realised by this rune within your very spirit. It will exert a strong influence on the Óðr <-> Fylgja interactions, as well as enable you to make a strong connection with the familial Dísir. By doing so, both the paternal and maternal ancestral influences can be brought into your spiritual 'home', which will be greatly enriched.

This rune's power is not all about the Self; once the spiritual part of you has been established and gained its new foothold on the spiritual, you can use the other side of its power, namely the familial. Using ᛟOthala, it is possible to extend the reach of 'you' with others, effectively building a type of mingling spot for spirits that are compatible with you. The best way to think about this is in terms of a community and radiating a spiritual energy wave outwards, which acts as an invitation. It will attract those spirits that are compatible with your own nature and bring them in. Because ᛟ Othala is a rune of solidity and stability, this type of 'gathering' is solid as well – in other words, it would not be what, here on Earth, one would consider temporary or short-term.

Mind & Mental Reality

ᛟOthala is a critically important rune and power for the mind and memory. It helps you stabilise any changes in your mind and the linked adaptations in your awareness. Working with the runes and Seiðr causes sometimes subtle, other times not-so-subtle changes in our way of thinking and our capabilities in general. Such changes on the mental side of things can be very fickle and a nice boost in ability one minute can be totally unobtainable the next. ᛟOthala enables you to root those within your mind and memory systems; it strengthens and solidifies them, not only temporarily, but also on a long-term basis. Using this rune provides a great helping hand when you want to firm up and gain better control of all these shifts in mind capabilities. For example, ecstatic trances and evolution of consciousness are notoriously difficult to reproduce. Often times, you can have deep, even life-changing experiences and then it might take years to replicate the heightened state of mind that enabled this type of experience. By mastering ᛟ Othala, then using it immediately after such experiences end, with the intent to anchor them in your mind, or energy body (when it's a shift of awareness, for awareness is housed and rooted in the energy body, not the mind), you can facilitate and speed up the process to trigger them again and again.

By the same principle, some states of mind are anchored in a place rather than in you. You must have surely experienced such a thing: you walked into a place, a room, an event and you not only felt different but your mind started racing. Suddenly, your thoughts raced, ideas flowed effortlessly, a type of mental excitement took hold. Using ᛟ Othala, you can build an anchor into wherever this happened and then by simply using its energy at a later time, shift into that anchored place to re-trigger the same state of mind. The same runs true for memory: some places are environmentally conducive to recall. Students should take note here: by studying in the same place each time and then anchoring with ᛟ Othala at a later point in time (for instance, during an examination), all it takes is to visualise yourself in that same place and using the rune. This will facilitate recall of whatever you were studying in your chosen space. It is really very helpful. The same can be achieved for other types of recall, such as establishing an anchor to a happy place, to somewhere where you shared a special moment, and so forth. Likewise, it is possible to use ᛟ Othala to de-anchor from spaces and experiences that were traumatic. Memories are enhanced by frequency of recall, and ᛟ Othala enhances such recall; it is a simple matter to de-anchor using this rune and weakening recall, until the memory fades away totally (if you combine with this ᛞ Dagaz to process that memory into its essence, it helps the shedding of the painful memories even more).

It would not be a discussion of ᛟ Othala if ancestral memories were not mentioned. These are stored in the energetic components of our DNA. Using this rune, it is possible to recall all of these and with the help of ᛞ Dagaz, bring them right into the remit of your consciousness. Doing this is very much like recalling yourself living through the ancestor whose memories you are experiencing. This is what people often confuse when they talk about past lives and past life regression; there are no past lives – each Spark of Self embodies itself once in an energy body, whether or not the Self fails to realise its essence and memories, skills and experiences, knowledge and power, which is passed onto the next generation for realisation. Some fragments of a shattered Self can hang around, and they are that: just fragments, like pieces of a broken mirror reflecting parts of what that Self was in life. What you will be recalling are those very things your ancestors left in your genetic makeup. Do be cautious because such recall in effect integrates all those memories and experiences into you. It is a type of side-effect of the anchoring or rooting capabilities of ᛟ Othala. Guilt, emotional problems and blocks of all types, as well as the positive aspects of all those memories will surface, and unless processed properly, they will haunt you just as your own experiences in life do. This is why this type of work is left until the Self has completed its formation and is now ready to anchor.

Energy Body & Energy Reality

ᛟ Othala can be used in many ways when it comes to the energetic side of things. As with all other levels of reality, all things ancestral come within its remit, be it the accessing of ancestral energy, prosperity or authority, or using ancestral energy patterns and traditional abilities, knowledge or wisdom. ᛟ Othala also governs all the roots running through the energy body, the billions upon billions of thin threads that root themselves throughout the body are a product of this rune. It also maintains the forms and patterns in operation in it. The unique configurations you inherit from your family, your cultural background and your Self are all expressed in your energy body by the underlying ᛟ Othala force.

When it comes to shape, this too is inherited and part-formed by the Self (or rather, to be more precise, by the Spark of Self's radiation, which forms the spirit, which in turn patterns the mind and energy, and then shapes the energy body in accordance to the rules set by the ancestral inheritance and fate). However, ᛟ Othala goes further than just this; using it allows you to master the energy body's shape and even to start moulding it. The re-shaping can be learnt once this rune is mastered and is mentioned in countless Eddas, ranging from adopting the Fylgja's animal form, and other human forms – even that of the opposite sex and importantly, the geometric Fyljga for inter-dimensional travel. All these fall within the realms of mastery of this body and this rune.

Since awareness is rooted in the energy body and it is the result of crystallisation of billions of threads of universal light through our hvels, ᛟ Othala in combination with ᛜ Ingwaz and ᛚ Laguz can be used to manipulate it and even grow it (use ᛟ Othala and ᛞ Dagaz for that).

Another important use of this rune's power is the establishment of a personal sacred space. By allow its energy to spread through an energetic or even physical location, you will be able to immediately delineate a specific space as yours. It becomes dedicated to you (well, the higher parts of you) and your entire being (that includes all the ancestral, as well). From such a space, you gain immediate protection from external non-compatible or unwanted energy beings, and a solid ground upon which you can build. It is the direct manifestation of your personal inner universe in some external space. Be creative with it and follow the guidance of this rune in order to learn how to make use of such a space. This will be discussed further at a later point in time, so mastering this is important.

In terms of emotions, this rune plays a very positive role. It promotes stability of emotion, maturity and playfulness of character. Its energy's effects strengthen loyalties and long-lasting bonds between individuals, and protects those bonds from interference by outsiders.

Physical Body & Physical Reality

ᛟ Othala is the rune of the physical body. Energetically speaking, this body is the sum total of all the ancestral and Self's work. It is the crystallisation of the Self in matter and is a direct reflection of the hidden true Self within the Spark of Self. It is also the sum total of the three energetic bodies (the energy body, the shadow and finally the physical). All that which one is, can be or will be is based on or around this body. In other words, it is the root of all the (current) manifestations of the Self and is also the foundation from which all further development arises. Yes, parts of the Self do exist and did before, or outside of the body, but those parts only become functional as a life form once they are brought together within it. This, of course, only applies to us human beings; other forms of existence have different structures and bodies as their foundation, but the underlying principles are the same: they too will have parts of the Self which are brought together into one whole functioning unit. By the same principle, when the physical dies, if one has not made full use of this foundation to grow the Self, it shatters into parts, most of which are dissolved or reabsorbed to be reused in another manifestation of a new part of the Self's journey.

All that aside, ᛟ Othala is the rune of this body. It can be used to influence any of its structures and functions, and as such, when it comes to healing, a rune mystic specialising in this rune has what can be described as an unimaginable range of powers and influences they can use. Everything from the root-like blood system and vessels, nervous system, muscle structures, organ make-up, down to the energetic functions of organs and the interconnections of the physical with the energetic and wider non-physical. It is also important to keep in mind the real ancestry of the human being (see *The Blood of Lóðurr Awakens* for more info). Using ᛟ Othala, this can be connected with through your very physicality. The Giants, Æsir, Vanir and beyond are all rooted within.

Consciousness is also born from the physical. ᛟ Othala gives you the unique capabilities to make full use of it, to adapt it, change it and mould it into new heights of functioning. Combine this rune with others to achieve interesting trance states and expand your conscious capabilities. Keep a focus on using this rune's power to bridge your consciousness to the biological awareness and intelligence within your physical body. This is a very important skill to gain, both in terms of physiological development and in terms of its energetic development as well. Carrying over your physicality and anchoring it in the energy body itself is made possible, once you have achieved this and mastered this rune's powers. Men, take heed: this rune is especially important to you; it is anchored in the Y-chromosome for good reason! Use it.

On the more daily focus, this rune's power influences our homes, our home lives and the 'castle'(or foundations) in our lives. Our familial and cultural traditions are rooted in its power and so is our current identity. It is important to learn its lesson, not because the first reaction should be to automatically discard it – quite to the contrary; there is a reason why this forms part of our very selves – but it should be mastered. Its lesson learnt, its ancestral power mastered, it is only then that we can move onto the non-physical. By the same principle, ᚷ Othala is also responsible for governing all things that are foundational in our lives. This is one of the main reasons why it is so strongly connected with ancestral wealth and non-mobile wealth. It is that which accumulates, provides security and belonging. Its energy will help you succeed in your ventures but also shield you from forces which might try and disrupt, if not negating their effects then most certainly diminishing them to the point where they become manageable. Through its roots, you can establish yourself and build a domain of your own, into which you can welcome those whom you would have as part of your life, your family and your friends (in total, a modern-day clan of your own, if you prefer), offering all whom you cherish the safety and power of your foundations. It is, as a general rule, a rune of prosperity and bringing people together under one roof for the furtherance of common goals, and an increase in everyone's success. A space from which all can undertake new journeys, but also a space to which everyone can return. The inverse is also possible – a space delineated as yours can keep out any who seek to harm you, and it is possible to set up the runic power in such a way that no intruder can ever step into its remit. It shields, it protects, it endures, and even time loses its entropic power when faced with a regenerating and renewing ᛟ Othala current.

HÁVAMÁL RUNE SONGS

Insights into the Hávamál Rune Songs

Having gone through the runes and the practices of High Galdr, it is worth taking a final stop (for this title, in any case) at the Hávamál. With your new knowledge and insights into the runes, it is easy to understand Oðinn's rune poem (or songs, as he calls them – remember the runic vibrations and the dances of frequencies and vibrations of the runic forces in the universe?). Let us take a quick dive in. You can find the rune songs/poems in the *Hávamál* 146 to 163.

In the 1st song (146), Oðinn mentions it is not known to the chief's wife or the child of men, that its name is 'help' and that it will provide assistance against accusations (this is a more accurate term to use instead of 'lawsuits'), sorrows and every affliction. This refers to the ᚠ Fehu rune. It hints at the 'help' aspects of the rune – in other words, its ability to regenerate megin or 'luck' power, which can then be used to fix or withstand all these problems. Additionally, note that every affliction is mentioned; we know from our work on megin that its primary use is for healing purposes.

In relation to sorrows, things are a little different – this hints at the activating and fiery aspects of the rune, which can liven things up with an uplifting power like ᚠ Fehu.

The 2nd song (147) talks about the sons of men needing to know this rune if they wish to live – or an equally suitable word here would be 'study' – as physicians. This refers to ᚢ Uruz and the rune's healing properties, as well as pointing to the fact that the rune itself can be the teacher of the skills needed to become a physician.

In the 3rd song (148), Oðinn talks about the cases where he is in need of binding an enemy and blunting their weapons. It is important to note he mentions weapons and staffs. This implies physical combat and magical tools (staffs and wands were the tools of Seiðr, priests and monarchs). This fits in nicely with the functions of ᚦ Thurisaz, where its thorns can bind the enemy and blunt the weapons.

In the 4th song (149), he discusses freeing himself of bonds and breaking free of fetters and cuffs. These fit the functions of ᚨ Ansuz perfectly in its capacity as the rune of freedom and breaker of bonds.

In the 5th song (150), Oðinn discusses seeing a shot of baleful intent, a shaft shooting into the crowd, and mentions how if he catches sight of it, he can stop it. It is interesting to see him discuss the physical (shaft shoot) and the non-physical (baleful intent) attacks. Both of these are projectiles travelling from a source to destination. Oðinn hints at how he can change their course using ᚱ Raidho's power.

The 6th song (151) looks at what could be termed as cursing, where Oðinn mentions that the one who lays the curse or spell on him is, by virtue of this rune's power, made to suffer it instead. This is not a rebound of the curse; rather, it is the transformation of the initial curse or spell to rewrite its target as its source. Such things always run their course, whether you want them to or not. Using the ᚲ Kenaz rune, Oðinn can cause it to recoil back on its sender.

The 7th song (152) – here the translation is a little off, but still encapsulates the essence of the song. It tells of a hall set aflame, but not burning too brightly, that it cannot be and how, by using the rune of ᚷ Gebo, the force of the fires is by virtue of its exchange siphoned of power and swapped for another. Doing so, the flames diminish until eventually they are extinguished.

In the 8th song (153), we have a translation issue; the word 'nema' is translated as 'take' but 'to study' is a more accurate term. 'Hildings', translated as 'war-chief', could also be 'dwarf'. It talks about the hatred of the dwarfs growing, and that they are the guardians of the gateways between worlds and considered to be evil, associated with death and damage to the mental wellbeing of humans, and sexual predators after the goddesses and the maggots from Ymir. This song is useful when the hatred of the dwarf increases and their power to inflict ill on mankind grows. By using ᚹ Wunjo, it is possible to keep them and their 'evil' at bay, ensuring the places of human habitats are strong and safe against them.

In the 9th song (154), Oðinn tells of calming the sea, the wind and the waves when he is on his boat. This fits nicely with the powers of ᚺ Hagalaz; it can be used to control the destructive and threatening power. It also hints at the stillness this rune can induce.

The 10th song (155) also suffers in translation. Here, Oðinn talks of the hedge-riders playing in the sky. This refers to Seiðr sorceresses flying in the skies. He mentions how ᚾ Nauthiz forces them to change paths, to go home or down a certain path. This rune constrains the freedoms of the mind or its activity which are inducing distress. He uses ᚾ Nauthiz to induce this type of distress between their bodies and project non-physical parts (which are flying in the skies). This in turn forces them to go back home (into their bodies).

The 11th song (156) talks about going into battle with long-time friends, where Oðinn Galðrs under their shields will keep them safe from all harm and from everywhere. ᛁ Isa is the power of stasis able to stop all things in their track and brings all places to a standstill, ensuring the safety of his friends.

In the 12th song (157), Oðinn talks of finding the corpse of a hanged man and mentions how he cuts the runes to allow the hanged man to walk and talk with him once again. This is where ᛃ Jera, as the ruler of time, comes into its own. A rune that can reverse the flow of time for a specific human being can, in theory, achieve this when combined with two other runes.

The 13th song (158) talks of Oðinn casting water on a young man going to war, preventing him from falling in battle. This is one of the facets of ᛈ Pertho, which is both wet and has dominion over the flow of fate. Oðinn is using this rune in order to change the flow of the young man's fate, to prevent him from falling in battle.

The 14th song (159) talks of Oðinn recounting the victories of the Æsir and the Álfr to an assembly of men. The translation is a bit vague at the end of this song. Oðinn says that he knows 'everyone' of the Æsir and Álfr, rather than knowing the 'details' as translated. Essentially, this does not affect our understanding of the song; it clearly refers to ᛇ Eihwaz which bridges spirit and matter, unlocks knowledge of the mysteries, develops skills of communication across realities and enhances perceptions. This gives Oðinn wisdom of all Æsir and Álfr.

The 15th song (160) outlines how Þjóðrerir, using galðr, gave power to the Æsir, ability to the Alfar and insight to Oðinn himself. When looking at ᛉ Elhaz, you see that this is possibly by virtue of its expression of absolute divinity. There are manifestations of the higher spiritual powers of ᛉ Elhaz, embodied not in an event or rune, but in fundamental shape of the species (which transmits to all those live forms shaped alike).

In the 16th song (161) and the next, there is an uncomfortable statement for many. The term 'mans' (here) and 'man' (in 17) are both gendered masculine terms in old Norse. Yet they often get translated as 'maid', whereas if we are being precise, should be 'man' instead. The thought of Oðinn trying to seduce a man makes many readers in this day and age uncomfortable, yet in Norse times, it was a non-issue. Regardless, what this song talks about is ᛋ Sowilo. He wants to have the wise man with all physical and mental pleasures (is a better fit for the original meaning than heart and just pleasure; there is no emotional component here). He achieved this by changing the outpouring of the Self and twists it into the direction he desires it. He is not changing the nature of the man's Self, rather he is changing its directionality of expression.

In the 17th song (162), the father and ruler rune ᛏ Tiwaz comes into play, where he talks of ensuring the youthful man (see notes above) is slow or reticent to leave him. The young seeking the wisdom and protection of the elder, their company and the guidance through life is a well-known phenomenon even in our times. Note there are no sexual undertones in this text. It is purely companionship.

The 18th song (163) relates to ᛒ Berkano, which Oðinn says should never be made known to a maiden or man's wife. He mentions how everything is better for one man to know and how only the one he holds in his arms or his sister should be told. This is the mother rune, which he hints should be known only to her who will be the mother of one's children (hence the exclusion of the maiden, and another man's wife – but he does include the sister, because she too might be trying to become a mother).

This, ladies and gents, completes this High Galdr title. Many more practices will be covered in future titles, but for this one, the aim is to provide you with the foundational practices needed for mastery of the runes. This has now been done. You now have the groundwork from which you will be able to build. Master these practices well because they are the basis of all advanced work. I do hope you have exciting and successful work with the runes and learn to wield them.

> I would like to thank you all for joining me in this exciting adventure.

Frank A. Rúnaldrar

- High Galdr: Runes & Rune Secrets -

APPENDIXES

APPENDIX A

- Appendixes -

Table of Runic Names in Icelandic & Germanic

Rune	Numeric Value	Icelandic Name	Germanic Name
ᚠ	1	Fé	Fehu
ᚢ	2	Úr	Uruz
ᚦ	3	Þurs	Thurisaz
ᚨ	4	Óss (Ás)	Ansuz
ᚱ	5	Reið	Raidho
ᚲ	6	Kaun	Kenaz
ᚷ	7	Gjöf	Gebo
ᚹ	8	Vin	Wunjo
ᚺ	9	Hagall	Hagalaz
ᚾ	10	Nauð	Nauthiz
ᛁ	11	Íss	Isa
ᛃ	12	Ár	Jera
ᛈ	13	Perð	Pertho
ᛇ	14	Jór	Eihwaz
ᛉ	15	Ýr	Elhaz
ᛊ	16	Sól	Sowilo
ᛏ	17	Týr	Tiwaz
ᛒ	18	Bjarkan	Berkano
ᛖ	19	Eykur	Ehwaz
ᛗ	20	Maður	Mannaz
ᛚ	21	Lögur	Laguz
ᛜ	22	Ing	Ingwaz
ᛞ	23	Dagur	Dagaz
ᛟ	24	Óðal	Othala

APPENDIX B

References & footnotes

1. Strange Footprints on the Land (Author: Irwin, Constance publisher: Harper & Row, 1980) ISBN 0-06-022772-9)

2. Snorri Sturluson. 'The Prose Edda: Tales from Norse Mythology', translated by Jean I. Young (University of California Press, 1964)

3. Frank A. Rúnaldrar (2018), "The Blood of Lóðurr Awakens", London: Bastian & West, ISBN: 978-0-9955343-6-0

4. Frank A. Rúnaldrar (2017), "The Spirit of Húnir Awakens - Part 1", London: Bastian & West, ISBN: 978-0-9955343-2-2 and Frank A. Rúnaldrar (2017), "The Spirit of Húnir Awakens - Part 2", London: Bastian & West, ISBN: 978-0-9955343-3-9

5. Frank A. Rúnaldrar (2017), "The Breath of Oðin Awakens", London: Bastian & West, ISBN: 978-0-9955343-4-6

6. Frank A. Rúnaldrar (2019), "Roadmap to High Galdr", London: Bastian & West, ISBN: 978-0-9955343-7-7

7. Literal translation of Hávamál-80, accessed from: http://www.voluspa.org/literal/havamal.htm

8. Literal translation of Hávamál-145, accessed from: http://www.voluspa.org/literal/havamal.htm

9. Image is licensed under the Common Creative License 2.5, from the Swedish National Heritage Board downloaded: http://kmb.raa.se/cocoon/bild/show-image.html?id=16000300013409

10. Author added quotes.

11. Literal translation of Hávamál-144, accessed from: http://www.voluspa.org/literal/havamal.htm

12. Literal translation of Hávamál-162, accessed from: http://www.voluspa.org/literal/havamal.htm

FORTHCOMING TITLES

DreamWalking
The Art of Runic Dreaming

Dreaming, everyone does it, yet not everyone remembers it, some like it others fear it but no one can agree on what dreaming actually is and why we all dream. Science argues it is a result of the brain consolidating daily information and memories, Psychology argues it is a reflection of the inner state of being and mental balance, mystics argue it is a separation of the spirit from the body and so forth.

In Runic dreaming we explore and learn how to both use dreams and grow through them. Combining High Galdr with the Arts of the Völva (Old Norse Prophetess or Seeress) the full power of dreaming is unleashed as a transformation or awakening tool, an essential in reclaiming the full power of human awareness as it takes its first steps across creation.

Learn about runic energy and its impact on dreams, how to remember your dreams and use memory as a gauge of development, how to imbue the Minni (memory) to enhance dream capabilities, how to increase energy via dreams, how to experience the other Nine Worlds through dreams and how to bridge the dream and daily realities to shape the one through the other and vice versa...

Secrets of the Norse Fylgja
Inter-dimensional Travel Vehicle, Animal Totem & Spirit Guide

Animal totem, spirit guide and inter-dimensional vessel, the Fylgja is one of the nine constructs of the Norse Self, the carrier of ancestral memories, experiences and potential with the sole aim of guiding us in our evolution both physically and spiritually.

Overseeing the development of the Self and weaving the personal (and ancestral) Ørlög, the Fylgja plays a vital role in our lives and unfolding inner potential as we move towards our divine birth-right, yet is often unnoticed and unacknowledged.

Commonly referred to in the Eddas in animalistic forms, sometimes in humanoid ones and only ever hinted at secretly and briefly in geometric form, gaining mastery of the Fylgja opens up countless possibilities and opportunities for the development of the Self.

Speeding up evolution, allowing for conscious travel out of the physical (faring forth), storing memories and experiential learning beyond the limitations of the brain, and many more fascinating possibilities are all within reach of those mastering it.

Amplified Manifestation
Norse Sexual Mysteries for Women

For time immemorial, female sexuality has been restricted solely to childbearing and more recently for pleasure or pastime. Almost nothing has been revealed about the mysteries, the dynamics or potential of female sexuality.

Women have an innate ability to amplify, manifest and give form to creation that has been a revered and sacred sexual art which lies at the foundation of the female sexual current.

The mastery of female sexual energy, to the exclusion of the male, allows women to manifest their true potential, causing their minds and perception to span across boundaries of realities, to shape energy into creation, weave events into our reality and enhance each and every part of reality. The secrets of becoming physical, of grounding the divine in flesh and form, of sustaining the physical reality all fall within the grasp of the female sexual mysteries.

Now is the time to unlock the full potential of female sexuality, to awaken the shaper's mysteries within, to unlock the spirit dormant in the flesh, to increase your spiritual gravity, and become a great weaver of reality!

For Adults Only (18 years+)

Accelerated Evolution
Norse Sexual Mysteries for Men

For a long time, male sexuality has been the subject of great controversy. Its mysteries have only ever been taught to the select few who have kept them secret and hidden. Discover why these practices were historically confined to a small elective, what they were and how they were used to enhance those who wielded them. Discover the secrets of Oðinn and Loki's ventures and what their adventures in the depths of the night.

The mastery of male sexual energy, empowering and evolving one's Self and the Self of other men are but a few of the birth-rights every male carries deep within himself. Discover the power of the Y-Chromosome and how harnessing its potential allows us to evolve faster, how the runes empower the masculine current and most importantly how to take advantage of this phenomenal evolutionary opportunity.

Unleash the sexual secrets of the Fylgja, ancestral powers, quantum consciousness, sexual galdr, spiritualisation of the flesh and combine them with the male creative sexual current in order to accelerate and enhance your evolution across multiple realities.

Channel that inherent sexual prowess that is locked deep within, surfacing only for the briefest moments during sexual ecstatic release, and alight your Divine Spark.

Seize the moment, awaken the sleeper in the glory of physical and spiritual explosive ecstasy...

For Adults Only (18 years+)

- HIGH GALDR: RUNES & RUNE SECRETS -

www.ingramcontent.com/pod-product-compliance
Lightning Source LLC
Chambersburg PA
CBHW020940230426
43666CB00005B/101